Developmental dyslexia in adults: a research review

Michael Rice with Greg Brooks

CONTENTS

This report is funded by the Department for Education and Skills as part of **Skills for Life**: the national strategy for improving adult literacy and numeracy skills. The views expressed are those of the authors and do not necessarily reflect those of the Department.

Preface

A rigorous review of research on dyslexia is long overdue. 'Developmental Dyslexia in Adults: a research review' aims to generate and share new knowledge, based on evidence from sound research, to add to all that is already known about dyslexia from practice, informed advocacy and research and development work by organisations which have been active in the field over several decades. So NRDC is pleased to publish this report from a rigorous, peer-reviewed research project. The report can inform policy development and teaching and learning practice by enhancing the evidence base on which decisions are taken and new directions pursued. We believe it will deepen and enrich our knowledge of dyslexia and in addition inform literacy provision for other groups of *Skills for Life* learners.

It is important to emphasise that this is a review of research, not a review of practice or policy. However, we believe that a strong partnership based on the combined approaches of researchers, practitioners, dyslexia organisations and policy makers can make a real difference for the learners whose needs this report highlights – people with dyslexia. The major project: 'A Framework for Understanding Dyslexia' conducted recently by LSDA and NIACE has identified existing approaches to the teaching and learning of adults with dyslexia. Wherever good approaches could be found, they have been bought together to illuminate possible strategies for people whose learning needs, as with most learners of literacy, numeracy and language, can be better identified and met by carefully designed and focused teaching and learning strategies. NRDC's recent report 'Adult Numeracy: review of research and related literature' analysed research on dyscalculia. These new pieces of work, adding to the large body of work already carried out by dyslexia organisations, LLU+ at South Bank University and others, have the potential to raise significantly the quality of educational opportunities for people with dyslexia, whose learning needs can be better identified and met by carefully designed and focused teaching and learning strategies.

We hope the report will interest organisations and teachers working with dyslexic adult learners. We strongly believe the messages here can also speak to many practitioners engaged in wider literacy provision for young people and adults. It is critical to improve learning opportunities and focus sharply on the best methods of teaching to help learners overcome the obstacles they face, achieve more and progress in life and work.

The report indicates that the work done in the field of dyslexia to help dyslexic people learn has much to offer literacy practitioners working with learners who are not dyslexic. This is because dyslexia practice has developed structured, explicit approaches to teaching, which are geared to the assessed needs of individual learners and which are successful in helping many learners.

There is evidence that the approaches to teaching developed for the field of dyslexia might well be appropriate for other groups of people learning to improve their literacy. The findings of this study connect interestingly with other NRDC research into effective teaching and learning. We are finding out from research projects on reading, that much literacy teaching does not systematically use explicit teaching strategies in the blend of teaching and learning activities in the classroom. We also know that, for many adult literacy learners, significant progress is elusive. We are now carrying out five extensive linked studies of Effective Teaching and Learning Practice: in reading, writing, ESOL, numeracy and ICT. These studies, based on assessments and detailed observation of classrooms and other settings, are investigating which strategies do make a difference to learners' progress and achievement.

'Developmental Dyslexia in Adults: a research review' also finds that there are many reasons why people find it difficult to learn to read and write and suggests that we should find out much more about why different groups of people find reading and writing, language and number difficult to learn, for a range of different reasons. It seems likely that we are not looking at a simple straightforward divide between people with dyslexia and people whose education has been unfulfilling and unrewarding, whether because of lack of support at school or home, poverty or other external factors. This is why we have placed phrases such as 'ordinary poor readers', which are used commonly in the scientific literature in speech marks: this review questions such a divide. The reasons adults have difficulty with literacy and numeracy are multiple and complex and we should begin to explore them thoroughly so that we can help people to overcome them, and achieve.

At NRDC we would very much like to work with partner organisations in the field of dyslexia and related areas to discuss the findings of this review and to look at priorities for further research and development so that we can better match the needs and difficulties learners have with teaching strategies which will enable them to achieve. Please contact us if you would like to work with us.

Ursula Howard
Director, NRDC

Foreword

This is a critical review of the extensive and complex *research* literature on developmental dyslexia as it might apply to adults participating in courses which offer literacy, numeracy, and English for speakers of other languages (ESOL). By using electronic databases, including the Science Citation and Social Science Citation Indexes, ERIC and Medline, by making visual inspections of library holdings at the Institute of Education, University of London and elsewhere and by searching the Internet, we identified a large number of potentially relevant book chapters or papers published in peer-reviewed journals. Although we set our watershed at 1987, we included earlier items when continuing citation underlined their importance. From more than three thousand items initially identified, we selected 1,800 items for inspection. We obtained reprints or made photocopies of 1,220 items, which we then read and annotated. Because very few of the items deal specifically and exclusively with adults and even fewer dealt with adults in basic education, we have needed to make cautious inferences from the literature on childhood dyslexia. In our review, we consider the major explanatory theories of dyslexia and their implications for practice. We also consider some recent alternative perspectives on developmental reading difficulties. A draft version was reviewed by a panel of academic experts and this version incorporates nearly all of their suggested amendments and additions.

We conclude that there is no evidence from research to support a policy of differentiating dyslexic from non-dyslexic students in adult literacy, numeracy and ESOL. We offer five main reasons for our conclusion. First, both dyslexic and non-dyslexic students need to acquire the same knowledge and skills in literacy and numeracy. Second, structured and explicit tuition is appropriate for both groups. Third, individual differences between students occur along many dimensions, while all classification schemes entail overlapping categories. Fourth, diagnostic protocols for dyslexia in adults cannot be used with any confidence either to ascertain the causes (as opposed to the symptoms) of literacy or numeracy difficulties or to predict the outcomes of interventions. Fifth, the construct of developmental dyslexia is insufficient for a systematic and thorough appraisal of learners' difficulties in adult education. With respect to adult literacy, we also conclude that successful teaching is informed by the tutor's understanding of 'normal' language and literacy acquisition.

Our conclusions are not to be taken to mean that 'nothing works'; practitioners know many things that have 'worked' for particular learners. However, that is professional wisdom based on experience and an analysis of that knowledge was not part of our remit. Nevertheless, there is a clear need for research which draws on practitioner knowledge and wisdom and investigates whether there are grounds for categorising learners as either 'dyslexic' or as 'ordinary' adult learners with literacy, numeracy and language needs. As our research shows that there are multiple reasons why adults find learning literacy, numeracy and ESOL difficult, we should extend our knowledge of the diversity of causes and the strategies needed to help adults improve their skills.

Michael Rice
Dr Michael Rice (University of Cambridge, formerly Senior Research Officer, NRDC Institute of Education)
with
Greg Brooks
Research Director, NRDC Sheffield, and Professor of Education, University of Sheffield

Acknowledgements

We are grateful to:

- the seven academic experts who responded to our invitation to comment on either the complete draft or specific sections of it. Two of the seven are themselves the parents of young dyslexic adults;
- library staff at the Institute of Education, University of London, the University of Cambridge Institute of Education, Cambridge University Library and the Department of Experimental Psychology at the University of Cambridge; and
- Felicity Rees, who edited an earlier draft and provided a first draft of an executive summary.

Project team and authorship

Greg Brooks was the project director, gave advice and edited the final draft.

Michael Rice was the Senior Research Officer. The rest of the project and this report, was his work, including authorship of the entire text.

Executive summary

Synopsis

The *Skills for Life* strategy is committed to addressing the needs of learners with learning difficulties such as developmental dyslexia. The term 'dyslexia' is problematic: there are many definitions, with varying degrees of overlap. For the purposes of this review, 'dyslexia' has been interpreted widely, to embrace most if not all of the ways in which the term has been used by scientists and educationalists.

This is a research review. It was undertaken to establish the evidence base for developmental dyslexia in adults. It began by searching electronic data bases, exploring library holdings, and following citation trails. This process identified a large number of potentially relevant book chapters and papers published in peer-reviewed journals, which were then read critically.

The review draws attention to a range of methodological and interpretational problems in the literature, with particular respect to sampling and research design. It presents a detailed account of phonological awareness. Four explanatory theories of dyslexia are summarised and their implications for teaching practice are assessed. Three alternative perspectives on developmental reading difficulties are described. The language in these accounts reflects, where necessary, the terminology used in their sources.

Key points

The research review found that:

- There are many reasons why people find it difficult to learn how to read, write and spell. Some causes of reading difficulty are located within society and some are located within the individual.
- There are many definitions of dyslexia but no consensus. Some definitions are purely descriptive, while others embody causal theories. It appears that 'dyslexia' is not one thing but many, in so far as it serves as a conceptual clearing-house for a number of reading skills deficits and difficulties, with a number of causes.
- There is no consensus, either, as to whether dyslexia can be distinguished in practice from other possible causes of adults' literacy difficulties. Many 'signs of dyslexia' are no less characteristic of non-dyslexic people with reading skills deficits. In our present state of knowledge, it does not seem to be helpful for teachers to think of some literacy learners as 'dyslexics' and of others as 'ordinary poor readers'.
- Learning to read in an alphabetic system helps, and is helped by, the development of phonemic awareness.
- Reading fluency is a complex process, and research is needed for this process to be better understood.
- The most inaccurate readers are not the most likely to be dyslexic, as most scientists use the term.
- Teachers of both initial reading and adult literacy need to be well-informed about language and its acquisition.
- The teacher's aim must be to impart declarative knowledge (or knowledge that) and to ensure that the learner transforms it into procedural knowledge (or knowledge how) in order to be able to draw upon it without conscious attention.

- Reading interventions need to address both the cognitive and the emotional needs of adult students.
- Adult literacy learners need to be taught how their writing system works.
- The research does not indicate that 'dyslexics' and 'ordinary poor readers' should be taught by different methods. However, the methods promoted as specialist interventions for dyslexic people are well suited for mainstream teaching, which is how they originated.
- Good practice in this field rests almost entirely on professional judgement and common sense, rather than on evidence from evaluation studies. The review found no experimental evidence comparing the group outcomes between dyslexic adults and the wider population of adults with reading skills deficits.
- Many people who have difficulty in learning literacy skills can be helped by a curriculum that is both structured and explicit, with methods that reinforce their learning. However, a minority of learners do not respond to structured and explicit reading intervention programmes, and ways of helping them have yet to be developed.
- Students will not become proficient without repetitive practice.
- Computer-supported instruction can make repetitive practice acceptable to adult students.
- Findings from research with middle-class groups of mother-tongue speakers may create misleading expectations about the needs and abilities of learners in adult literacy classes.

Background and rationale of the research

The research was undertaken as part of the NRDC's programme of research reviews into key aspects of adult basic skills teaching and learning. The aim was to identify ways in which adult literacy practitioners could more effectively meet the particular needs of some of their students.

More generally, it was intended to establish a sound theoretical basis for adult literacy teaching and learning. The review was based on a robust analysis of the scientific research literature on developmental dyslexia as it affects adults. It was then the aim to establish what implications, if any, the literature holds for teaching of adults with literacy needs.

Main elements of research

By searching electronic databases, making visual inspections of library holdings and following citation trails, a large corpus of potentially relevant book chapters and papers published in peer-reviewed journals was identified. More than 3,000 items were initially selected and from this number 1,800 were inspected and over 1,200 were read and annotated.

The studies reviewed were then analysed under the following major topics:
- conceptual issues, including definitions of dyslexia and of dyslexics;
- methods of identifying dyslexic people and of distinguishing them from others with literacy difficulties;
- research and interpretational issues;
- the prevalence rate of dyslexia;
- evidence from brain imaging and autopsy studies;
- possible subtypes of dyslexia;
- explanatory theories of dyslexia (e.g. the phonological deficit theory and the double-deficit hypothesis); and
- intervention and evaluation studies.

This report is also available in PDF format from the NRDC's website at www.nrdc.org.uk

Part one
Key issues in dyslexia research

Introduction

Why do some people find it so difficult to learn how to read, write and spell? Are their difficulties part of a normal continuum of human opportunity, aptitude and motivation, or are they caused by innate and circumscribed brain abnormalities? Can the research on developmental dyslexia in children help adult literacy tutors to respond to the needs of these students? Is it helpful for tutors to think of some of their students as dyslexics and of others as non-dyslexics, or ordinary poor readers? Do the categorical distinctions embodied in terms such as 'dyslexic' and 'non-dyslexic' correspond to distinct realities? If there are categorically distinct realities for dyslexic and non-dyslexic students, in what way or ways do those realities differ? Would it be helpful to screen adult students for dyslexia? Are the limitations of screening fully appreciated? Even if it would be helpful to screen adult students, would it be feasible to do so? How does a diagnosis of dyslexia affect students and their tutors? Should dyslexics have a different curriculum from that followed by ordinary poor readers? If so, what differences should there be? Should dyslexics be taught by a different method? Is dyslexia one thing or many? If dyslexia is more than one thing, do different explanations of dyslexia indicate different responses for different dyslexic students?

All of these questions are debatable and at times the debate becomes animated. Part of the explanation for this might be that while research into dyslexia generates all of the excitement of the California Gold Rush it also stirs up much of the heat and dust. For a number of years, it has been 'commonplace to bemoan the state of confusion and disagreement in the field' (Stanovich, 1988). A prominent researcher has referred to 'the competitive viciousness that so characterises the dyslexia ecosystem', describing it as 'an explosive mixture of high numbers of the affected, high parental emotion, yet poor understanding of the condition, hence poor definition and unreliable methods for judging the outcome of treatments' (Stein, 2002).

As in any gold rush, fool's gold is found everywhere. A standard textbook on remedial education observes that 'the term *dyslexia* is overused in the popular press, which gives an inaccurate impression that everyone with reading or literacy problems has dyslexia' (Kirk et al., 1993). Overuse of the term in the press, which may reflect and perhaps encourage both mistaken diagnoses by practitioners and face-saving explanations by poor readers and their families, has led to redefinitions that are now much broader than their equivalents of a hundred years ago. This breadth takes many directions, resulting in 'the vast dimensionality of the terminological space in which dyslexia exists' (Grigorenko, 2001) and 'the current chaos in the field' (Frith, 1995), where dyslexia may strike observers as 'the equivalent of a Rorschach test' telling more about the researcher than about dyslexia itself (Fawcett & Nicolson, 1994).

If it is still true, as it often appears to be, that 'most of what we can say about dyslexia is tentative, speculative, and controversial' (Ables et al., 1971), that 'the standard diagnostic criteria for diagnosing dyslexia cast much too wide a net' (Seidenberg et al., 1986) and that 'dyslexia carries with it so many empirically unverified connotations and assumptions that many researchers and practitioners prefer to avoid the term' (Stanovich, 1994), then it should be no surprise that 'the body of research associated with reading disability is unusually complex and confusing' (Spear-Swerling & Sternberg, 1994) and that the confusion is widespread in almost every quarter. Teachers in schools are likely to be familiar with the argument that 'dyslexia' has become a diagnostic label of convenience (Smith, 1997), applied to learners 'who are so confused by their poor reading instruction that they can't overcome it without special help' (McGuinness, 1998).

In adult education, the perplexity may be greater. Adult life-histories are more complex than those of children. Although every developmentally dyslexic adult was once a dyslexic child, the dyslexic adult is not simply a child with a learning disability grown up (Ott, 1997). Among teachers and providers in adult basic education, a survey into attitudes and beliefs about dyslexia has revealed 'almost universal, and very considerable, confusion and uncertainty as to what dyslexia might be, what might indicate it, what might cause it, what to do about it and even whether it existed at all' (Kerr, 2001)—which is an astonishing state of affairs after a decade of dyslexia awareness campaigning.

Confusion among members of the general public is made worse by policy-makers' inability to resolve the tension between value-driven submissions from advocacy groups and evidence-driven submissions from scientists. The evidence itself is problematic because the actual mechanisms of dyslexia 'are still mysterious and currently remain the subject of intense research endeavour in various neuroscientific areas and along several theoretical frameworks' (Habib, 2000). Elucidation of those mysteries may take a long while, since 'one of the difficulties that significantly impedes progress in the field of dyslexia is the absence of consensus over the "correct" research questions' (Richards et al., 2002). Therefore, for the time being, the field of learning disabilities may be 'more than ever dominated by advocacy rather than science' (Stanovich, 2000), with 'an ongoing power struggle' (Tønnessen, 1997) in an atmosphere of 'highly-charged melodrama' (Nicolson, 2002).

Pupils, parents, politicians and professionals might be 'well-advised to learn to live with legitimate doubts' concerning the nature, identification, prevalence, prognosis and alleviation of dyslexia (Pumfrey, 2001). Meanwhile, it is sometimes unclear whether 'dyslexia' is used as a term of diplomacy or of science.

What is clear in all the copious literature on dyslexia is that most of it concerns reading and reading difficulty; a little concerns spelling; and very little concerns other aspects of literacy – handwriting, punctuation and above all writing as composition, hardly figure. In much of what follows, therefore, 'reading' is discussed and even when 'literacy' is being discussed, reading is usually, although not always, meant.

In the wider fields of learning to read and reading difficulty beyond dyslexia, there has been debate for more than half a century. At issue have been questions of culture (Feagans & Farran, 1982; Luke, 1988; Olson, 1994); social exclusion (Cox & Jones, 1983; Davie et al., 1972; Hurry, 1999; Locke et al., 2002; MacKay, 1999; MacKay & Watson, 1999); teacher training (Brooks et al., 2001a; Brooks et al., 1992; Mather et al., 2001; Moats, 1994; Morris, 1993); curriculum and teaching method (Adams, 1990; Byrne, 1998; Coles, 2000; Department for Education and Employment, 1998; Goodman, 1978; McGuinness, 1998; Rayner et al., 2001; Smith, 1978, 1997; Stuart, 1998; Turner, 1990); and remedial practice (Fawcett, 2002; National Reading Panel, 2000).

In the teaching of reading, many positions are partisan, not least those positions taken with respect to phonics and whole language (Carrier, 1983; Dudley-Marling & Murphy, 1997; Liberman & Liberman, 1992; Postman, 1970; Rayner et al., 2001; Stanovich, 1999). As elsewhere in politics, partisans tend to confuse values with facts. Even so, a mature science of reading instruction can reconcile the opposing positions (Beard & McKay, 1998); its basis of reconciliation will be an agreement that 'to get started one may need phonics, to get fluent one needs practice, to keep practising one needs enjoyment' and 'to have enjoyment one needs a real book' (Nicolson, 2002).

It is a judgment of value—endorsed by the national strategy for improving adult literacy and numeracy skills, **Skills for Life** (DfES, 2001)—that people who struggle with reading, whatever the origin of their problems with reading, should be helped to read to the best of their ability and to adopt coping strategies where their reading ability proves insufficient for their social and economic well-being and personal fulfilment. It is an assertion of fact—critically examined in this review—that developmental dyslexia, *stipulatively* defined as a specific learning disability with a biological origin, largely accounts for the skills deficits of some adult literacy learners whereas the skills deficits of others are largely accounted for by experiential factors. A successful intervention policy for poor readers will avoid confusing facts with values. Both are important, but they are important in different ways.

Either way, a general theory of adult reading skills problems is as likely a prospect as a general theory of holes. Even for deficits with a neurological origin, 'given the complexity of the task and the kinds of capacities it involves, it would be very surprising if reading disability did not have multiple causes' (Seidenberg, 1992). However, despite a common assumption to the contrary, not every reading skill deficit has a neurological origin, even though it necessarily has neurological consequences. There may be a parallel here with research in other fields of enquiry, where theoretical developments have been driven by cognitive neuropsychological models in which the disorder ceases to be simply a useful way of thinking about the world and instead becomes reified as something with an independent existence, which then needs to be explained as an innate psychological dysfunction caused by a specific brain abnormality (Sonuga-Barke, 2002).

Yet, in addition to possible biological causes of reading difficulties, there are possible experiential causes (Bryant & Bradley, 1985; Cashdan, 1969; Chall, 1967; Chall et al., 1990; Clay, 1987; Cox & Jones, 1983; Ellis & Large, 1987; Gough & Tunmer, 1986; Jackson & Coltheart, 2001; Lawton, 1968; MacKay, 1999; Maughan & Yule, 1994; P. Mortimore et al., 1988; Ravenette, 1968; Rutter et al., 1975; Share et al., 1984; Snowling, 1991, 1998; Spear-Swerling & Sternberg, 1996; Stubbs, 1980; Vellutino et al., 1996; Vernon, 1957). One of the experiential causes may be inexplicit teaching, especially teaching that fails to appreciate the student's problems in understanding concepts expressed in particular ways (Marcel, 1978). Whatever the balance of biological and experiential causes in any individual case, their interaction in the course of development leads to ever more complex outcomes (Bronfenbrenner & Ceci, 1994; Gottlieb & Halpern, 2002; Sroufe, 1997; Thomas & Karmiloff-Smith, 2002), so that by adulthood it may be impossible to apportion the causal influences retrospectively (Rack, 1997).

This review acknowledges the association between low literacy attainment and social exclusion, which has both cultural and physiological dimensions and which will characterise the majority of students in adult literacy classes, including most of those who may be identified—however questionably—as 'dyslexic' on the widely used assessment criteria published by the Basic Skills Agency (Klein, 1993). It might well be that 'the key to treating reading disability lies in the effectiveness of the instruction received rather than the categorisation of reader type' (Pogorzelski & Wheldall, 2002). While there might be valid distinctions between dyslexic and ordinary poor readers in theory, 'there are few compelling reasons for attempting to make such distinctions in practice' (Fowler & Scarborough, 1993), since emphasis on a phonics-based curriculum and multisensory methods may benefit all poor readers, not dyslexics alone (Davis & Cashdan, 1963).

There are many reasons why students in basic skills classes have low reading skills and there are many possible outcomes for education programmes that address their problems (Brooks et al., 2001b; Sheehan-Holt & Smith, 2000; Strucker, 1995). For intervention programmes, an appropriate guiding principle may be assimilation (Fowler & Scarborough, 1993), namely, the avoidance of any attempt to separate dyslexic and 'ordinary' adult learners with reading difficulties. However, tutors need to bear in mind that the over-diagnosis of dyslexia might neglect other types of special educational need (Thomson, 2002). By contrast with intervention, the guiding principle in scientific research is not assimilation but differentiation. Between research and practice there is no exact alignment, neither should we seek one: 'models of etiology and models of treatment bear no necessary relation to one another' (Sroufe, 1997).

We shall explore the implications of this observation in the following section. Meanwhile, we note that:

- Scholars agree that difficulty in learning to read can have many causes.
- They agree that some causes of reading difficulty are located within society.
- They agree that some causes of reading difficulty are located within the individual.
- Scholars do not agree as to the relative importance of those causes.
- They do not agree as to whether dyslexia is a valid concept.
- Among the scholars who believe that dyslexia is a valid concept, there is no agreement as to precisely what it is, or whether it is subsumed by or distinct from ordinary poor reading.
- Scholars do not agree as to whether dyslexic and non-dyslexic poor readers require different intervention programmes.
- Scholars who believe that dyslexic people require different interventions from those needed by 'ordinary' adult learners with reading difficulties do not agree about the nature of those interventions.

Conceptual issues

The context

Dyslexia is associated with problems of great complexity. These problems are fundamental; they cannot be dismissed as semantic quibbles. It may be helpful to begin by asking a few elementary questions, in order to outline *possible* ways in which they might be answered. By looking at different uses of the word 'dyslexia' and by asking which, if any, of these uses might be currently supported by scientific evidence, we will be brought face-to-face with some of the conceptual problems. After that, we can go on to consider the practical difficulties that follow from the conceptual problems.

In many other fields of enquiry, there is a consistency in the use of words that makes this strategy unnecessary. In dyslexia research and practice, there is a degree of inconsistency verging on anarchy, as the opening paragraphs of the introduction reveal (and as *Appendix 1* illustrates).

How can dyslexia be defined?

This section sets out a range of theoretical possibilities. Answers to the practical question 'Who do we describe as 'dyslexic'?' will be reviewed in the next section.

The pathway of possibility divides at the start of the journey. The word 'dyslexia' might represent either a natural kind, that is, part of the reality of the world that we perceive directly; or it might represent a construct, an idea that people have developed to help them theorise about the workings of the world—in short, a tool for thinking with. Constructs themselves are neither true nor false. Instead, they are useful or otherwise, depending on our purpose. What is useful for research might not be useful for intervention and vice versa.

If 'dyslexia' is a construct, rather than a natural kind, our path divides again. The construct of 'dyslexia' might derive from a single behavioural feature, or it might derive from a set of behavioural features. If 'dyslexia' derives from a set of behavioural features, the path divides once more. Either 'dyslexia' derives from a set of behavioural features, or 'signs', all of which are both necessary and sufficient for identifying a person as 'dyslexic', or it derives from a set of behavioural features, none of which is necessary or sufficient by itself, although a specified number of those features might be sufficient for identifying a person as 'dyslexic' (Bailey, 1973). The definitions collected in *Appendix 1* and the analysis in *Appendix 2*, suggest that there is a 'dyslexia' in every one of these possible categories.

> Dyslexia can be defined in more ways than one, but each definition outlines a different concept.

Who do we describe as 'dyslexic'?

Not surprisingly, then, there is no consensus as to who might be described as 'dyslexic'.

- Either people are 'dyslexic' if they have alphabetic skills deficits (Seymour, 1986; Stanovich, 1996).
- Or people are 'dyslexic' if they have severe and persistent difficulty in acquiring alphabetic skills, even though their difficulties might be attributable to moderate learning difficulties or sensory impairments (British Psychological Society, 1999).
- Or people are 'dyslexic' if they experience difficulty in attaining fluency by automatising word-recognition skills, so long as that difficulty can be attributed, at least in part, to a constitutional factor (Gersons-Wolfensberger & Ruijssenaars, 1997).
- Or people are 'dyslexic' if their difficulty in acquiring alphabetic skills cannot be attributed to any more probable explanation (such as moderate learning disability or sensory impairment), especially if that explanation relates to experience or opportunity; and this definition is 'exclusionary' (World Federation of Neurology, 1968).
- Or, with a difference of emphasis, people are 'dyslexic' if their difficulty in acquiring alphabetic skills is accompanied by specific neurological impairments, no one of which may be necessary or sufficient for diagnosis; and this definition is 'inclusionary' (Miles, 1982).
- Or people are 'dyslexic' if they show a characteristically uneven pattern of facility and difficulty; this definition, too, is inclusionary (Miles, 1983).
- Or people are 'dyslexic' if they share a secondary characteristic with others who have difficulty in acquiring alphabetic skills, even if they do not experience this difficulty themselves (Miles, Wheeler, & Haslum, 2003).

The various possible answers to the question 'Who do we describe as 'dyslexic'?' imply, in their turn, a variety of causal assumptions. But before we consider the causes of dyslexia, we need to remind ourselves that exclusionary definitions of dyslexia are primarily research definitions (Vellutino, 1979). Although exclusionary definitions relying upon a discrepancy between measured IQ and attainment may be crucially important in developing the theory of dyslexia, their sole justification is to identify potential research participants (Nicolson, 1996; Torgesen, 1989). Otherwise, the observed differences between dyslexics and non-dyslexics may simply reflect differences in intellectual ability and so tell us nothing about dyslexia itself (McCrory, 2003).

Inclusionary definitions may be misleading in a different way. A 'pattern of difficulties' approach (Miles, 1983) is sometimes assumed to imply an absolute distinction between impaired and normal abilities, by analogy with the 'holes in the mind' found in stroke or brain injury patients. However, the presence of fully-realised abilities in other domains cannot be taken for granted in developmental disorders. If there is a genetic abnormality, then it is possible that the whole of a person's development will be atypical (Karmiloff-Smith et al., 2003), so that their 'pattern' of difficulty is one of muted contrasts.

For the purpose of intervention, several studies have questioned the validity of the IQ-discrepancy criterion (Aaron, 1997; Fletcher et al., 1992; Gustafson & Samuelsson, 1999; Hatcher, 2000; Klicpera & Klicpera, 2001; Siegel, 1992). Contrary to what people may sometimes assume, IQ is not a measure of intellectual potential (Stanovich, 1999); neither is it a measure of ability to benefit from intervention (Vellutino et al., 2000). Meta-analysis has shown that 'any classification of poor readers based on IQ-discrepancy is an artefactual distinction based on arbitrary subdivisions of the normal distribution' (Stuebing et al., 2002). On measures of decoding ability, there is no great difference between IQ-discrepant and non-discrepant poor readers (Vellutino, 2001).

Given a conjectural association between dyslexia and 'right-hemisphere' abilities in a 'pathology of superiority' (Geschwind, 1984), it is unlikely that the last word has been written on this topic. On anecdotal evidence (Davis, 1994; West, 1997), the belief that 'difficulty in learning to read is not a wholly tragic life sentence but is often accompanied by great talents' (Stein & Talcott, 1999) may seem attractive. However, systematic investigation has found little if any support for it (Adelman & Adelman, 1987; Everatt, 1997; Thomas, 2000; von Karolyi et al., 2003; Winner et al., 2001).

Adult literacy tutors need to be wary of any reading disability construct with its origins in a 'folk psychology' based on conjecture, correlation and inferences from anecdotal evidence. 'Folk' taxonomies differ greatly from scientific, theory-based taxonomies (i.e. principled classification schemes) in the overall patterns they see in nature (Ziman, 2000); folk taxonomies may be ecologically valid, but reasoning about them as if they were theory-based often leads people into error (Atran, 1998). (To take an analogy, the frog, the eel and the elephant seal are each viable on land or in water. Ecologically they have something in common, but no taxonomic theory can make their association meaningful.)

It will become evident in the course of this review that current methods of identification of who is (or can be described as) 'dyslexic' map loosely, if at all, to current theories. This is entirely proper. Although the research programmes in cognitive psychology, physiology and genetics are exciting, they may need to continue for many years before their findings inform methods of diagnosis or prevention. The scientists themselves advise that much of their work is, in the nature of scientific enquiry, conjectural. While the research must be supported, too much should not be expected of it too soon.

People can be described as 'dyslexic' on a variety of criteria, not all of which are compatible.

What kind of causal process might result in dyslexia?

Once more, the theoretical pathway divides. There might be either one cause or more than one cause of 'dyslexia'. If there is only one cause, it has to be either biological or experiential. However, if there is more than one cause, the causes might be either biological, or experiential, or part biological and part experiential. If there is more than one cause, the causes might take effect separately or in combination. If the causes take effect in combination, they might do so independently, in a 'main effect' model; or one cause might mediate the effect of another cause, whether by exacerbating it or by alleviating it, in a static 'interactional' model; or there might be continuing and progressive interplay over time between biological and experiential causes, in a dynamic 'transactional' model (Gottlieb & Halpern, 2002; Gottlieb et al., 1998; Sameroff & Chandler, 1975).

These causes may take effect at different developmental stages. They may be immediate or remote, with respect to learning how the alphabet encodes the spoken language. A cause at one stage in development might be supplemented by a second cause at a later stage. One cause might mediate the effect of another. At every stage from conception onwards, some event might affect a person's acquisition of alphabetic skills, to their benefit or detriment. There can be many different courses of individual development before a learner reaches the final common pathway of failure to acquire alphabetic skills at the expected age and with a fluency that makes reading for meaning both informative and enjoyable.

In short, there may be no single causal process. If it turns out that there is indeed no single causal process, then no single theory of reading failure can explain *every* individual failure. Indeed, it might be that no single theory could fully explain *any* individual failure or, at the extreme, that a fully-developed theory might explain one case only.

This analysis has used the metaphor of a dividing pathway. In an ideal world, there would be only a single pathway. On the landscape of 'dyslexia', however, there are many pathways, and it seems that almost every one is—rightly or wrongly— signposted to our destination.

Samples of the evidence for these observations can be found in *Appendices 1* and *2*.

Dyslexia might be a final pathway common to many causal processes.

What is the prevalence of dyslexia?

Although people sometimes speak of the 'incidence' of dyslexia, incidence is the frequency with which new cases occur and are diagnosed over a period of time (Barker et al., 1998). The proportion of dyslexic individuals in a population at any one time is properly called the 'prevalence rate' (Everitt & Wykes, 1999), although 'prevalence' is the term in general use.

The previous section implies that any estimate of the prevalence of dyslexia will reflect the chosen definition and how it is operationalised. No two of those definitions could possibly identify the same individuals, or the same number of individuals, in any population. It has been shown that prevalence estimates for dyslexia are susceptible to definitional manipulation over a wide range (Snowling et al., 2000a). In the absence of a definition that provides unequivocal identification criteria, all statements about prevalence are guesses; they are value judgements, not scientific facts (Kavale & Forness, 2000). All the same, there can be no doubt that the higher the estimate is, the more likely it will be to confound dyslexia with ordinary reading difficulty.

The British Dyslexia Association's prevalence estimates of either 4 per cent for severe dyslexia or 10 per cent to include mild dyslexia have been described as 'both theoretically and technically contentious' (Pumfrey, 2001). Lower, but possibly no less contentious, are the estimate of 2.29 per cent for (what was then called) 'specific reading retardation' obtained from the Child Health and Education Study cohort (Rodgers, 1983) and the figure of 2.08 per cent given not as a prevalence estimate but as representing 'the children in the cohort about whose dyslexia one can have the most confidence' (Miles et al., 1993). In the original standardisation sample for the British Ability Scales (BAS), 8.5 per cent were defined as showing general reading backwardness, while a further 3.2 per cent were defined as showing 'specific reading retardation' (Tyler & Elliott, 1988). Because 'specific reading retardation' is a wider concept than developmental dyslexia, the prevalence of dyslexia must have been less than 3.2 per cent in the BAS standardisation sample.

However, where dyslexics are identified by IQ-discrepancy methods, prevalence estimates may be particularly sensitive to teaching techniques; reading difficulty rates are higher with whole-language methods than with systematic and explicit phonics and highest of all among socially disadvantaged learners (Chapman et al., 2001; Nicholson, 1997). With all such estimates, unstable diagnoses raise further doubts about their reliability (Badian, 1999; Haslum, 1989).

It may well be that in asking about prevalence we are posing an inappropriate question. If we take the perspective that 'developmental disorders are not diseases that one does or does not have but are behaviorally defined dimensional traits along a continuum with fuzzy edges and a wide range of severity' (Rapin, 2002), then questions about prevalence are misconceived; 'there is no crisp partition between normalcy and disorder ... even when there is no controversy regarding the identification of prototypic exemplars' (Rapin, 2002).

None of these difficulties should worry adult literacy tutors. If a reliable estimate of the prevalence of dyslexia in the general population were ever available, tutors should not expect to find the same rate among their students, nor is it likely that any student rate would be stable over place, time and first-language status.

Adult literacy tutors may nevertheless appreciate a word of warning about the high prevalence sometimes reported for dyslexia among offenders (e.g. Alm & Andersson, 1997; Davies & Byatt, 1998; Kirk & Reid, 2001; Morgan, 1997; Turner et al., 2000). As the studies in question do not differentiate dyslexics from ordinary poor readers, their prevalence estimates must be inflated (Rice, 2000; Samuelsson et al., 2003; Snowling et al., 2000). A history of childhood disadvantage is more frequent among prisoners than it is in the general population (Dodd & Hunter, 1992; Social Exclusion Unit, 2002); between childhood disadvantage and low literacy, a causal association is well-documented (Cox & Jones, 1983; Davie et al., 1972; Kolvin et al., 1990; MacKay, 1999; Mortimore & Blackstone, 1982; Nicholson, 1997; Richman, Stevenson, & Graham, 1982; Tough, 1982). Accordingly, it is reasonable to expect that prisoners' reading skills will reflect their social circumstances and ability levels (Putnins, 1999), which is what systematic enquiries have found (Black et al., 1990; Haigler et al., 1994).

In passing, tutors are advised that the frequently cited ALBSU study is an unreliable guide to prisoner literacy, because of its haphazard sampling and poor data quality — problems that were not reported on publication (ALBSU, 1994).

After social and educational background variables have been taken into account, there appears to be no support for the belief that either dyslexics or ordinary poor readers are over-represented in prison populations. It follows that, as careful investigations have shown, the correlation between low literacy and offending does not indicate a causal relationship (Farrington, 1998; Fergusson & Lynskey, 1997; Flood-Page et al., 2000; Gottfredson, 2001; Maguin et al., 1993; and see Malmgren et al., 1999; Maughan et al., 1996; Smart et al., 2001).

The topic of screening and its implications for the determination of prevalence, is discussed in *Appendix 8*.

Prevalence estimates for dyslexia are arbitrary and may owe more to politics than to science.

High estimates of the prevalence of dyslexia in prisons are inflated by the inclusion of 'ordinary poor readers' and are likely to be gross over-estimates.

Research issues

Four issues in dyslexia research follow directly from the conceptual issues.

1. Choosing the concept

The first issue concerns the concept itself. The choice of concept may or may not be reflected in the term chosen to identify it, whether it is 'dyslexia', 'specific reading retardation', 'reading disability', 'unexpected reading difficulty', 'learning disability', or even 'low literacy'. The concepts have varying degrees of overlap and entail different causal assumptions (or none at all), although it is not always the case that the causal assumptions reflect those implied by the chosen term. 'Dyslexia', for example, implies a biological cause (see *Appendix 1*), although this is not always clear from the way in which the term is used. By contrast, while 'reading disability' and 'specific reading retardation' embrace 'dyslexia' they are concepts that do not embody any causal assumptions.

Unlike the concepts of 'reading disability' and 'specific reading retardation', the concept of 'dyslexia' embodies a causal theory—namely, that the origin of the difficulty is biological.

2. Making the concept a reality

The second issue concerns the method by which the chosen concept is applied in practice (or 'operationalised'). Practitioners and researchers have employed a number of methods to identify their target group for intervention or comparison:

- The simplest method is possibly age-discrepant performance on a standard attainment test.
- An alternative is IQ-discrepant performance on a standard attainment test, sometimes but not always adjusted by a regression formula. (Either or both of these methods, used informally, will prompt referral for assessment in everyday life. However, it needs to be recognised that a statistically significant difference between two groups does not necessarily imply that the difference between them is categorical; it may only be a matter of degree.)
- A third course is the use of a behavioural screening instrument, sometimes but not always followed up with an educational psychologist's assessment using a psychometric test battery with an intelligence scale.
- A fourth course is to determine a discrepancy between reading comprehension and listening comprehension.

- A fifth course is to undertake differential diagnosis by exclusionary conditions, so that the target group consists of people whose poor reading skills cannot otherwise be explained.
- A sixth course is to identify the target group by neurological soft signs and associated characteristics, whether or not those 'signs' only co-occur with poor reading.
- A seventh course is effectively to delegate the selection in some way, by identifying the target group on the basis of attendance at some form of special education or at a clinic.
- An eighth course is to carry out a programme of 'conventional' (i.e. explicit and systematic) instruction in the alphabetic principle with an undifferentiated group of poor readers and to identify the 'treatment-resisters' as the true dyslexics on the ground that response to 'conventional' instruction fails to meet one of the exclusionary criteria and thus identifies the treatment-responder as a 'false positive'.

None of these methods is problem-free. For example, the choice of cut-point on a dimensional scale needs to be guided by norms, but opinions may differ as to whether those norms should be for the entire country, for the institution attended by the test-taker, or for the test-taker's social background and opportunities (Alexander & Martin, 2000). With IQ-achievement discrepancy as with age-discrepancy, the choice of cut-point is largely arbitrary. No cut-point on any continuum serves to demarcate causal explanations. While a person's learning need may be reflected by the severity of their difficulty, there is no clear relationship between the cause of a reading difficulty and its severity and neither is there a clear relationship between the severity of difficulty and the prospect of successful learning.

Many researchers would agree with the conclusion that 'the concept of discrepancy operationalised using IQ scores does not produce a unique subgroup of children with [reading difficulty] when a chronological age design is used; rather, it simply provides an arbitrary subdivision of the reading-IQ distribution that is fraught with statistical and other interpretative problems' (Fletcher et al., 1994). Perhaps the most important objection to using IQ may be that it is a combined measure of both innate and acquired ability, not a measure of purely innate ability (Ceci, 1991; Mackintosh, 1998); it is necessarily affected by any neurological defect involved in a learning problem (Rie, 1987).

The problems of quantitative approaches to identifying the target group are not resolved by qualitative methods of identification using behavioural correlates or 'signs' of dyslexia. Among the problems here are the difficulty in establishing which, if any, of a number of correlates may be causal and what (given a causal relationship) is the main direction of causality. 'Soft signs', in particular, are found in some people without learning problems and absent in others who experience learning difficulties; a moderate number of minor 'signs' is quite compatible with normality. Some 'soft signs' point in more than one direction; they may indicate a lack of motor learning, rather than any inability to learn. They are as likely to indicate the exclusionary conditions normally eliminated by differential diagnosis as they are to indicate dyslexia.

However, the point at issue is not the validity of any of these identification techniques but their variety. This variety has implications for the research literature; even where researchers use the same conceptual term, it cannot be assumed that they have understood it in the same way. (*Appendix 3* shows that variety may be the rule here, too.) Less obvious, but no less important, is the variety of ways in which the concepts have been operationalised; for example, the same causal explanation is not necessarily valid for all scores in the lowest range of any dimensional test. If assumptions like these are questionable in research involving children, they are much more questionable in research involving adults.

Researchers use at least eight different methods to identify people with dyslexia.

Their choice of method determines which people will be identified as dyslexic.

A participant who is dyslexic in one research study would not necessarily be dyslexic in another.

3. Choosing the comparison group

Just as the identification of target groups is problematic, so is the identification of their normal comparisons:

- A researcher may choose to compare dyslexic people and superior readers of the same age (the 'age-level' match).
- To compare dyslexic people with a younger but normally-reading group (the 'reading-level' match). Implicit (if not explicit) in these comparisons are two assumptions: that all poor readers are dyslexic and that all dyslexics are poor readers.
- A third strategy is to take an undifferentiated group of people with low reading skills and subject their test scores to factor analysis or a similar technique in order to identify sub-groups of dyslexic and non-dyslexic people. This strategy is essential for investigating claims that dyslexic people can be distinguished from 'ordinary poor readers'.
- A fourth strategy, albeit an uncommon one, is to compare discrepancy-defined dyslexic people with non-discrepant, age-matched 'ordinary poor readers'.

Where reading-level matches are involved, there is a choice of measures, some of which might be more appropriate than others. For example, word recognition skills might provide a more appropriate match than reading comprehension level does; the two measures may identify different although overlapping target groups. In word recognition, a measure of decoding accuracy for regular words or pseudowords might conceivably identify a different comparison group from that identified by measures of irregular-word reading or reading rate. Given that readers make strategy choices or trade-offs between speed and accuracy, the composition of these groups might—and probably will—change over time.

Where researchers attempt to match groups on IQ, they have a choice between full-scale, non-verbal, or verbal measures and this choice, too, will influence the selection of comparison group members. If no attempt is made to match the groups on demographic measures, they may nevertheless be found to differ in terms of socio-economic status and all that this difference implies with respect to language development and educational opportunity.

Whether and how dyslexic people differ from non-dyslexic people depends on the researcher's choice of comparison group.

Researchers have at least four options for choosing comparison groups.

Within those options, there are further sources of variation.

4. Choosing the strategy

The fourth issue concerns research strategies.

Although the options are seldom discussed, the decision to study groups rather than individuals is another strategy choice for the researcher. It is a matter of serious debate whether group studies are the appropriate method for investigating mixed populations in either developmental or acquired disorders (Bates & Appelbaum, 1994; Caramazza & McCloskey, 1988; Martin, 1995). Case studies, which 'address the problem of false generalisation from heterogeneous group means to individual group members', are not without problems of their own, such as that of comparing the actual performance of an impaired subject with the theoretical performance of a 'normal' subject (Ellis & Large, 1987). However, in developmental dyslexia, by contrast with loss of reading ability through a stroke or head injury, single-case studies are both rare and untypical.

Groups are often studied in a contrasting-groups research design, but this design is flawed whenever the groups are obtained by cutting a continuous distribution. Small-scale studies in which the groups differ on a single measure ('univariate contrasting-groups studies') commonly claim 'significant' between-group differences on the measure of interest, despite an appreciable overlap. However, only a minority of the target group may cause the differences. As researchers sometimes discover, controversy may be an inevitable consequence of applying a research strategy based on univariate contrasting-groups methods when the experimental group is not homogeneous and the basis for the disability is multivariate in nature (Fletcher & Satz, 1985). The most defensible position may be a pragmatic one: that group comparisons are justified only when the number of participants is large enough to permit statistically significant differentiation on all theoretically important measures, so that the most probable causes of group differences can be identified.

Many studies of reading difficulties have a cross-sectional design; that is to say, they take place at a single point in time. This is not the most obviously appropriate design for research into development. Evidence from longitudinal research shows that differences between individuals are unstable over time, which implies that variations in development may invalidate some of the conclusions drawn from cross-sectional studies of developmental disorders. Longitudinal studies of reading development have shown that individuals' non-heritable influences may change over time (de Jong & van der Leij, 1999; Snowling & Nation, 1997; Sprenger-Charolles et al., 2001; Wright et al., 1996), although the genetic influences shaping their development appear to be stable (Wadsworth et al., 2001).

The choice of research method has significant implications for the research findings: different methods applied to the same study population can lead to markedly different conclusions, not all of which are likely to be valid.

Interpretational issues

Do 'dyslexic' brains differ from 'normal' brains?
Introduction
By now it will be clear, both from the preceding sections on conceptual and methodological issues and also from *Appendixes 1, 2* and *3* (dyslexia definitions and their operationalisation in research), that the interpretation of evidence for a qualitative distinction between developmental dyslexia and 'ordinary' problems with literacy learning is anything but straightforward. Could it be true that researchers have 'misconstrued their object of study—unexplained underachievement—interpreting it neurologically and ignoring classroom practices and events' (Carrier, 1983), so that the theory masks societal forces as they affect academic performance? Are people justified in believing that the neurological studies validate dyslexia as a qualitatively distinct condition? How should the neurological evidence be interpreted? Also, can we afford to forget that 'the diagnosis of dyslexia is itself a theory, distinguishing reading failure arising ultimately from internal rather than solely external reasons, but a rather unspecified one' (Frith, 2001)?

For a long time, most of our knowledge about the workings of the brain was gained in the course of autopsies on people whose previously normal abilities had been compromised by head injuries or strokes. These findings suggested that people are born with a brain rather like a Swiss Army knife, with a modular component for every purpose—an analogy that now seems false (Karmiloff-Smith, 1992; Quartz & Sejnowski, 1997). Accordingly, loss of function was not a good guide to what happens in developmental disorders (Alarcón et al., 1999; Karmiloff-Smith, 1998; Thomas & Karmiloff-Smith, 2002). In any case, there have been very few autopsy studies of people who had experienced difficulty in learning to read, write and spell.

Over the past 15 years, a number of brain imaging (or 'scanning') techniques have been introduced. So there are now two sources of evidence for differences between 'dyslexic' and 'normal' brains. From *post-mortem* studies, there is evidence of differences in brain structure; from brain imaging studies of living people (or *in vivo* studies), there is evidence of differences in brain structure and function. To date, the *in vivo* studies are almost without exception cross-sectional. However, in future, prospective longitudinal imaging studies may show how brains change as people acquire complex skills.

The table and figures in *Appendix 10* may help readers to locate the brain areas named in the following sub-sections.

Evidence from post-mortem studies
Structurally, the brains in the autopsy studies reveal anomalies at two levels of analysis (Galaburda et al., 1989). At the microscopic (or neuronal) level, researchers have found abnormal outgrowths known as 'ectopias' and abnormal infoldings known as 'microgyria', visible on the surface of the brain (Galaburda et al., 1989). In addition to these abnormalities in the outer layer of the brain, or cortex, researchers have found a magnocellular defect within the inner chamber of the brain, in a part of the thalamus known as the lateral geniculate nucleus, which is activated during visual processing (Livingstone et al., 1991). At the macroscopic level, researchers have found an unusual symmetry in that part of the temporal lobe known as the *planum temporale* (Galaburda et al., 1989), which is normally larger in the left hemisphere, where it is activated in tasks related to language, than in the right hemisphere (Shapleske et al., 1999).

The causes of these outgrowths and infoldings have yet to be determined. Their origin does not appear to be directly genetic (Galaburda et al., 2001). Possible environmental causes include the adverse effects of testosterone upon fetal neuronal development (Geschwind & Galaburda, 1985), viral inflammation from influenza (Livingston et al., 1993) and toxic substances such as lead or alcohol (Hynd & Semrud-Clikeman, 1989). Although it is possible that individual differences in susceptibility to environmental hazards could be heritable and although some developmental abnormalities are heritable in the form of genetic mutations or chromosomal defects (Baraitser, 1997; McKusick, 1994; Weatherall, 1991), there is no need to assume that every developmental abnormality is heritable.

Ectopias and microgyria develop before birth, at a late stage of neuronal migration (Galaburda et al., 2001). They are associated with higher degrees of connectivity, both within their own cerebral hemisphere and between the two hemispheres (Galaburda et al., 1989). The effect that these microscopic abnormalities have upon human cognitive functioning must be inferred from laboratory experiments with rats and mice, where there is evidence that they impair both auditory processing (Galaburda et al., 2001; Peiffer et al., 2002) and the normal balance of arousal and inhibition (Gabel & Turco, 2002; Redecker et al., 1998).

Cerebral asymmetries have an ancient ancestry in primate evolution (Steele, 1998). Perhaps for this reason, they may be related more closely to handedness than to language lateralisation (Annett, 1985; Corballis, in press; McManus, 1999). In the course of individual human development, planar asymmetries (differences between the brain hemispheres in the *planum temporale*) are established before birth (Wada et al., 1975). While the extent to which asymmetries are influenced by heredity and environment is unclear (Eckert et al., 2002), it is plausible that genes are the major cause of asymmetric neural tissue development (McManus, 1999).

However, there is no uniform pattern of asymmetry. In the general population, about three in four people have left-greater-than-right asymmetry, whereas about one in 12 have no detectable asymmetry and about one in eight have right-greater-than-left asymmetry (Shapleske et al., 1999). Language functions may not always be lateralised in the cerebral hemisphere with the larger *planum temporale* (Moffatt et al., 1998). The degree of planar asymmetry appears to be reflected in individual differences between verbal and nonverbal ability (Riccio & Hynd, 2000), in which case it could represent normal variation rather than a pathological state. However, a reduction in planar asymmetry has been found in schizophrenics (Saugstad, 1999), where it is associated with disordered language but not with difficulty in learning to read.

The significance of abnormalities in the magnocellular system is particularly difficult to determine in relation to dyslexia. For a more detailed consideration of the evidence, readers are referred to the later section on dyslexia and processing speed.

However, some words of caution are appropriate. Although evidence from the post-mortem studies could be interpreted to support distinctions both between dyslexics and 'normal' readers and also between dyslexics and ordinary poor readers, there are three reasons why this interpretation is tenuous.

First, the post-mortem research involves few brains. The numbers vary from one study to another, but studies typically involve between three and seven brains. From small samples like these, the findings are at best suggestive rather than definitive.

Second, it is unclear whether the brains in the post-mortem studies are representative of dyslexic brains in general (Beaton, 2002). Even if that were the case, it would be unsafe to assume that the abnormalities in those brains are specific to dyslexia, because the full nature and extent of the cognitive and behavioural problems experienced by their donors was not identified before they died (Bishop, 2002). The specificity of the post-mortem brain abnormalities is questionable with respect to *planum temporale* symmetry, since it is possible that dyslexia (defined as a phonologically-based reading disability) might be associated with asymmetrical brain structures, whereas symmetrical brain structures might be associated with the linguistic deficit known as Specific Language Impairment (Leonard et al., 1998).

Third, the evidence from brain imaging studies offers no support for the notion that there is a causal relationship between dyslexia and an absence of left-greater-than-right asymmetry of the *planum temporale*: one non-dyslexic brain in three shows similar symmetry or reversed asymmetry; some researchers find abnormally large right plana, while others find abnormally small left plana; patterns of symmetry or asymmetry vary from study to study; and it has not been established that deviations from normal asymmetry are exclusive to dyslexia (Beaton, 2002; Cossu, 1999; Habib, 2000; Heiervang et al., 2000; Robichon et al., 2000b; Rumsey et al., 1997a; Shapleske et al., 1999).

Whether 'dyslexic' brains differ in structure from 'normal' brains is not a question that can be determined on the evidence of the post-mortem research. While there are undoubted abnormalities in the autopsied brains, their relationship to dyslexia is open to question. Although the post-mortem findings have suggested interesting new lines of investigation, lack of convergence with findings from more recent *in vivo* studies is an obstacle to their acceptance.

Evidence from in vivo *studies: structural differences*
Although no consistent morphological correlates have been associated with developmental dyslexia in children or in adults (Cossu, 1999), there is broad agreement about the main regions of interest. Thus, *in vivo* studies of 'dyslexic' and 'normal' brains examine two kinds of structural anomaly. They consider both the patterns of symmetry in the temporal lobes and the cerebellum and also the connectivity between left and right cerebral hemispheres. At the time of writing, magnetic resonance imaging (MRI), the technique employed for this purpose, cannot be used to resolve details as fine as the microscopic abnormalities reported in the post-mortem studies.

The question of symmetry in the temporal lobes has typically focused on the *planum temporale*, which is considered above. Additionally, dyslexia appears to be associated with lack of normal asymmetry in the cerebellum, which may also be associated with mixed handedness in ways that have yet to be explained (Rae et al., 2002).

Connectivity between the two sides of the brain is a function of the *corpus callosum*, the mass of white-matter fibres that connects the brain's two hemispheres. The issue of the link between anatomical observations and clinical abnormalities in the *corpus callosum* remains fundamentally unresolved (Habib & Robichon, 2002). Atypical development of the *corpus callosum* may be characteristic of dyslexics (Hynd et al., 1995; Rumsey et al., 1996; von Plessen et al., 2002), although the evidence is conflicting (Habib et al., 2000a). While it is possible for qualitative differences in *corpus callosum* morphology to have biological origins (Robichon et al., 2000a), it is also possible that they could be caused by atypical experience

(Moffatt et al., 1998), including experiences associated with childhood deprivation (De Bellis, 2001).

However, reports of anatomical differences between 'dyslexic' and 'non-dyslexic' brains must not be taken to imply that they are causes rather than consequences of reading problems. People who have never learned how to represent speech in writing cannot perform mental functions requiring an ability to spell (Castro-Caldas & Reis, 2003). These mental functions have a biological counterpart in the anatomical development of the brain (Carr & Posner, 1995; Castro-Caldas & Reis, 2003). A developmental pattern can thus be the consequence rather than the cause of atypical learning activity and not only in the representation of speech (Hsieh et al., 2001).

Consider two examples. Exceptional developments in the brain area associated with spatial awareness have been shown in London taxi-drivers, who need to master 'the knowledge' of routes and destinations in the capital (Maguire et al., 2000) and both functional and structural differences have been shown between the brains of musical instrumentalists and non-musicians (Schlaug, 2001). In each case, it is a reasonable assumption that these differences develop as adaptations to experience; for, although the ability to adapt is present in the cradle, the taxi-driver's 'knowledge' and the abilities to play the xylophone or spell its name are not.

The structural imaging literature contains many inconsistent findings. They can be accounted for by the use of a variety of scanning protocols and image analysis methods, by small study populations, by wide variations in the diagnostic criteria used to define dyslexia, by heterogeneous samples, by non-uniform matching of controls and by lack of routine analysis for sex, handedness, socio-economic status, psychiatric co-diagnoses, intellectual ability and educational background (Filipek, 1995, 1999).

There are two further grounds for caution when the findings from structural imaging are interpreted. To begin with, simple comparisons between 'dyslexic' and 'non-dyslexic' subjects may imply categorical distinctions where the differences are really points on a continuum. Then, the abnormalities seen in 'dyslexic' brains might be assumed to be typical of dyslexia, or exclusive to dyslexia, when they are neither.

Structural findings from the imaging studies, like those from the post-mortem studies, are at best suggestive, not definitive. Indeed, it is possible that the neurological anomalies in developmental dyslexia are task-specific; that is to say, they are not structural at all but functional (McCrory et al., 2000).

Evidence from in vivo *studies: functional differences*
Certainly, the most compelling evidence for neurological anomalies in dyslexia comes from functional imaging. Both positron emission tomography (PET) and functional magnetic resonance imaging (fMRI) techniques directly relate behaviour to brain activity. They allow researchers to contrast patterns of brain activation in impaired and unimpaired readers.

Functional neuroimaging has demonstrated that reading entails much more complex patterns of activation than had been suspected on the basis of findings from post-mortem studies of stroke and brain injury patients. Formerly, reading was conceptualised in terms of two localised and self-contained components, known as Broca's area and Wernicke's area, in the dominant cerebral hemisphere (Pickle, 1998). Now, reading is known to entail a wider repertoire of distributed processes in both cerebral hemispheres (Binder et al., 1997; Price, 2000), functioning as neural networks in which Broca's and Wernicke's areas might be analogues of Crewe and Clapham junctions in the railway network. It is also evident that patterns of activation emerge and are transformed in the course of learning to read and write (Booth et al., 2001; Petersson et al., 2000).

It appears that the *normal* process of reading has a characteristic neural signature —or rather, that each linguistic subprocess has a neural signature of its own (Cabeza & Nyberg, 1997; Wise et al., 2001). For example, normal silent reading activates the left inferior parietal cortex, the right posterior temporal cortex, both sensorimotor cortices and the supplementary motor areas (Cossu, 1999). Additionally, non-word reading activates the left inferior temporal region the left inferior frontal area, and the supramarginal gyrus (Cossu, 1999). Viewing words in alphabetic script (by contrast with viewing word-like forms in false fonts) activates bilateral language areas, including the left inferior prefrontal regions and the left posterior temporal cortex (Cossu, 1999). Reading aloud and making lexical decisions also entail bilateral activation of the mid-to-posterior temporal cortex and mainly left-hemisphere activation of the inferior parietal cortex (Cossu, 1999).

Evidence for a neural signature of reading *impairment* is provided by studies reporting differential activation patterns in three key areas: the inferior frontal gyrus (Broca's area); the dorsal parieto-temporal region, incorporating the superior temporal gyrus (Wernicke's area) and angular and marginal gyri; and the left posterior inferior temporal area, incorporating the fusiform gyrus and middle temporal gyrus (McCrory, 2003).

However, these neural studies of reading impairment are not without interpretational problems (McCrory, 2003). One study reports reduced activation in Wernicke's area (Rumsey et al., 1997b), but leaves open the possibility that the same reduction might be seen in ordinary poor readers, in which case it could be interpreted as secondary to some other difficulty (McCrory, 2003). A similar reduction in activation (Shaywitz et al., 1998) might be explained as a reflection of lower levels of reading accuracy, again leaving open the possibility that it might also be characteristic of ordinary poor readers, a possibility made all the more likely in this case by a lower level of intellectual ability in the group designated as 'dyslexic' (McCrory, 2003).

Reduced activation reported in the parietal-temporal-occipital association cortex (Brunswick et al., 1999) may indicate a more robust difference (McCrory, 2003), and this finding has been replicated in a cross-linguistic comparison (Paulesu et al., 2001).

Across these and other studies, the most consistent discrepancies between the activation patterns of dyslexic and non-dyslexic participants have been in three areas: the posterior inferior temporal cortex, the left angular gyrus and the left inferior frontal cortex (McCrory, 2003).

Reduced neural activation by dyslexics in the posterior inferior temporal cortex is consistent with difficulty in retrieving phonological forms from visual stimuli, perhaps including dyslexics' frequently-reported difficulty in picture-naming (McCrory, 2003). Reduced neural activation by dyslexics in the left angular gyrus, however, might possibly be a secondary and nonspecific effect of inefficient phonological processing (McCrory, 2003). In the left frontal and precentral regions, the neural activation seen in dyslexics is greater, not less, than that seen in efficient readers and may correspond to effortful compensatory strategies involving inner speech (McCrory, 2003). Nevertheless, activation in Broca's area is not specific to dyslexia: all poor readers work harder to uncover the gestures underlying the phonological structure of words (Mody, 2003).

Differences in brain activation observed in functional imaging studies could occur for a variety of reasons (McCrory, 2003; Pennington, 1999). Even where there are consistent differences across studies, a causal association with dyslexia cannot be taken for granted (McCrory, 2003). Atypical functioning may point to nothing more 'pathological' than an unusual brain organisation set up earlier, adaptively, in response to atypical experience (Locke, 1997). An individual might exhibit contrasting responses to the same stimulus by attending to different aspects of it on separate occasions (Kuhl et al., 2001). Group differences may reflect primary cognitive deficits, but they might also reflect secondary consequences of those deficits, compensatory processing, some other behavioural impairment, or more general differences such as intelligence (McCrory, 2003). The cross-sectional nature of most functional imaging studies might also invite misinterpretation, as the pattern of impairments at an early stage of development may not resemble any pattern observed at a later stage (Bishop, 1997).

Nonetheless, functional neuroimaging is an invaluable technique for evaluating cognitive theories of dyslexia and testing their implications (McCrory, 2003). Importantly, the dynamic changes in regional cerebral blood flow challenge the established notion that phonological representations are 'located' in a particular brain area and thus sequentially accessed, as opposed to being 'activated' in parallel computational processes that are distributed across a number of brain areas (McCrory, 2003). This insight into the competitive nature of the computational process in reading, where many prospective candidates may need to be considered before a word is finally identified (Pulvermüller, 2003), suggests that the central difficulty in dyslexia could be conceptualised as a difficulty in resolving the phonological competition (McCrory, 2001).

What do the brain studies tell us?
Many adult education practitioners have grown up at a time when 'nurturism' prevailed over 'nativism'—except (paradoxically) in linguistics (e.g. Chomsky, 1957). Now, it is well understood that individual differences are joint and interactive outcomes of random genetic recombination at conception and subsequent experience (Gottlieb, 1992; Michel & Moore, 1995; Rutter, 2002). In this process as in so much else, timing is all: 'The effects of a particular set of genes depend critically on the environment in which they are expressed, while the effects of a particular sort of environment depend on the individual's genes' (Bateson & Martin, 1999).

The differences between 'dyslexic' and 'non-dyslexic' brains revealed by the autopsy and imaging studies are unquestionably biological in nature. This does not amount to proof that the differences are biological in origin. There are grounds for caution in our understanding of the brain's 'plasticity'—its capacity for adaptation and development. This understanding should lead us to prefer a 'neuroconstructivist' view of language development (Bates, 1999; Johnson, 2003; Karmiloff-Smith, 1998) to a 'nativist' view (Pinker, 1994); that is to say, to prefer a view of language ability emerging in the course of development to a view of language as an innately modular capacity. A neuroconstructivist approach to developmental disabilities (e.g. Snowling, 2000) is supported by the interpretation of findings from imaging studies that 'learning to read and write during childhood influences the functional organisation of the adult human brain' (Castro-Caldas & Reis, 2003).

From this perspective, atypical brain functioning may not be 'pathological' but rather an adaptive response to atypical experience (Locke, 1997), representing variation within the normal evolutionary range (Levelt, 2001). The discovery of a neural signature for this atypical functioning—differential activation in the three brain areas identified above—does not establish that dyslexic brains are inherently and categorically different from other brains.

Dyslexic brains differ by definition from non-dyslexic brains.

It has not been established that the observed differences are either inherent or categorical.

Is there a gene for dyslexia?
Introduction
We have seen that a careful interpretation of the brain imaging research does not— or not yet, at any rate—validate the belief that 'dyslexic' and 'non-dyslexic' brains are inherently and categorically different, as many people believe them to be. In the face of unwarranted accusations of stupidity or laziness, the dyslexic person's need for self-vindication cannot be met by findings from imaging studies. Can this need be met by research in genetics?

Modes of inheritance and their implications
From time to time the media report that 'Scientists identify dyslexia gene' (BBC), or that 'Dyslexia found in genetic jungle' (Reuters), but such reports are potentially misleading: there is no 'gene for dyslexia' in the same way that there is a gene for, say, cystic fibrosis. Although single-gene inheritance once seemed a possible mode of transmission (Smith et al., 1990) and has been reported to occur in some families (Fagerheim et al., 1999; Nopola-Hemmi et al., 2001), it now appears unlikely that dyslexia could fit a single-gene, single-disease model in which a simple genetic mutation results in failure to synthesise an essential protein (Pennington, 1999).

In one single-gene model—namely, autosomal dominant transmission—where only one parent has to transmit the gene for it to be expressed, the explanation would be consistent with the observed prevalence rate, but inconsistent with the observation that some reading-disabled individuals have no affected relatives (Plomin et al., 2001). In a second single-gene model—namely, X-linked recessive transmission—either parent can transmit the abnormal gene, but it will be expressed only if the son or daughter lacks a normal copy of it from the other parent, so that a dyslexic son would need to have a dyslexic mother whereas, for a dyslexic daughter, both parents would need to be dyslexic. This explanation is consistent with a higher reported prevalence among males, but inconsistent with the observation that reading disability passes as often from father to son as it does from mother to son (Plomin et al., 2001).

A single-gene model of heritability does not fit the observations about dyslexia, not least because of the problems it creates by assuming that dyslexics differ categorically from non-dyslexics. A better fit is offered by a multiple-gene model, which assumes that poorer readers differ dimensionally from better readers both in their genetic constitution and also in the environmental risk factors to which they are exposed (Pennington, 1999). According to this model, which currently dominates research into the genetics of reading difficulty (e.g. Cardon et al., 1994; Fisher et al., 2002; Fisher et al., 1999; Grigorenko et al., 2001; Wijsman et al., 2000), a quantitative behavioural trait could be the effect of a number of genes—perhaps dozens, perhaps hundreds—the variation in each of which adds a small difference to a wide range of outcomes in the population (Plomin et al., 2001).

Within such a multiple-gene model, it no longer makes sense to think of individuals as 'dyslexics' or 'non-dyslexics', unless in the sense that their scores fall either side of a pragmatic threshold on a reading ability test. Accordingly, it does not appear that any genes 'for dyslexia' could be simply abnormal variants of genes for normal reading (Davis et al., 2001).

Abnormalities in myelination and the synthesis of fatty acids in the brain have been proposed as explanations of processing difficulties in dyslexia and other disorders (Horrobin et al., 1995; Richardson & Ross, 2000; Stordy, 2000; Taylor et al., 2000), but the links between dyslexia and any genes coding for errors in protein synthesis are still conjectural (Francks et al., 2002; Habib, 2000). For example, a link between dyslexia and an abnormality in a gene that codes for a protein found in myelin has been suspected but not so far confirmed (Smith et al., 2001), although it cannot yet be ruled out (Turic et al., 2003).

The complexities in this field of enquiry are challenging (Ahn et al., 2001; Asherson & Curran, 2001; Gilger et al., 2001; Grigorenko, 2001; Grigorenko et al., 1997; Rutter, 2002; Wood & Grigorenko, 2001) and repay greater consideration than is possible in this review. As elsewhere, the interpretation of research findings is made difficult by the inconsistency of protocols for identifying research participants, in both quantitative genetics and molecular genetics studies. These protocols, which not infrequently employ IQ-discrepancy methods, may limit the applicability of research findings so far as adult literacy students are concerned. Although it has long been recognised that dyslexia may be familial, a familial trait may also be transmitted culturally (Pennington, 1991). Thus, contrary to what practitioners may sometimes suppose, family relationship ('familiality') alone is not a reliable indicator of genetic heritability. (As the Mitford daughters observed, whether by nature or nurture, they'd had it.)

Familiality in reading disability may have a stronger genetic component among abler people but a stronger cultural component among the less able, where the two groups also differ in terms of parental education, books in the home and the extent to which the parents read to their children (Wadsworth et al., 2000). In any population, the degree of genetic influence on individual differences depends partly on the range of the relevant environmental influences (Gayán & Olson, 2003). Reading disability studies where the participants come from the white-collar classes will produce higher estimates of heritability than would be expected from more broadly representative studies with both white- and blue-collar participants.

Policies to optimise home and school environments for learning how to read and write cannot eliminate all differences between individual outcomes and might not even narrow the range of outcomes, although they will unquestionably raise the average level of achievement. Meanwhile, in many countries the single most powerful predictor of literacy achievement is the number of books in the home (Elley, 1994). This is ostensibly an environmental measure, although it is doubtless influenced by parental genes.

Although reading difficulties are heritable, no single gene creates a qualitative difference between dyslexic and non-dyslexic people.

Instead, a number of genes may be involved, each making a quantitative contribution to the variance in reading and writing ability in the population.

The processes by which these genes take effect are not yet understood.

Do 'dyslexics' and 'non-dyslexics' differ in kind or in degree?

The statistical evidence

It might be thought that all the analysis above points to the conclusion that dyslexics and non-dyslexics differ in degree rather than kind. The question whether 'dyslexics' differ in kind (categorically) or in degree (dimensionally) from 'non-dyslexics' remains nevertheless one of the most controversial in this field (Ellis, 1985; Fletcher et al., 1994; Fredman & Stevenson, 1988; Frith, 2001; Jorm et al., 1986b; Rutter, 1978; Share et al., 1987; Tyler & Elliott, 1988; van der Wissel & Zegers, 1985). It may be a question that is best answered by reference to complex models of reading development (e.g. Ellis & Large, 1987; Jackson & Coltheart, 2001; and Stanovich, 1988).

It is important to specify whether the 'non-dyslexics' in the comparison group are good readers or 'ordinary' poor readers. Much confusion appears to derive from failure to provide this specification. The critical question in dyslexia research is not whether dyslexic people in particular differ from 'normal' readers, neither is it how 'poor' readers in general differ from "normal" readers. It is *whether dyslexic people differ from other poor readers*. Yet the designs of many research studies leave this last question open. To test the hypotheses that developmental dyslexics differ from both normal readers and 'ordinary' poor readers, researchers need two control groups, not one. They also need to take both psychometric and demographic measures, so that they can control for the effects of potentially confounding variables. Without those controls, the effects of dyslexia are likely to be confounded with those of conditions explicitly excluded from the concept of dyslexia (Chiappe et al., 2001).

In the Isle of Wight study, the presence of two categorically distinct traits in reading ability was suggested by a bimodal distribution of reading ability—one with two peaks or humps, like a Bactrian camel (Yule et al., 1974). However, while such a distribution might be interpreted as evidence for a discrete phenomenon of specific reading difficulty it cannot be interpreted as evidence for a genetically distinct syndrome of dyslexia, since methods of teaching as well as biological differences could create a bimodal distribution (Rutter & Yule, 1975).

No evidence for a bimodal distribution in reading ability was found in the Child Health and Education Study of the 1970 birth cohort (Rodgers, 1983), although the same data-set has been analysed to investigate—but, as the investigators made clear, not to determine—the prevalence of dyslexia (Miles et al., 1993). The Child Health and Education Study findings are tentative with respect to both the lack of consensus for the criteria by which the dyslexic cohort members were identified and also the uncertain sensitivity and specificity of the chosen method of identification (Haslum, 1989).

By contrast, in the Connecticut study, a unimodal distribution—with a single peak or hump, like a dromedary—suggested that reading ability is a single, dimensionally-distributed trait in the population and that 'dyslexics' are those at the lower end of the continuum, not a discrete group (Shaywitz et al., 1992). However, the logic of this interpretation has been questioned on the ground that, although a dip in the observed distribution implies a mixture of underlying processes, the converse does not necessarily hold. What is more, the failure to find a dip could be due to both the obscuring effects of measurement error (Abelson, 1995) and the presence of a few etiologically distinct factors (Pennington et al., 1992) one of which might be rapid naming ability (Meyer et al., 1998; Wood & Grigorenko, 2001).

The statistical findings are mixed and do not present irrefutable evidence for differences in either kind or degree between dyslexic and non-dyslexic people.

The psychometric evidence

Although 'dyslexics' are easily shown to differ from good (or even adequate) readers on a number of reading-related assessments, we need to ask whether the same assessments differentiate 'dyslexic' from 'non-dyslexic' (i.e. ordinary) poor readers (Stanovich, 1988). It now seems that a number of reading-related characteristics once thought to be specific to dyslexia are shared with other novice readers (Ellis, 1985; Taylor et al., 1979). These characteristics include reversal errors with letters of the alphabet (Fowler et al., 1977; Mann & Brady, 1988; Worthy & Viise, 1996), directional sequencing errors (Vellutino, 1979), pseudoword reading difficulties (Bishop, 2001), phonemic segmentation difficulties (Cole & Sprenger-Charolles, 1999; Metsala, 1999) and spelling of sight vocabulary (Scarborough, 1984). The characteristics are also shared with neurologically normal people who have had no opportunity to learn how to read (Castro-Caldas et al., 1998; Kolinsky et al., 1994; Lukatela et al., 1995; Morais et al., 1979). Moreover, between-group differences on those measures are also associated with differences between phonics-based and whole-word methods of teaching reading (Alegria et al., 1982; Thompson & Johnston, 2000). Students tend to perceive words in the way that they are taught to perceive them (Huey, 1908). This appears to be the case whether or not they are taught in a transparent orthography (Cardoso-Martins, 2001), where each phoneme is always or almost always represented by the same grapheme, as in Finnish (always) or Italian (almost always).

Although dyslexic people are believed by some scholars to differ dimensionally rather than categorically from non-dyslexics (Shaywitz et al., 1992), this may not mean that the most impaired readers are dyslexic (see also page 61). When IQ-discrepancy criteria have been used to distinguish dyslexics from ordinary poor readers, the ordinary poor readers have obtained lower scores than dyslexics on memory span, segmentation, and rhyme tasks (Fawcett et al., 2001) and also on a pseudoword repetition task (Jorm et al., 1986a).

With respect to differences unrelated to reading, a number of apparently interesting associations between 'dyslexia' and other variables (such as blue-collar social status, inconsistent left-handedness and autoimmune disorders such as hay fever) have been found to disappear when subject to the scrutiny of multivariate techniques of data analysis (Haslum, 1989). This finding is an example of a general warning seldom heeded in folk psychology: namely, that simple bivariate correlations do not establish a causal relationship and cannot determine a causal direction. A more specific warning, against reification, is also appropriate: 'Categorical diagnoses do not refer to real discrete entities; they are only meaningful as approximate descriptions that remind the clinician of prominent characteristics of specific combinations of quantitative traits' (Cloninger, 2000).

Psychometric findings suggest that differences between dyslexic and non-dyslexic readers are differences in degree, not differences in kind.

Are diagnoses of dyslexia stable across methods of ascertainment?

A sample of dyslexic people defined by IQ-discrepancy using a cut-off of one standard deviation (1 SD) below the mean on a continuous measure of decoding skill will be about three times as large as a sample identified in the same population by a cut-off of 2 SD below the mean on the same measure. Because human traits are distributed in multidimensional space (Cloninger et al., 1997), the two groups will also differ in kind as well as in size (Ellis, 1985). In neither case will extreme scores indicate a reason for their extremity (Frith, 2001). Groups defined on quantitative measures such as IQ-discrepancy are by their nature heterogeneous and different patterns of heterogeneity result from different definitions. Diagnostic criteria inferred from one group may thus be too broad, or too narrow, for the other group.

Some problems in making IQ-related identifications have been analysed in a study of children with 'specific reading retardation' (Bishop & Butterworth, 1980), a construct which despite its similarity to 'dyslexia' carries no implication as to cause and does not imply a single cause (Yule & Rutter, 1976). The argument runs like this (Bishop & Butterworth, 1980):

- If learners with 'specific reading retardation' are defined as those with a *nonverbal* IQ of 90 or more who are reading 12 months or more below age level, then, since reading is strongly related to verbal IQ, poor readers would generally have low verbal IQs. However, since verbal IQ and nonverbal IQ are positively correlated, most specifically reading-retarded learners would have low nonverbal IQs, yet the definition would exclude those learners.
- If, on the other hand, specifically reading-retarded learners are defined as those with a *full-scale* IQ of 90 or more who are reading 12 months below age level, then the poor readers by this definition (who have a low verbal IQ as poor readers) would have a relatively high nonverbal IQ and so there would be a larger proportion of learners with verbal-nonverbal discrepancy among the specifically reading-retarded group.
- Alternatively, if specifically reading-retarded learners are defined as those with a *verbal* IQ of 90 or more who are reading 12 months or more below age level, then there would be no verbal-nonverbal discrepancy relationship with specific reading retardation. What is more, if verbal IQ were the basis for selection, it would increase the proportion of males classified as specifically reading-retarded.

Learners might be most appropriately described as specifically 'reading-retarded' only if their reading ability is disproportionately poor in relation to their verbal (rather than nonverbal or full-scale) IQ, but such people are rare and their rarity would frustrate researchers (Bishop & Butterworth, 1980). Nevertheless, to define specific reading retardation in terms of poor reading relative to nonverbal IQ would include many learners whose reading is quite consistent with their low verbal ability and could not, on this account, be regarded as 'unexpected' (Bishop & Butterworth, 1980).

This is not merely a matter of fine-tuning. In a study in which several different methods of identification were compared, the criteria for dyslexia were progressively relaxed until every poor reader was included, at which point the lowest and highest estimates of prevalence were found to differ by a factor of seven (Snowling et al., 2000).

In brief, people may be 'dyslexic' according to one method of identification but not according to a different method. In as much as 'dyslexia' is a construct, the characteristics of 'dyslexics' are necessarily artefacts resulting from the identification procedures; they may not necessarily reflect an *innate* cognitive dysfunction in the people identified by those procedures. Most research findings reflect statistical tendencies, not systematic rules; the given effect is sometimes present in only a minority of subjects and caution is needed in drawing explanatory models from such studies (Habib, 2000).

Thus, if it is a valid observation that 'standards of clinical practice in the learning disabilities field have, at various times in its history, reflected more than 50 per cent pseudoscience or unverified, virtually armchair speculation about human abilities' (Stanovich, 1999), there can be scant justification for expecting any consistency in the diagnoses that adult 'dyslexics' may have received as children. The evidence for inconsistency is overwhelming—unsurprisingly, given the difficulty of operationalising any definition of dyslexia so as to exclude all ordinary poor readers—and false positives may outnumber true positives severalfold.

Diagnoses of dyslexia are unstable across identification methods.

A diagnosis of dyslexia may be a ticket of eligibility for a particular form of learning provision rather than a scientific statement.

Are diagnoses of dyslexia stable over time?

In cases where the method of identification is held constant, there is no guarantee that it will identify the same people as 'dyslexic' over time, even though dyslexia is conceptualised as a lifelong condition. This is particularly likely to be so where identification has been limited to measures at the behavioural level (Frith, 1999). Several serious problems confront the researcher or clinician seeking to evaluate adults who report childhood reading and writing problems: they are often self-selected volunteers, potentially unrepresentative of the population at large; their elementary school records are not available to document their school-age reading achievement; diagnostic techniques designed for children may have norms that are unsuitable for adults; and adults with childhood reading problems might have adopted compensatory strategies as a result of remedial teaching or self-instruction (Scarborough, 1984).

So, while the concept of dyslexia assumes that there is a stable group of people who are underachieving in literacy and whose classification is neither age- nor test-specific, this kind of stability may not exist (Wright et al., 1996). Some of the apparent change over time may be attributable to measurement error (Fergusson et al., 1996). As with specific language impairment (NICHD, 2000), a nonlinear developmental path, with spurts and plateaux, may lead to unstable perceptions of 'impairment' and 'recovery'. Where the concept of 'reading disability' embraces all poor readers, detailed assessment of 'recovered' and 'non-recovered' readers has suggested that intelligence, language ability, working memory and the adoption of a 'word decoding' approach to reading and spelling may play a role in 'recovery' (Waring et al., 1996). However, change is not always for the better: in a cohort of children with specific language impairment, the prevalence of 'specific reading retardation' has been found to increase between the ages of eight-and-a-half and 15 years (Snowling et al., 2000).

Stability of classification is a separate issue within the underachieving group. The question of subtypes will be examined at greater length in the following section. Meanwhile, it is sufficient to take note of findings that the characteristics commonly used as a basis for the classification of developmental dyslexia into 'phonological' and 'surface' subtypes may reflect differences in teaching method and strategic choice rather than differences in learning aptitude (Baron, 1979; Hendriks & Kolk, 1997; Zabell & Everatt, 2002) and that over a two-year period, readers have been observed to move from one of these subtypes to the other (Snowling & Nation, 1997). Proportions in the subtypes may also vary, not only according to the language in which subjects are assessed but also according to the method used to classify them and, in a given language, according to the measure used; furthermore, longitudinal data have shown that over time the two subtypes are inconsistent in their relative proportions (Sprenger-Charolles *et al.*, 2001).

Diagnoses of dyslexia are unstable over time.

Are there phonological and surface subtypes of dyslexia?

Before the term 'dyslexia' was used in a developmental context, it had been applied to alexia, or traumatic loss of the ability to read (Anderson & Meier-Hedde, 2001). Implicit in the new application was a belief that the difficulties of developmental dyslexics could be conceptualised in the same way as the difficulties of previously-competent readers whose abilities had been impaired by a stroke or other brain injury. Since traumatic loss of reading ability was associated with focal damage (Pickle, 1998), the dysfunction in developmental dyslexia was attributed 'most probably to defective development of that region of the brain, disease of which in adults produces practically the same symptoms' (Morgan, 1896).

The appearance of two distinct kinds of selective impairment in stroke patients meanwhile suggested a 'dual route' model of normal reading in which words are recognised either as wholes (the 'semantic' or 'lexical' route) or as letter-strings in which the graphemes have to be converted into phonemes before recognition is possible (the 'phonological' or 'nonlexical' route). At best, the subtypes represent trends; even among stroke patients, no 'pure' cases of selective impairment have been reported (Coltheart & Davies, 2003).

Just as selective impairments in either the ability to read 'irregular' or 'exception' words with an atypical spelling-sound relationship ('surface' alexia) or the ability to read 'regular' but unfamiliar letter-strings ('phonological' alexia), or both, may be caused by traumatic loss of function, it has been argued that a similar pattern of dysfunction, while lacking such specific impairments, might be found in developmental dyslexia (Castles & Coltheart, 1993). However, although 'surface' and 'phonological' subtypes are consistent with the 'dual route' model of reading, they can also be explained within connectionist models (Harm & Seidenberg, 1999; Manis et al., 1996; Plaut et al., 1996). A 'connectionist model' is a computational, neural network model of parallel distributed processing by which a great deal of information latent in the environment can be derived, using simple but powerful learning rules (Elman et al., 1996). If, in addition, connectionist models can account for different kinds of alexia, then the notion of *selective* disorders of reading among stroke patients also comes under challenge (Patterson & Lambon Ralph, 1999).

Does this then represent a challenge to the concept of selectivity in developmental dyslexia and with it a challenge to the idea of 'surface' and 'phonological' subtypes? How persuasive is the evidence for a widespread belief that visual (or orthographic) and phonological mechanisms represent equivalent alternatives for acquiring skilled word recognition (Share, 1995)? What is the role of phonic and whole-word methods of teaching word identification (Snowling, 1996)? How should we understand the distinctions drawn between 'dyseidetic' and 'dysphonetic' subtypes of disabled readers (Boder, 1973), or between 'Phonecian' and 'Chinese' readers (Baron & Strawson, 1976)? How valid is the analogy between developmental difficulty and later loss of function? Could it be true that 'the whole question of subgrouping of dyslexics has arisen because we have not been working empirically and inductively, but rather deductively and intuitively' (Tønnessen, 1997)?

Theoretical arguments against the analogy between developmental difficulty and later loss of function are compelling. Cerebral specialisation depends as much on specific experiences as on 'pre-wiring', so that researchers need to explain a complex pattern of associated impairments, not a highly selective deficit (Bishop, 1997; Gilger & Kaplan, 2001). The assumption of residual normality against a background of normal development is difficult to maintain when both compensation and disruption result from initially undamaged cognitive functions developing in untypical ways (Karmiloff-Smith, 1998; Thomas & Karmiloff-Smith, 2002).

Empirical evidence, too, suggests that the analogy is invalid (Ellis, 1985; Snowling et al., 1996). An early study reported that developmental dyslexics resembled 'surface' but not 'phonological' alexics in that they were qualitatively similar to younger, normal readers (Baddeley et al., 1982). Some later studies have reported a phonological-to-surface continuum (Bryant & Impey, 1986; Ellis et al., 1996; Rack et al., 1993), which is also seen in 'normal' readers (Bryant & Impey, 1986; Ellis, 1985) and reports of distinct phonological and surface subtypes of developmental dyslexia (e.g. Curtin et al., 2001) might be explained as outcomes of teaching method and strategic choice, not as outcomes of biological constraint (Hendriks & Kolk, 1997; Manis et al., 1996; Murphy & Pollatsek, 1994; Thomson, 1999).

There is further evidence for rejecting the assumption that 'surface' and 'phonological' dyslexia are alternative or complementary manifestations of an organic dysfunction. 'Surface' dyslexics are characterised by developmental delay, whereas 'phonological' dyslexics are characterised by a cognitive deficit (Griffiths & Snowling, 2002; Gustafson, 2001; Sprenger-Charolles et al., 2000; Stanovich et al., 1997). Unlike 'surface dyslexia', 'phonological dyslexia' is associated with naming-speed deficits (Wolf & Bowers, 1999) and also with deficits in the transient visual system (Borsting et al., 1996; Spinelli et al., 1997).

In theory, the 'surface dyslexia' profile could be caused by any or all of lead exposure, prenatal exposure to alcohol, influenza viruses and other causes of congenital malformation, or by intensive instruction in phonological processing (Castles et al., 1999). Empirical evidence suggests that it might be explained by insufficient exposure to print (Griffiths & Snowling, 2002; Gustafson, 2001; Sprenger-Charolles et al., 2000) and lower verbal ability (although not necessarily less potential for intellectual development). This might offer a parsimonious explanation for the association between 'surface dyslexia' and socio-economic adversity (Bishop, 2001; Samuelsson et al., 2000), since higher and lower IQ groups of reading-disabled children differ significantly on several home literacy variables, including parental education, books in the home and being read to (Wadsworth et al., 2000), all of which relate to print exposure.

Whether reading difficulties are attributable to delay (the 'surface' subtype) or to deficit (the 'phonological' subtype), they are of equally high priority for intervention. However, if the 'phonological' dyslexia profile alone is robust in reading-level comparisons (Sprenger-Charolles et al., 2000; Stanovich et al., 1997), then perhaps most developmental 'surface' dyslexia should be thought of as ordinary poor reading, leaving only the 'phonological' subtype to be properly considered as an organic dysfunction. Such a change would have important implications for estimates of the prevalence of developmental dyslexia, should it be conceptualised as a discrete condition. Although this change would have no implications for estimates of the overall numbers of people with reading skills deficits, it might affect estimates of the cost and duration of preventive measures and remedial interventions and their probable outcomes, by a downward adjustment of the numbers estimated to require intensive remediation over a long period or to need support in other ways.

Dyslexia subtypes do not occur naturally; they are artefacts of research and teaching strategies.

Is there any bias in our perception of dyslexia?

In literacy practices there are cross-cultural differences. Some, like differences between English and Chinese writing and spelling systems, are obvious (Gleitman & Rozin, 1977); others, like differences between English and Chinese readers in brain morphology and function, are not (Hsieh et al., 2001). In dyslexia, too, there are cross-cultural differences reflecting differences between writing and spelling systems (Habib et al., 2000; Paulesu et al., 2001); there are also cross-cultural similarities (Ho et al., 2000; McBride-Chang & Kail, 2002). In passing, it deserves mention that not even the Chinese are 'Chinese' (as opposed to 'Phonecian') readers, since Chinese characters contain not only semantic but also phonetic elements (McBride-Chang & Ho, 2000). However, dyslexia is more evident in alphabetic writing systems than it is in nonalphabetic systems, like Chinese. It is also more evident in a morphophonemic spelling system with complex relationships between phonemes and graphemes, like English, than it is in a phonemic system with simple relationships between phonemes and graphemes, like Finnish. In these respects, there is cultural bias.

Writing systems are not the only potential sources of cultural bias in dyslexia. Differences in socio-economic status—the standard proxy measure of differences in educational and social opportunity—have long been implicated in the debate about dyslexia. Here, there is a paradox. Some parents may believe that exceptional abilities in music or mathematics are 'innate' when their children have no obvious flair for them, but if their children are found to be deficient in a skill such as reading they will blame environmental influences such as poor teaching (Bateson & Martin, 1999). Other parents accept personal responsibility even while denying it, as they embrace the social cachet of dyslexia (which might be heritable) while disclaiming the social stigma of low intelligence (which is also heritable). A clinical psychiatrist has observed that when mothers are asked what makes their children tick, they 'plump for whichever nature or nurture theories most conveniently let them off the hook—largely, of course, to avoid guilt' (Oliver James, in *The Guardian*, 25 September 2002, G2, page 8).

It is probable that there is a white-collar or class bias in reporting dyslexia; it would be very surprising if there were not. However, reporting bias could be expected in clinic (or special school) samples, but not in community (epidemiological) samples, because epidemiological sampling is less likely to be affected by the economic and social factors that bias clinic referral and special school enrolment. A systematic study has investigated this question in a community sample, avoiding the use of an IQ-discrepancy formula. It found that the prevalence of dyslexia—and 'any attempt to determine the prevalence of dyslexia should be treated with caution' (Miles & Miles, 1999)—varied only at the extremes of the social scale (Miles et al., 1994). Because of the uneven distribution of IQ scores across the social spectrum (Mackintosh, 1998; Neisser et al., 1996; Sternberg, 2000), a prevalence estimate based on an IQ-discrepancy operationalisation of the dyslexia concept would necessarily be higher for middle-class than for working-class groups (e.g. Wadsworth et al., 2000) and this would reflect identification bias but not cultural bias. Nevertheless, it may be that the literacy difficulties in most children, even those from middle-class backgrounds, are caused by experiential and instructional deficits, not by basic deficits in cognitive abilities (Vellutino et al., 1996).

Differences between languages and their writing and spelling systems create a form of cultural bias in dyslexia.

Differences in discriminative criteria for educational failure between the social classes create a reporting bias in dyslexia.

Differences in the effects of IQ-discrepancy operational criteria create an identification bias in dyslexia.

Can the research findings be applied to adults in literacy and numeracy classes?
Adult dyslexic people taking part in research carried out in cognitive psychology and neuroimaging laboratories tend to be either university students or mature adults who had attended specialist schools or clinics as children. Both scientific exclusionary criteria (Vellutino, 1979) and cultural self-selection have thus led to a research population which is, by destination if not by origin, predominantly white-collar. Research with greater numbers of working-class participants has indicated important socio-economic differences in the nature of reading skills deficits. Even if that were not the case, it would be rash to generalise research findings to populations dissimilar from those involved in the research. As it is, recent findings suggest that such generalisations may often be misleading. To the extent that adults in basic skills classes are working-class or second-language speakers of English, the research literature on dyslexia (as distinct from that on reading disability) may not apply to most to them.

Findings from research with participants from middle-class groups may create misleading expectations about the needs and abilities of learners in adult literacy classes.

The crux of the problem

Heterogeneity in 'dyslexia' is generally acknowledged. It may reflect the fact that complex systems break down in complex ways (Seidenberg, 1992). It may also reflect differences in concepts and methods of identification (Filipek, 1999). In the latter case, it would reflect laboratory practice, since most research into developmental dyslexia 'seems content to lump together individuals with grossly different reading profiles in a way that would never be accepted in the field of acquired dyslexia' (Ellis et al., 1997a).

The consequence of heterogeneity is that no generalisation is valid for each and every member of the population of adults who have been identified (or who have identified themselves) as 'dyslexic'. Diagnoses (and self-diagnoses) are unstable, both across methods of identification and—in the case of diagnoses if not self-diagnoses—over time. Some of these diagnoses, including allocation to subtypes, are artefacts of research and teaching methods. Some, especially in the case of people whose literacy ability is discrepant in relation to their perceived intelligence because they have been poorly taught or because they have grown up in an environment where schooling and literacy are under-valued, may be more appropriately replaced by diagnoses of ordinary poor reading', which has also been referred to as 'pseudodyslexia' (Morton & Frith, 1995; Perfetti & Marron, 1995).

Does this mean that we cannot define developmental dyslexia? Or that, once we have defined dyslexia, we cannot operationalise the concept? Does it mean that, although we can operationalise the concept of dyslexia, we can do so only in an arbitrary manner? Or does it mean that we can operationalise some concepts of dyslexia but not all of them and that feasibility of operationalisation necessitates both a broadening of the concept and a corresponding reduction in its unique explanatory potential?

As is clear from *Appendices 1* and *2*, there are many definitions of dyslexia and the differences between them are striking. In the stipulative definition that we have adopted in this review, the guiding concept is widely if not universally agreed: dyslexia is 'a neurodevelopmental disorder with a biological origin, which impacts on speech processing with a variety of clinical manifestations' (Frith, 1999). However, we cannot prove a biological *origin* in any individual case. We must take care not to confuse correlation with causation; at best, we can think only in terms of probability. We have to establish the exact degree of probability by reference to a base-rate for the prevalence of dyslexia. To determine a base-rate, we need to operationalise the concept. As yet, there is no agreement as to how this should be done. That is the crux of the problem.

A diagnosis of dyslexia is a theory, but the diagnostician cannot estimate the likelihood of its being correct.

Part two
Explanatory theories of Dyslexia

Caveat 1 'The history of dyslexia research, the well-known heterogeneity of dyslexic children and the very complexity of the reading process argue against any single unifying explanation for reading breakdown' (*page* 432). Wolf, M. and Bowers, P. G. (1999). The double-deficit hypothesis for the developmental dyslexias. **Journal of Educational Psychology,** 91(3), 415–438.

Caveat 2 'A difficulty in learning to read, or dyslexia, should not be viewed as a condition in itself, but as a symptom of a breakdown in one or more of the various processes involved' (*page* 460). Farmer, M. E. and Klein, R. M. (1995). The evidence for a temporal processing deficit linked to dyslexia: a review. **Psychonomic Bulletin & Review,** 2(4), 460–493.

Caveat 3 'Some of the seeming confusion in the study of dyslexia may simply reflect the fact that complex systems may break down in complex ways' (*page* 260). Seidenberg, M. S. (1992). Dyslexia in a computational model of word recognition in reading. In P. B. Gough & L. C. Ehri & R. Treiman (Eds.), **Reading Acquisition.** Hillsdale, NJ: Laurence Erlbaum Associates.

Introduction

The theories reviewed here are attempts to describe what is going wrong for people who have difficulty in learning to read and write and to explain why it is going wrong for them. Not all of the theories attempt both tasks. Nevertheless, the different kinds of theory can be fitted into an inclusive causal model entailing three levels of analysis, one of which is descriptive, one of which is explanatory at the proximal level and one of which is explanatory at the distal level— behavioural, cognitive and biological explanations. The original model was developed at the Medical Research Council's former Cognitive Development Unit (Morton & Frith, 1995) at about the same time that the comparable biobehavioural systems model was proposed in the USA (Fletcher et al., 1995). It has been adopted in accounts of dyslexia in adults (Lee, 2000, 2002) and its usefulness as an explanatory framework is widely acknowledged (Nicolson et al., 2001a; Richards et al., 2002; Snowling, 2000). It has recently been elaborated in a general model of reading and the influences on reading development (Jackson & Coltheart, 2001). In this form (see *Appendix 4*), it offers useful points of reference for the present review.

Reading, as most dyslexia theorists use the term, refers to the decoding of single words, but this is only one stage in the acquisition of literacy. A more elaborate account describes reading as a cognitive activity accomplished by a mental information-processing system made up of a number of distinct processing subsystems or component skills (Carr et al., 1990), where the input is print and the processes applied to the input yield output in the form of word meaning, syntactic representations of sequences of words and pronunciations (Jackson & Coltheart, 2001). This is not to suppose that anyone believes the ability to recognise and pronounce words—'word calling', or 'barking at print'—is the final aim of reading instruction; if the *basic* skill is to derive meaning from print, then reasoning and discourse are ultimately what make literacy *functional* (Rayner et al., 2001). That being so, it may help to follow the 'simple model' of reading (Gough & Tunmer, 1986) with the observation that the critical difficulty in dyslexia lies in decoding at the single-word level rather than in comprehending passages of text (Snowling, 1991). It is worth bearing in mind that word recognition difficulties are not exclusive to dyslexia; they are also characteristic of poor readers who do not meet the diagnostic criteria for dyslexia and of good readers who are beginning to read (Seidenberg et al., 1986).

Nevertheless, while locating the critical difficulty in dyslexia at the level of word recognition, commentators acknowledge that adult dyslexics also have problems with reading comprehension and other aspects of literacy (Nicolson et al., 1993). Comprehension is made more difficult for all people with poor reading skills when they have to allocate attentional resources to the task of decoding (Sabatini, 2002); it can be difficult enough for 'good' readers when they are faced with unusual texts (like the present one). Listening comprehension, despite the belief that it is unimpaired in dyslexia, will inevitably become more difficult when the spoken language uses vocabulary normally acquired through reading or when it employs the more complex syntax of the written language—two difficulties either created or exacerbated by low exposure to print—or when utterance length makes greater demands on verbal memory. There may be a case for locating the core difficulty of dyslexia not in word recognition without further specification but in *rapid* and *automatic* word recognition, where impairments have serious implications for reading comprehension.

Similarly, this account of reading does not imply that difficulty in decoding is the only problem for poor readers in general: for these people, especially, comprehension is an important independent source of difficulty (Cornoldi & Oakhill, 1996). Neither does it imply that, where comprehension is the critical difficulty in low literacy, any failure of comprehension is necessarily accompanied by difficulties in decoding regular words, as there is more than one point at which the acquisition of literacy can founder (Spear-Swerling & Sternberg, 1994).

Although phonological awareness is a good predictor of reading development at the outset (McBride-Chang & Kail, 2002), it may be a much less efficient predictor of reading ability in later years (de Jong & van der Leij, 1999), when readers come to rely on it less and less because of their increasingly automatised (or 'direct route') word recognition (Doctor & Coltheart, 1980). Of special concern is the 'slump' observed in children who have succeeded in learning to decode familiar, regularly-spelled words but who lose momentum when they encounter less familiar words, particularly when those words are irregularly spelled or have abstract meanings (Chall et al., 1990). This slump is associated with socio-economic disadvantage, where the quality of language in the home may be a less than optimal preparation for schooling (Bernstein, 1971; Feagans & Farran, 1982).

Although the difficulties of dyslexic people do not stop at single-word decoding, the present review confines its attention to this problem.

Phonological awareness

'Understanding normal development is a prerequisite to understanding abnormal development' (*page* 411). Michel, G. F. and Moore, C. L. (1995). **Developmental Psychobiology: an interdisciplinary science.** Cambridge, MA: MIT Press.

'Developmental dyslexia should ... be understood in relation to a theory of how learning to read normally takes place and how it fails to proceed in certain cases' (*page* 444). Snowling, M. J., Bryant, P. E. and Hulme, C. (1996). Theoretical and methodological pitfalls in making comparisons between developmental and acquired dyslexia: Some comments on A. Castles & M. Coltheart (1993). **Reading and Writing,** 8(5), 443–451.

Background

In spite of the evolutionary recency of literacy, it is now expected that everyone who is given the opportunity to do so will learn to read and write. Some people learn quickly when formal instruction begins, irrespective of the teacher's method or lack of one (Meek, 1991; Smith, 1978), while others need a longer period of instruction and a few make very little progress despite extensive remedial intervention (Fawcett, 2002). The latter group are sometimes said to lack phonological awareness. What is now the central theory of reading difficulty implicates phonology at more than one level of analysis with respect to cause, symptom and treatment (Nicolson, 2002). Teachers sometimes speak of a deficit in phonological awareness as if it were a trait like colour-blindness or a hearing impairment. But is that an appropriate way to conceptualise it? Does the term tell us anything we did not know already?

What is phonological awareness?

Though there have been other, subtly different definitions, phonological awareness has been defined as 'conscious access to the component sounds of speech within words and the ability to manipulate these sounds...involv[ing] primarily the sound units of onset and rime...and phonemes (Walton & Walton, 2002, *pages* 79-80).' ('Onset' refers to the opening consonant phoneme(s) of a syllable, if any; 'rime' refers to the rest of the syllable, the obligatory vowel plus the closing consonant phoneme(s), if any. For 'phonemes', see below.) While phonological awareness does not appear to be a complex construct (Schatschneider et al., 1999, but see Hulme, 2002), it may be associated with at least three component skills, namely general cognitive ability, verbal short-term memory and speech perception (McBride-Chang et al., 1997).

Phonological awareness is an important prerequisite, but it is not sufficient, for learning to read (Bus & van IJzendoorn, 1999); it needs to be supplemented by knowledge of letters and of the sounds they represent (Treiman, 2000). When learners have both phonological awareness and letter-sound knowledge, they are in a position to grasp the alphabetic principle: the idea that letters in printed words represent the sounds in spoken words in a manner that is more-or-less regular (Treiman, 2000), depending on the transparency of the spelling system.

Phonological awareness does not come free of charge with language acquisition (Shankweiler, 1999). Although the ability to develop phonological awareness is necessarily innate, phonological awareness itself is not, as it were, pre-programmed for any specific language (Nittrouer, 2001). Just as with reading and spelling, where learners do not simply change from a state of not knowing a rule to knowing it (Bryant, 2002), so with phonological awareness; it is a dynamic construct, in which abilities develop over time (Anthony et al., 2002; Norris & Hoffman, 2002).

Over time, too, the most appropriate measures of phonological awareness may change (Schatschneider et al., 1999). Learners begin to acquire phonological awareness when they learn to separate word units in the speech continuum, to hear the two parts of a compound word, to separate the syllables of a word, to select rhyme-words and to hear which words start with the same or different sounds (Goswami & Bryant, 1990; Sodoro et al., 2002). In its most complete sense, phonological awareness is neither innate nor acquired spontaneously in the course of cognitive development (Morais et al., 1979). 'Discovering phonemic units is helped greatly by explicit instruction in how the system works' (Ehri et al., 2001); moreover, it is optimally taught in the context of reading instruction (Hatcher et al., 1994).

The importance of tuition becomes clear when we acknowledge that *phonemic* awareness— the insight that every spoken word can be conceived as a sequence of phonemes (the smallest units of language that distinguish one word from another) —differs from less fine-grained aspects of phonological awareness (such as syllable counting and rhyme recognition). To develop the phonemic awareness that reading and writing call for, students must learn to put their attention where it had never had to be and learn to attend to meaningless phonemes, not meaningful morphemes and words: 'Speech does not require phonemic awareness for the same reason that it does not produce it' (Liberman & Whalen, 2000). Our acknowledgement is underlined by the recognition that discovering phonemic units is helped by, or even conditional upon, explicit instruction in their isolation, identity, categorisation, blending, segmentation and deletion (Alegria et al., 1982; Cardoso-Martins, 2001; Ehri et al., 2001) and explicit instruction in letter-sound relationships.

Phonemes themselves are abstractions: they do not exist as part of the acoustic speech signal (Baudouin de Courtenay, 1895; Liberman & Whalen, 2000; Nittrouer, 2002). While it is true that speech is a stream of vocal sounds, we learn to analyse this sound-stream as a sequence of linguistic units; in the normal course of events, we learn to recognise words and syllables before we first go to school and we learn to recognise phonemes as we are taught to read and spell. Each phoneme is a set of similar (but audibly different) sounds, or 'phones', like the sounds represented by the letter 'p' in 'pot' (where it is followed by a puff of air) and in 'spot' (where it isn't), so that a phoneme is both a percept and a concept (Gleitman & Rozin, 1977). For reading and spelling, it is less a noise in the ear than an idea in the mind (Baudouin de Courtenay, 1895).

In English, especially, the correspondences between phonemes and graphemes (the letters or letter-groups used to transcribe phonemes) are complex (Jackson & Coltheart, 2001). For most people, learning to read offers the only opportunity to gain insight into the phonological structure of speech; if people are not taught, they may never intuit this structure (Liberman, 1998; Morais et al., 1979). The method by which learners are taught to read may influence the development of phonemic awareness (Alegria et al., 1982), but the whole-word method is not incompatible with the development of phonemic awareness (Leybaert & Content, 1995) and neither do phonics methods guarantee that development (Vellutino et al., 1996).

A useful distinction can be made between sensitivity to phonemes and the ability to analyse (or manipulate) them (Mann, 1987). Then, if phonemic awareness is defined as *conscious* access to the phonemic level of the speech stream (Stanovich, 1986), a lack of phonemic *awareness* need not imply any substantial inferiority in phonemic *sensitivity* (Adrián et al., 1995) and would not be sufficient evidence for a cognitive dysfunction. Indeed, the growth of phonemic *sensitivity* is a developmental imperative. Since the acoustic signal of speech lacks invariant physical correlates to phonetic segments and the ability to recognise segmental structure is not present from the start of language learning, the beginning reader must learn how to process the complex, generally continuous acoustic speech signal so that the phonetic structure of language can be derived (Nittrouer, 2002). This process may last for a period of several years (Nittrouer, 2002).

Phonological awareness is both the explicit knowledge that words are made up of sounds and the ability to manipulate those sounds.

The ability to develop phonological awareness is innate but development is not spontaneous.

Phonological awareness develops over time and is helped by language games and nursery rhymes.

Phonemic awareness is a fine-grained version of phonological awareness, with the insight that each spoken word is made up of phonemes.

Because phonemes are ideas in the mind, not noises in the ear, a lack of phonemic awareness need not imply a lack of phonemic sensitivity.

Most people do not develop phonemic awareness without being taught.

Individual differences in phonological awareness

Phonemic awareness is not a unitary process (Ackermann et al., 1997; Ivry & Lebby, 1998). Neither is phonological awareness an all-or-nothing quality: the ability to isolate and combine sounds in words is part of a continuum stretching from unexpectedly poor to unexpectedly good readers (Bryant & Bradley, 1985). Lower levels of phonological sensitivity (Bowey, 1995) and phonemic segmentation (Duncan & Seymour, 2000) have been associated with socio-economic disadvantage, to the extent that the difference between middle-class and socially disadvantaged children's ability to read single words may be reduced or even eliminated after controlling for differences in phonological awareness (Raz & Bryant, 1990). Moreover, children from socially-disadvantaged homes respond to training in phonological awareness (Blachman et al., 1994).

Low levels of phonological awareness in people from socially disadvantaged backgrounds are more likely to reflect early language experience than to indicate innate learning difficulties, because general language backgrounds shape the way that people learn to weigh the acoustic properties of speech in their decisions about phonemes (Nittrouer, 2002). This will be the case, whether linguistic disadvantage is experienced at home (Hecht et al., 2000) or at school (Raz & Bryant, 1990). Nevertheless, any correlation between a measure of socio-economic disadvantage and a measure of phonological awareness could have multiple explanations, relating to both environmental and biological factors.

Socio-economic disadvantage predicts linguistic disadvantage.

Linguistic disadvantage impedes the development of phonological awareness.

The reciprocal relationship between phonological awareness and reading ability

Phonological awareness clearly influences the acquisition of alphabetic skills. Is it true, as we might assume, that this influence travels in a single direction? Evidence suggests that the relationship is interactive, in that early phonological skills are crucial in learning to read (Goswami & Bryant, 1990; Rayner et al., 2001), while learning to read in an alphabetic system enhances phonological awareness (Morais et al., 1987); and similarly, phonemic awareness assists learning to spell (Caravolas et al., 2001), while learning to spell enhances phonemic awareness (Ventura et al., 2001). The relationship between phonological awareness and reading ability thus involves reciprocal causation (Korkman et al., 1999; Snowling et al., 1996b; Tunmer & Chapman, 1996).

However, a pattern of interaction between reading ability and phonological awareness is not inevitable. People may learn to read without fully grasping the fundamental structure of the writing system (Byrne, 1998), in which case their reading ability could depend more on sight-word recognition and contextual clues than upon the decoding skills associated with phonological awareness. Such readers will have no difficulty in reading either regular or irregular words so long as these words are familiar, but they will have difficulty with pseudowords and unfamiliar real words. While spelling can be learned implicitly through exposure to print (Bryant, 2002), learning to read is usefully supplemented by explicit instruction in spelling (Caravolas et al., 2001; Viise, 1996).

The identification of unfamiliar words by playing 'psycholinguistic guessing games' (Goodman, 1970) is seldom a viable alternative to decoding: context may help (Archer & Bryant, 2001) and it may be especially useful to readers with low levels of literacy skill (Snowling, 1996), but it depends on existing semantic and syntactic knowledge (Rego & Bryant, 1993) and accurate guessing may require a high level of predictiveness in the word to be guessed at (Gough & Wren, 1999). For less skilled readers, psycholinguistic guessing games are inadequate, both because there is an extraordinary number of synonyms or near-synonyms in English and also because successful prediction is possible only where the predicted word violates the basic communicative convention of conveying non-redundant information. Natural language does have a built-in level of redundancy (sufficient to infer what is said against a background of some noise and what is written when text has been to an extent degraded), but this level is almost always too low to predict individual words uniquely.

Although early research suggested that skilled readers recognise words without noticing the letters that compose them (Huey, 1908), we now know that this is not so (Rayner, 1998; Reichle et al., in press); if it were so, then proof-reading would be impassible—as readers now see. Psycholinguistic guessing games are at best an emergency strategy; they are not a substitute for learning about the alphabetic principle (Chapman et al., 2001; Liberman & Liberman, 1992). Moreover, reliance on *conscious* predictions from context in word reading may reduce available working memory capacity and thus impair comprehension (Bruck, 1998). The routine use of context as a strategy to compensate for poor decoding skills may well lead to future reading difficulties (Liberman & Liberman, 1992; Nicholson et al., 1991).

Learning to read and write in an alphabetic system helps and is helped by, the development of phonemic awareness.

Are there any impediments to the acquisition of phonemic awareness?
The most critical consideration for adult learners is whether age itself is an impediment to the acquisition of phonemic awareness. However, since a small-scale experimental study has shown that neurologically normal illiterate adults may display rapid improvements in performance when explicit instruction and continuous corrective feedback are provided in a phoneme deletion task, it appears that maturity should not impede the acquisition of this skill (Morais et al., 1988). Neither does it appear to do so: in an intensive adult literacy programme in Turkey (where the orthography is transparent), 'neoliterates' have been reported to show significant improvement in letter and word recognition, phonological awareness and spelling levels (Durgunoglu & Öney, 2002). Similarly, among adults who have previously learned to read in a nonalphabetic script, specific instruction in phoneme deletion has led to improvements not only in phonemic analysis but also in word reading in an additional, alphabetic language (Cheung, 1999).

These findings may be valid for people with normal speech perception, but are they valid for people whose speech perception is now impaired or was impaired when they were first learning to read and write? Moreover, are the findings valid for people whose perception is unimpaired but for whom the phonetic or acoustic features of the language most familiar to them at a critical period in their development were different from those of the language they now seek to read and spell? It appears that the findings may not be valid in two distinct circumstances.

The first of these circumstances concerns hearing ability. Generally speaking, a perceptual impairment early in life may be sufficient to cause a phonological disorder which persists even after the perceptual impairment has resolved (Bird & Bishop, 1992). Children with mild-to-moderate sensorineural hearing loss are as impaired as normally-hearing children with specific language impairment on tests of phonological discrimination (Briscoe et al., 2001). Children who have otitis media with effusion ('glue ear') may have difficulty in making fine discriminations between speech sounds (Singleton et al., 2000), although the otitis media may need to be both chronic (Nittrouer, 1996) and bilateral (Stewart & Silva, 1996) for speech perception and articulation to be compromised, with effects that may then persist into mid-adolescence (Bennett et al., 2001), long after the hearing problem itself has cleared up. In this case, the impairment can be described as having a biological origin.

However, in the case of pre-school children, any linguistic difficulties attributable to otitis media may be outweighed by the difficulties associated with social disadvantage (Paradise et al., 2000; Vernon-Feagans et al., 2002; Wallace et al., 1996), when language development may be impaired irrespective of hearing difficulty (Tough, 1977; Walker et al., 1994).

The second circumstance concerns the phonetic or acoustic features of language in childhood. From a connectionist perspective (see above, p.36), it has been suggested that speech perception involves the integration of multiple acoustic properties, so that learning how best to weight these properties may then be prerequisite for recognising phonetic structure (Nittrouer, 1996). Individual perceptual weighting strategies have been found to differ not only according to the quality of perception but also according to the quality of the signal (Nittrouer, 1996). In the latter case, learners from disadvantaged backgrounds—where language may be suboptimal in both quality and quantity—have been found to perform even less well on phonemic awareness tasks than learners with chronic otitis media (Nittrouer, 1996). Nevertheless, disadvantaged learners with speech segmentation deficits may respond well to alphabetic instruction (Duncan & Seymour, 2000). In the case of such learners, who may lack skill in phoneme analysis but have no deficiencies in auditory discrimination (Wallach et al., 1977), the impairment is properly described as having its origin in experience.

Neurologically 'normal' adults are not too old to acquire phonemic awareness.

People who have had 'glue ear' in early childhood may continue to have difficulty on phonemic awareness tasks, even after their hearing problem has resolved itself.

People from disadvantaged backgrounds may respond well to alphabetic instruction.

Summary

There are at least two distinct but compatible explanations for a deficit in phonological awareness, although only one of them requires a biological impairment. For this reason, it might be more accurate to explain the phonemic awareness deficit as a *perceptual* problem in the case of hearing impairment and as a *conceptual* problem in the case of socio-economic disadvantage. (This distinction is not the same as the distinction between biological and experiential impairments: in a person of low intellectual ability, a phonemic awareness deficit may be both perceptual and conceptual and, in so far as it is conceptual, at least partly biological in origin.) But, whatever the explanation of a student's deficit in phonological awareness, it is axiomatic that such a deficit entails difficulty in the acquisition of alphabetic skills.

Dyslexia and alphabetic skills: the phonological deficit theory

The phonological deficit theory

After such a lengthy preamble, the phonological deficit theory of dyslexia (Bradley & Bryant, 1978; Rack, 1994; Vellutino, 1979) can be stated succinctly: 'Dyslexic children have an impairment in the ability to detect and process speech sounds and this impairment critically limits the skills which are a prerequisite for reading, such as the ability to detect rhymes and later, the ability to "sound out" words and "blend" sounds when trying to decipher the written word' (Fawcett & Nicolson, 1994).

Succinct though it is, the statement can be clarified. The abilities to detect and to process speech sounds can be distinguished from one another. Whether or not a person is sensitive to differences in speech sounds is by definition a perceptual question; it follows that an impairment in detection may lead to difficulties in processing. However, as we have already seen, there is evidence that for some people, particularly those from disadvantaged backgrounds, the processing of speech sounds may be more a problem of analyticity than a problem of sensitivity (Mann, 1987); that is to say, the question is not about percepts but about concepts (Marcel, 1978; Rozin & Gleitman, 1977), because writing systems are not so much portrayals of linguistic *behaviour* as codifications of linguistic *knowledge* (Rée, 1999). The problem may be more a question of the teacher's ability to teach than a matter of the student's ability to learn.

In spite of this proviso, it should be noted that the phonological deficit theory of dyslexia is a theory mainly at the cognitive level. Biological origins of the phonological deficit have been a matter for conjecture (Rack, 1994). One suggestion has been that weak connectivity between the anterior and posterior language areas of the brain is caused by a dysfunctional left insula, which may normally act as an anatomical bridge between Broca's area, the superior temporal cortex, and the inferior parietal cortex (Paulesu et al., 1996). How this might occur is unclear; in the light of current knowledge, it is unlikely that it occurs at all (Lieberman, 2000).

Further research is indicated, because of the possibility that specific explanations, even if they do not apply to every instance, might lead to specific interventions. However, any search for a single neural substrate of dyslexia may be misguided if, when the term 'dyslexia' is used to denote an otherwise inexplicably severe and persistent difficulty in learning to read, it is understood as a symptom—or a 'final common pathway'—of more than one cause of developmental abnormality in the neural system.

> According to phonological deficit theory, dyslexic people are specifically impaired in their ability to detect and process speech sounds.

> The phonological deficit theory is a cognitive theory, which assumes a biological explanation but does not propose one specifically.

What does the phonological deficit theory explain?
The phonological deficit theory has been described as a 'near-complete explanation of the problems dyslexic children face when learning to read' (Fawcett & Nicolson, 1994). For this and other reasons, it became 'the consensus view of most dyslexia researchers' about 15 years ago (Nicolson, 1996). Within the domain of reading, the phonological deficit theory accounts for dyslexics' poor performances in short-term memory, long-term memory, picture naming and verbal repetition, all of which are consistent with a deficiency in the use of phonologically-based information (Rack, 1994).

However, the description 'near-complete' is circumspect in acknowledging that the phonological deficit theory may not account for all of the difficulties that dyslexic people experience in their efforts to become literate. The description is also circumspect in implying that dyslexic people may experience difficulties unrelated to literacy and which, for some, may cause more distress than is caused by their failure to achieve functional literacy.

> The phonological deficit theory offers an explanation of problems with accurate and fluent recall of phonologically-coded items in memory.

What does the phonological deficit theory not explain?
While providing a persuasive account of difficulties in reading, the phonological deficit theory predicts problems with only the phonological aspects of spelling and makes no predictions about the motor skill problems of handwriting (Nicolson, 1996).

With respect to spelling, the phonological deficit hypothesis has been understood to predict that poor readers will compensate for phonological deficits by relying heavily on their visual memorisation of orthographic patterns. Such students should produce a low proportion of spellings revealing sensitivity to phonological structure relative to the proportion of their spellings revealing sensitivity to orthographic structure (Bourassa & Treiman, 2001). Dyslexic people and non-dyslexic people may be statistically indistinguishable in terms of correct spellings of real words, performing at similar levels on measures designed to tap the phonological and orthographic processes involved in spelling (Bourassa & Treiman, 2003).

While this finding does not invalidate the phonological deficit hypothesis as a description of what for many practitioners and researchers is the central aspect of dyslexia, it offers no support for the phonological deficit hypothesis as an *explanation* of dyslexia.

Most, but not all studies, have failed to obtain evidence of reduced or absent spelling-to-sound regularity effects in dyslexia. This has been the case irrespective of whether dyslexia is defined by discrepancy or by low-end cut off scores. In other words, the overwhelming majority of spelling evidence appears not to support the prediction of the phonological deficit model (Metsala & Brown, 1998; Metsala et al., 1998). If the model were correct, dyslexic people would only be able to read by recognising the shapes of words (rather than the letter sequences they are composed of) and so there would be no difference in their ability to read regular and exception words. Since differences in the ability to read regular and exception words are reported in both dyslexics and reading age controls, this evidence appears not to support the phonological deficit model (Ellis et al., 1997a).

The phonological deficit theory does not explain problems with motor skill development.

The phonological deficit theory is challenged as an explanation (as opposed to a description) of dyslexia by the difficulty of distinguishing dyslexics and non-dyslexic people in terms of their spelling errors and their abilities to read regular and exception words.

Do phonological deficits differentiate 'dyslexics' from other poor readers?

With respect to spelling and handwriting, the phonological deficit theory of dyslexia is too narrow; with respect to reading, it is too broad. Implicit in the foregoing sections is the question of whether measures of phonological awareness can differentiate dyslexic people from 'ordinary' poor readers. It is a matter of definition that pseudoword repetition and other phonological measures differentiate poor readers from good readers. However, do they differentiate developmental dyslexic people from 'ordinary' poor readers? As an example, the task of pseudoword repetition requires accurate speech perception, efficient verbal working memory and the ability to keep phonological representations distinct (Holopainen et al., 2001). Task performance can be compromised by deficits in speech perception (Chiappe et al., 2001); in children with mild-to-moderate sensorineural hearing loss, serious difficulty with pseudoword repetition has been found to be compatible with normal literacy ability (Briscoe et al., 2001). Task performance can also be affected by vocabulary knowledge (Dollaghan et al., 1995), which is in its turn affected by knowledge gained from exposure to print. Otherwise-unimpaired adults who never had the opportunity to learn to read have been shown to experience difficulty in repeating pseudowords (Castro-Caldas et al., 1998).

In the light of these and other findings (e.g. Bishop, 2001), it appears that the pseudoword repetition task does not differentiate between those with dyslexia and ordinary poor readers, possibly because it assesses what is common to both groups, namely limitations in declarative knowledge that might normally have been acquired at home or at school (Thompson & Johnston, 2000).

It is also possible that the pseudoword repetition task might confound phonological awareness with general intellectual ability. Although children whose later reading ability was not discrepant with their assessed intelligence had performed less well at pseudoword repetition than those who were later considered to be 'normal' readers, children whose later reading difficulties were discrepant with their general ability could not be distinguished from the 'normal' readers on this task (Jorm et al., 1986a). If this is also the case with adults, then it might be that pseudoword repetition *does* have a discriminant function albeit, paradoxically, that errors in pseudoword repetition might identify not developmental dyslexics but 'ordinary' poor readers—perhaps because the task loads on verbal ability at least as much as it loads on phonemic discrimination and verbal short-term memory.

Comparable findings have been obtained in studies using other phonological awareness tasks. Here, too, previous experience of literacy appears to be an important condition for success, in that otherwise unimpaired but illiterate adults perform very poorly at the task of phoneme deletion (Adrián et al., 1995)—for example, saying 'boat' without the /b/. More specifically, as a predictor of success, previous experience of alphabetic literacy is better than previous experience of nonalphabetic literacy (Cheung et al., 2001).

Thus, while phonological awareness tasks are essential to help the adult tutor to plan a programme of teaching, a student's initial difficulty with these tasks need not indicate any biological abnormality since the ability to manipulate speech sounds is a taught skill, not an outcome of cognitive maturation or exposure to language (Read et al., 1987). Tasks such as phoneme deletion differentiate poor or beginning readers from accomplished readers; they do not differentiate dyslexic from non-dyslexic poor readers.

This discussion leads to an important issue in the logic of diagnosis. It may be true —although the assumption has been queried (Miles et al., 2003)—that everyone with dyslexia experiences difficulty on assessments of phonological processing. However, the inference that everyone with impairments in phonological processing must then be dyslexic is not a logical corollary. The error is a classic one: the deductive fallacy of 'affirming the consequent'. It is a fallacy which amateur (and professional) diagnosticians need to recognise and avoid—although that may prove difficult, since affirming the consequent is implicit in diagnostic materials published by the Prison Service (HM Prison Service, 1999) and the Basic Skills Agency (Klein, 1993) in the past and it reappears in the Agency's new *Skills for Life* Diagnostic Assessments in Literacy (Bradshaw et al., 2002).

One way of avoiding this fallacy might be to ensure that only those impairments which are 'persistent' after years of regular schooling qualify for consideration as 'dyslexic' (Herrington & Hunter-Carsch, 2001). How the tutor manages this situation needs to be guided by its ethical implications. Moreover, with respect to method and quality of early reading teaching strategies, the quest to identify whether or not there has been 'regular schooling' may be a fool's errand.

Phonological deficits do not permit dyslexics to be differentiated from other poor readers.

Limitations of the phonological deficit theory: the phonological-core variable-difference model of reading disability
The ability to detect and process speech sounds can be compromised for more than one reason and those reasons are likely to differ from one learner to another. In some cases, the dominant factor might appear to be experiential; in some, the dominant factor might appear to be biological; and, in the remaining cases, neither factor might predominate. The question then arises whether cases of reading disability form discrete clusters (or subtypes). From such an admittedly simplified account, a typology of reading-disability subtypes might be derived, with two questionably discrete categories and a residual category, thus illustrating a

problem occurring in other typologies: an unbridgeable gap between '(h) those that are included in this classification' and '(i) etcetera' (Borges, 2000). The problem arises even in a univariate classification; in a multivariate classification, it leads to increasing fractionation (Van Orden et al., 2001).

Is there a more persuasive way of classifying the observations? Need they be classified at all? Does it help to conceive of all the relevant distributions of reading-related cognitive skills as being continuously arrayed in a multidimensional space and not distributed in clusters (Ellis, 1985; Stanovich, 1988)? Does it help to consider the question quantitatively, in order to avoid 'the inherent connotations of discreteness carried by many natural language terms' (Stanovich, 1988)? In so far as dyslexia (or 'reading disability') is conceptualised as a difficulty in learning how to decode print, the phonological-core variable-difference model (Stanovich, 1988) not only recognises that phonological difficulties are common to both dyslexic and 'ordinary' poor readers but, by conceptualising differences in terms of dimensions, it also avoids the problems of discreteness and residual or mixed categories in dyslexia subtype analyses.

Although the phonological-core variable-difference model rests on a dimensional concept, it is claimed to be compatible with the categorical differences implied by subtypes (Morris et al., 1998). Nor are subtypes the only outstanding issue. The model proposes that the poor reader with dyslexia has an impairment localised at the phonological core whereas the ordinary poor reader has impairments extending into a variety of domains (Stanovich, 1988)—essentially the same distinction drawn between 'specific reading retardation' and general reading backwardness in the Isle of Wight study (Rutter et al., 1970). If the description 'specific' has any meaning at all, whether applied to 'reading retardation', learning difficulty, or dyslexia, things cannot be otherwise.

However, a concept of specificity is less easy to reconcile with the pattern-of-difficulties concept of dyslexia, where severe and persistent difficulty in learning to read is but one characteristic among many (Miles, 1983), or with the finding that shared problems may be more numerous and diverse than allowed for by the model (Hoskyn & Swanson, 2000). The concept of specificity is correspondingly difficult to reconcile with some of the items listed in behavioural checklists for dyslexia screening (see *Appendices 5* and *6*). It is also difficult to reconcile with our current understanding of human development (Gottlieb & Halpern, 2002) and its implications for reading (Stanovich, 1986).

> Challenges to the categorical assumption of the phonological deficit theory are addressed by the multi-dimensional phonological-core, variable-difference model of reading disability.

What does the phonological-core variable-difference model predict?
The phonological-core variable-difference model leads to the prediction that the dyslexic's impairment, while more localised, is more severe than that of the 'ordinary' poor reader and that because of its severity it will be more difficult to remediate (Stanovich, 1988). Consistent with this prediction is a recent finding, described by its authors as 'new, and perhaps controversial' (Rack & Hatcher, 2002), that dyslexics are actually less responsive to intervention than ordinary poor readers. Controversy? Almost certainly. Novelty? No. There is undoubtedly a conflict between robust findings that students with cognitive deficits in the domain of phonology are difficult to remediate (Vellutino et al., 1996), or even treatment-resistant (Chiappe et al., 2001) and claims that 'the effects of dyslexia can be largely

overcome by skilled specialist teaching' (Dyslexia Institute: see *Appendix 1*) and that the multisensory method, 'used early enough and by qualified practitioners, has every likelihood of eliminating the emergence of notable reading and writing problems' (Academy of Orton-Gillingham Practitioners and Educators: see *Appendix 1*).

Given that most 'ordinary' poor readers have deficits in the opportunity but not in the ability to learn, it is possible that the phonological impairments of treatment-responsive students are experiential, while those of the treatment-resistant students are caused primarily by fundamental deficits in the cognitive skills underlying reading ability (Vellutino et al., 1996). This distinction leads to a paradoxical conclusion—for advocates if not for scientists—that the intervention programmes for 'dyslexics' are successful in proportion to the number of 'ordinary poor readers' who take part in them. The conclusion accords with the conjecture that a phonologically-based intervention programme would be of greater benefit to an unimpaired learner from a disadvantaged background than to any learner with a structurally atypical brain (Eckert et al., 2001). With respect to at least one implemented programme, the Dyspel Pilot Project (Klein, 1998), which was funded for interventions with dyslexic prisoners and which was presented to the Prime Minister as a dyslexia-related scheme, the conclusion may be valid. Although the project has claimed success with dyslexic learners, an undetermined number of the participants, and possibly all of them, were 'ordinary poor readers' (personal communication, BDA Development Officer; personal communication, Education Manager at HMP Pentonville).

How well does the phonological-core, variable-difference model account for dyslexia in other languages? Where reading accuracy is the primary source of difficulty, the model is clearly valid and evidence from an imaging study suggests that the effect is universal (Paulesu et al., 2001), although the nature of the language being learned appears to play a part in the course of brain development (Habib et al., 2000). Where fluency rather than accuracy is the primary source of difficulty, the model's validity depends on whether or not fluency is understood as a measure of efficiency in phonological processing. Evidence suggests that people learning to read in nonalphabetic scripts may have deficits in processing phonological information, just like their alphabet-learning counterparts (Ho et al., 2000). Evidence from languages with alphabetic scripts suggests that a phonological deficit is a serious problem in more opaque spelling systems such as English and French but that it is less of a problem in German (Wimmer & Goswami, 1994), Greek (Goswami et al., 1997), Italian (Tressoldi et al., 2001) and Welsh (Ellis & Hooper, 2001), where the orthographies have greater spelling-to-sound consistency. In Finnish, where the spelling system is almost perfectly transparent, phonological awareness measures seem to be especially poor predictors of at-risk reading development (Holopainen et al., 2001). Perhaps languages that are readable at the syllabic level tend not to expose readers' difficulties in phonemic (i.e. sub-syllabic) analysis.

> The phonological-core, variable-difference model predicts that the dyslexic learner's impairment will be less responsive to intervention than that of the 'ordinary' poor reader.

> Intervention programmes for 'dyslexia' may be successful in proportion to the number of 'ordinary poor readers' who take part in them.

Is there an alternative to the phonological-core variable-difference model?
Despite an element of uncertainty about the role of identification methods in establishing different profiles in developmental dyslexia across languages, it appears that differences in

environmental factors can explain the observed differences in dyslexic behaviour better than differences in cognitive profiles might explain them (Sprenger-Charolles et al., 2001). Does this mean that, strictly speaking, the problems with phonological awareness represent a knowledge deficit rather than a learning disability? Or does it mean that one type of learning disability is activated only by 'non-transparent' orthographies and a second type of learning disability is activated by all orthographies? Genetic evidence appears to support the latter conjecture (Grigorenko et al., 2001) and thus to support the hypothesis that there are two independent sources of reading dysfunction, one related to phonological processing only and one related to lexical access, or naming speed only (Lovett, 1984)—the 'double deficit' hypothesis (Bowers & Wolf, 1993; Wolf & Bowers, 1999; Wolf et al., 2000a). If this is so, then it might suggest an alternative to the phonological-core variable-difference model.

The double-deficit model of reading disability is a further alternative to the phonological deficit model.

Dyslexia and lexical access: the double-deficit hypothesis

Introduction
A combination of deficits in accuracy (or phonological deficits) and fluency (or naming-speed deficits) appears to characterise students with the most serious and pervasive impairments in reading across various languages (Wolf & Bowers, 1999). The double deficit hypothesis represents an evolving, alternative conceptualisation of reading disabilities in which, in addition to a core deficit in accuracy, there is a second core deficit in fluency (Wolf & Bowers, 1999). Ultimately, the hypothesis could lead to a more differentiated view of reading failure and a more comprehensive approach to reading intervention (Wolf et al., 2000a).

The double-deficit model conceptualises dyslexia as entailing core deficits in both accuracy and fluency.

Is fluency distinct from phonological processing?
Fluency is the most salient characteristic of skilled readers (Fuchs et al., 2001). It can be viewed as a performance indicator of overall reading competence, achieved when efficient low-level word recognition frees up memory capacity for higher-level comprehension (Fuchs et al., 2001). However, there is some uncertainty as to whether rapid automatised naming, the conventional test of lexical access, is simply a phonological subprocess or whether it is a way of 'stressing' the phonological system through the demand for retrieval of phonological codes (Cutting & Denckla, 2001).

Evidence for two independent sources of reading difficulty might be provided by a double dissociation of accuracy and fluency, but not without the risk of circular argument: there is no theory-independent way to determine whether a given case is 'pure', since it requires in the first place a reliable theory of cognitive modules to guarantee that a 'pure' dissociation has been observed (Van Orden et al., 2001). From a behavioural perspective, oral reading fluency is a direct measure of phonological segmentation and phonological recoding (Fuchs et al., 2001). On the other hand, independent effects on reading achievement have been found for phonological awareness and rapid naming (de Jong & van der Leij, 1999). For separable effects, the evidence from psychometric research is supplemented by evidence from molecular genetics (Grigorenko et al., 2001).

Separate concurrent and predictive correlates have been found for tests of rapid automatised naming and tests of phonological segmentation and decoding (Meyer et al., 1998), providing support for the double-deficit hypothesis. Moreover, particular emphases on both processing speed and the integration of an ensemble of lower level, visual-perceptual processes with higher-level cognitive and linguistic subprocesses may distinguish naming speed from phonological processing (Wolf & Bowers, 1999).

Because rapid naming has predictive power only for poor readers, not for average readers, it might be that impaired readers are qualitatively different from the normal-reading population and are not simply the 'tail' of a normal distribution of reading ability (Meyer et al., 1998).

> The double-deficit hypothesis is supported by the finding that measures of accuracy and fluency have separate correlates.

Cognitive components of rapid naming

Naming speed has been conceptualised as 'a complex ensemble of attentional, perceptual, conceptual, memory, phonological, semantic and motoric subprocesses that place heavy emphasis on precise timing requirements within each component and across all components' (Wolf et al., 2000a). In a more detailed formulation, the components include: attention to stimulus; bihemispheric visual processes responsible for initial feature detection, visual discrimination and pattern identification; integration of visual feature and pattern identification with stored orthographic representations; integration of visual information with stored phonological representations; access and retrieval of phonological labels; activation and integration of semantic and conceptual information; and motoric activation leading to articulation (Wolf & Bowers, 1999). However, not all of the constructs have a precise definition, nor are the components of rapid naming tasks measured directly (Pennington et al., 2001). This is not to claim that they cannot be defined or that they cannot be measured. However, it is a reminder that the double-deficit hypothesis remains, pending further research, a hypothesis. It is not a dogma.

> Reading fluency is a complex process and further research is needed for these complexities to be better understood.

What causes the naming-speed deficit?

Slow naming speed persists as a characteristic of severely disabled readers (Bowers & Wolf, 1993). Automaticity of retrieval, not knowledge of names itself (as in confrontational naming tasks), appears to give rapid automatised naming its predictive power (Meyer et al., 1998). But is it then a marker of lexical encoding processes (Ellis & Miles, 1981), reflecting the precise timing mechanisms necessary to the development of orthographic codes and to their integration with phonological codes (Bowers & Wolf, 1993)? Do naming-speed deficits reflect a larger, systemic timing deficit (Wolf et al., 2000a)? These questions entail 'two highly complex and unresolved issues': whether naming speed represents the linguistic analogue of a larger, potentially domain-general timing deficit that goes beyond language and how such a broadened conceptualisation of processing-speed deficits would relate to reading processes (Wolf et al., 2000a).

When the hypothesis was first proposed, it was thought that slow naming speed could be predictive of reading difficulty by several interrelated routes: as an index of inefficient amalgamation of phonological and orthographic identities; as indicating an impaired timing mechanism affecting the quality of an orthographic code, or the amount of exposure and practice needed to achieve good quality representations, or both (Bowers & Wolf, 1993). Now, there are two broad conjectures. The first conjecture is that, if the magnocellular system is aberrant in the mid-brain area known as the thalamus, then the processing of lower spatial-frequency components will be slowed, potentially leading to slower visual discriminations, slower letter-pattern identification, slower naming speed for serially presented visual stimuli and delayed induction of orthographic patterns, so that slower naming speed is an index of lower-level problems that disrupt the smooth development of fluency in word identification and comprehension (Wolf & Bowers, 1999). The second conjecture is that naming speed might both indicate dysfunction in lower level processes and also contribute to pervasive reading failure as one manifestation of a cascading system of more general processing-speed deficits affecting visual, auditory and possibly motoric domains, in addition to orthographic and phonological processing systems (Wolf & Bowers, 1999).

Two broad explanations have been proposed for the naming speed deficit, but it is not yet clear how or whether we should adjudicate between them.

The diagnostic significance of naming speed tasks

Although there is evidence that rapid automatised naming tasks differentiate dyslexics from average readers, from ordinary poor readers and from readers with other learning disabilities (Wolf et al., 2000a), there is also counter-evidence in the cases of both ordinary poor readers (Swan & Goswami, 1997) and subjects with impaired executive functions (Rashid et al., 2001; Tannock et al., 2000). In particular, it is unclear whether the only people to show impairments in rapid naming are readers with persistent difficulty and additional impairments associated with the constructs of attention-deficit/hyperactivity disorder (American Psychiatric Association, 1994) or hyperkinetic disorder (World Health Organisation, 1992).

For most practitioners, the critical conflict of evidence is probably whether 'ordinary' readers with difficulties do (Swan & Goswami, 1997; Waber et al., 2000) or do not (Marcus, 1997, in Wolf & Bowers, 1999) have a naming-speed deficit. If they do not, then tests of rapid automatised naming like that in the Dyslexia Adult Screening Test (Fawcett & Nicolson, 1998) might be a useful way of differentiating dyslexic from ordinary poor readers. However, resolution of this conflict could entail a reconceptualisation of dyslexia that denies the assumption of specificity by incorporating deficits in both language and executive functions—that is to say, dysfunctions in both the temporal lobe and the frontal lobe of the brain. As recent research suggests that rapid automatised naming taps both visual-verbal (language domain) and processing speed (executive domain) contributions to reading (Denckla & Cutting, 1999), such a resolution is possible.

Performance on naming-speed tasks might distinguish dyslexic people from 'ordinary' poor readers.

If dyslexia can be distinguished in this way, then it may be a less specific impairment than it is sometimes believed to be.

Naming-speed deficits in other languages

There is evidence for a naming-speed deficit across a wide range of writing and spelling systems. It is a specific marker of reading disability in both opaque and transparent orthographies and in the presence or absence of attentional problems (Närhi & Ahonen, 1995). It appears in non-alphabetic systems such as Chinese, where beginning readers have naming-speed deficits and phonological memory deficits like their alphabetic counterparts (Ho & Lai, 1999). Significantly, in spelling systems such as German where there is little evidence of a phonological *awareness* deficit, dyslexics (i.e. dysfluent readers) exhibit a substantial naming-speed (or perhaps phonological *processing*) deficit (Wimmer et al., 2000). This distinction may be critically important for reading difficulties in English, too.

Naming-speed impairments appear to be a universal marker of reading disability, irrespective of writing and spelling systems.

The relation of naming-speed to psychometric and demographic variables

There is an interesting dissociation between good and poor readers when the relationships between speeded naming and other variables are compared. For poor readers in general, both naming speed and phonological awareness may be significantly associated with word reading, but verbal intelligence appears to have no association with it; in contrast, for good readers, phonological awareness and verbal intelligence, but not naming speed, may be significantly associated with word reading (McBride-Chang & Manis, 1996).

In all such comparisons, it has been suggested that attention should be paid to these variables when interpreting test scores: IQ and SES; differences in the variability of predictors over time; the quality and type of reading instruction; and the different rates of change of predictors at different ages (Wolf & Bowers, 1999).

The prognostic significance of naming-speed deficits in dyslexia

While some processes are believed to be innate and thus not amenable to training, motivation or arousal, others need practice before they become rapid, parallel and automatic; in contrast, effortful mental processes are slow, serial and subjectively controlled (August & Garfinkel, 1990). The exercise of a complex skill requires the co-ordination of many component processes within a brief time-frame; if each one required attention, then the exercise would become impossible because it would exceed attentional capacity (LaBerge & Samuels, 1974). Fluent reading therefore requires that word recognition is automatised in order to free learners' attentional capacity for comprehension, which cannot be automatised in the same way (Fuchs et al., 2001). Most readers attain a sufficient level of automaticity in word recognition to be able to concentrate on meaning. The critical question is whether all readers can do so or whether some people can learn how the alphabetic system works but then cannot apply that knowledge without effortful subjective control.

It has been suggested that readers with naming-speed and double deficits constitute some of the treatment-resisters described in intervention studies aimed at enhancing phonological awareness (Wolf & Bowers, 2000). Evidence from studies of dyslexics in higher education lends weight to this suggestion; although dyslexic university students may have developed sufficient compensation skills to attain average scores on untimed reading achievement measures, they may continue to demonstrate significant difficulty in rapid naming (Riccio et al., 1998).

With respect to adult 'ordinary' poor readers, who do not have a naming-speed deficit, there is evidence that fluency can be taught and that developing fluency can sometimes lead to increases in reading achievement (Kruidenier, 2002). However, whether a core deficit in visual naming speed will prove as amenable to treatment as a phonological deficit has not been thoroughly investigated (Lovett et al., 2000b). While intensive phonological interventions have led to improvements in reading accuracy, they have had little effect on fluency (Torgesen et al., 2001). However, there are indications that, at least for interventions involving children, teaching programmes can be designed to enhance fluency in participants with naming-speed impairments (Lovett et al., 2000a; Wolf et al., 2000b).

There is evidence that interventions can enhance fluency in adult ordinary poor readers.

We do not know yet if interventions can enhance reading fluency in dyslexic adults.

Limitations of the double-deficit hypothesis

The double-deficit hypothesis 'has never been conceptualised as a total explanation of dyslexia' (Wolf & Bowers, 1999). Like the phonological deficit hypothesis, it does not address all the problems experienced by some persistently poor readers. Meanwhile, conflicts of evidence as to the independence of naming-speed deficits from phonemic awareness deficits have yet to be resolved. The appearance of independence has been attributed to failure to control for letter-knowledge (de Jong & van der Leij, 1999), while the greater severity of impairment associated with a double deficit has been attributed in part to a statistical artefact caused by grouping children based on their performance on two correlated continuous variables, at least as far as some poor readers are concerned (Schatschneider et al., 2002).

Opinions differ widely as to the proportion of dyslexic people with a reading rate deficit, a difference that may reflect variation in the methods used to identify research samples. It may also be the case that differences between groups are invalid at the level of the individual: in one study, when individual participants were investigated, it was found that approximately 53 per cent of the dyslexic poor readers and 42 per cent of 'ordinary' poor readers had reaction times equal to or faster than those of the good readers (Catts et al., 2002). This finding might or might not be replicated; until the question is decided, we must suspend our judgement.

We are not yet in a position to assess the usefulness of the double-deficit hypothesis in explaining dyslexia.

Dyslexia and automaticity: the cerebellar deficit hypothesis

Introduction

Reading is a complex skill (Carr et al., 1990). When we read a single word, our brains make separate computations sustained by distinct neural areas, involving visual integration of the word, access to its phonological code, access to its semantic meaning, access to the structural form of the object that it represents (where that is applicable) and access to its learned output (Posner et al., 1997). If each of these component processes required attention, our attentional capacity would soon be overwhelmed (LaBerge & Samuels, 1974); decoding would then become laboriously slow and we would have little if any attentional capacity left for comprehension. Only when the basic skill of decoding print is so fluent as to be automatic does comprehension become possible—that is to say, we cannot properly understand what we read unless the act of decoding is involuntary, free from any demands on processing capacity and resistant to interruption from competing activity in the same domain (Yap & van der Leij, 1994).

For reading comprehension, it is necessary that word-recognition is automatic.

The dyslexia automatisation deficit hypothesis

The dyslexia automatisation deficit hypothesis attributes the reading deficits of dyslexics to a general failure to automatise skills (Nicolson & Fawcett, 1990). Since memory span is partly determined by reading rate and reading rate is determined by processing speed, which is in its turn partly determined by the degree of automatisation, the evidence from reading appears compatible with an automatisation deficit explanation (Nicolson & Fawcett, 1990). Where dyslexic people have problems in other motor and cognitive domains, as the hypothesis would predict, an associated 'conscious compensation' hypothesis suggests that these problems are masked by coping strategies and by active allocation of extra attentional resources (Nicolson & Fawcett, 1990). The resulting threefold prediction that dyslexic performance breaks down primarily for resource-intensive tasks, is particularly susceptible to stress and can be maintained only for relatively short periods, is consistent with the available evidence (Nicolson & Fawcett, 1990).

Taken together, the dyslexia automatisation deficit hypothesis (Nicolson & Fawcett, 1990) and the phonological deficit hypothesis can be viewed as twin components of the double-deficit hypothesis, in that they offer cognitive-level explanations of the two main difficulties of persistently poor readers—those involving fluency and accuracy. However, the dyslexia automatisation deficit hypothesis reaches beyond reading skills to offer a cognitive explanation of dyslexics' difficulties in automatising skills unrelated to reading (Nicolson & Fawcett, 1994), thus breaking new ground that the phonological deficit hypothesis could not cover and which the double-deficit hypothesis does not cover.

The dyslexia automatisation deficit hypothesis proposes an explanation of failure to automatise skills in word-recognition and other domains.

The cerebellar deficit hypothesis

Although, initially, the dyslexia automatisation deficit hypothesis proposed only a proximal, cognitive explanation of the dyslexics' difficulties in skill mastery, it was soon conjectured that a distal, biological explanation might be found in 'noisy neural networks' (Fawcett & Nicolson, 1991). Previously, there had been speculation that cerebellar function might be mildly impaired in dyslexia (Frank & Levinson, 1973). However, it was only with confirmation that the cerebellum—'the brain's autopilot' (Stein, 2001)—was involved in linguistic as well as motor skill acquisition (Ito, 1993) that there was reason to investigate cerebellar dysfunction as a possible cause of dyslexia (Nicolson et al., 1995). Brain imaging studies have since shown, for example, that the normal cerebellum is activated during speech perception (Dogil et al., 2002; Mathiak et al., 2002) and in reading (Fulbright et al., 1999) and that the patterns of activation are different for phonological and semantic tasks.

The cerebellar deficit hypothesis can be stated as a series of propositions. First, the behavioural symptoms of dyslexia can be characterised as difficulties in skill automatisation; this pattern of difficulties in cognitive, information-processing and motor skills would be predicted by cerebellar impairment; dyslexic adults show direct neurobiological evidence of such impairment; it is possible to explain the reading-related and other problems of dyslexic learners in terms of impaired implicit learning attributable to cerebellar abnormality (Nicolson et al., 2001a).

The cerebellar deficit hypothesis has been supported by a finding that dyslexic and non-dyslexic subjects do not overlap on measures of cerebellar impairment (Fawcett et al., 1996). Consistent with the cerebellar deficit hypothesis, subsequent investigations in a different laboratory found both biochemical (Rae et al., 1998) and morphological (Rae et al., 2002) abnormalities in the cerebella of dyslexic adults. At group level, poor readers whose reading levels are discrepant with measures of their intellectual ability have difficulty in static cerebellar tasks, whereas non-discrepant poor readers perform at near-normal levels (Fawcett et al., 2001). Interestingly, the non-discrepant poor readers (who are without cerebellar impairments) perform significantly worse than those with cerebellar impairments on memory span, segmentation and rhyme tasks (Fawcett et al., 2001), rather as ordinary poor readers performed worse than dyslexics at pseudoword repetition in the Geelong study (Jorm et al., 1986a). In other words, the most inaccurate readers are not the most likely to be dyslexic (see also page 34)

All in all, the cerebellar deficit hypothesis offers a potentially unifying framework for dyslexia, in that a cerebellar deficit can give rise to articulatory difficulties (leading to phonological problems), slowed central processing speed (and thus problems with reading rate), deficits in motor skills (and thus problems with handwriting) and reading skills deficits in consequence of impairments in learning new skills and automatising those skills (Fawcett et al., 2001).

The cerebellar deficit hypothesis proposes that the behavioural symptoms of dyslexia can be characterised as difficulties in automatising both cognitive and motor skills.

The hypothesis proposes that this pattern of difficulties is consistent with an impairment in cerebellar functioning.

Both structural and functional abnormalities have been found in the cerebella of dyslexics.

The most inaccurate readers are not the most likely to be dyslexic.

Limitations of the cerebellar deficit hypothesis

While the cerebellar deficit account of dyslexia is plausible, it is explicitly speculative (Nicolson & Fawcett, 1999; Nicolson et al., 2001a; Nicolson et al., 2001b). Whether the cerebellum simply reflects dysfunction elsewhere in the brain, or whether it makes a unique contribution to cognitive functioning, remains an outstanding question (Desmond & Fiez, 1998; Zeffiro & Eden, 2001). Until very recently, there has been no suggestion that remediating any cerebellar symptoms would have an effect on the primary educational difficulties relating to literacy; it might yet be established that cerebellar symptoms, literacy difficulties and phonological difficulties are all covariates of some as-yet-unidentified underlying cause (Nicolson & Fawcett, 1999).

Recent evidence from the *Dyslexia, Dyspraxia and Attention Disorder Treatment* (DDAT) study (Reynolds et al., 2003) that a cerebellar deficit in dyslexia is causal has far-reaching implications, not least for the reporting of scientific questions on television (Wilsher, 2002).

While the DDAT evidence might support the conjecture that a cerebellar deficit is causal, we have yet to find out whether the finding can be replicated with a more rigorous research design; the study has come under criticism from several quarters (e.g. Rack, 2003; Richards et al., 2003; Singleton & Stuart, 2003; Snowling & Hulme, 2003; Stein, 2003) although its methods have been defended (Nicolson & Reynolds, 2003a, 2003b).

If it should be established that the cerebellar deficit is not causal, it might nevertheless be the case that the cerebellum plays a *co-ordinating* role in the processing of speech production at the interface of cognitive and executive functions (Silveri & Misciagna, 2000), in which case a causal direction would need to be established for any functional abnormality (Beaton, 2002). Future research might also have to eliminate possible alternative explanations such as attentional difficulties, general language impairment, or less specific neurodevelopmental problems than the dyslexia construct implies (Bishop, 2002). Meanwhile, there appears to be no support for the cerebellar deficit hypothesis when causal theories are compared (Ramus et al., 2003a; Ramus et al., 2003b).

Importantly, we do not know yet how far cerebellar impairment might explain the problems of every person with dyslexia (Fawcett et al., 2001). As Aristotle was among the earliest to point out, with reference to the fallacy of division, what may be true of a group of people is not necessarily true of every member of the group. Among the individuals in one study, the dissociation between those with and without IQ-discrepancy on the static cerebellar tests was not complete (Fawcett et al., 2001). This suggests that, as the 'core' deficits predicted by other theories of dyslexia are not sufficient at group level to differentiate between dyslexics and ordinary poor readers (Fawcett et al., 2001), so evidence of a cerebellar impairment may not do so at the individual level.

It is unclear whether cerebellar abnormalities are causes or correlates of dyslexia.

Even if cerebellar abnormalities are found to cause reading difficulties for some people, they might not explain every case of reading difficulty.

Dyslexia and processing speed: the temporal processing deficit theory

Introduction

There is a plausible link between hearing impairments and reading problems. Hearing provides inputs to information-processing; this in turn yields phonemic categories, which are important to speech perception; damage to the auditory pathway leads to degraded signals, with a possibility of corresponding degradation in phonemic representation; and language problems with their roots in speech perception and production will be the result (Farmer & Klein, 1995).

In a hierarchy of temporal information-processing functions, timing may be critically important (Farmer & Klein, 1995). At the lowest level of the processing hierarchy are target detection and identification; at an intermediate level are individuation and temporal order judgement in both auditory and visual domains; at the highest level is complex sequencing in both perception and production. Deficits might be interpreted in terms of rate of processing, 'smudging' of encoded information over time so that mental representation loses crispness of input, or to 'temporal jitter' where the times assigned to events or their properties are variable (Klein & Farmer, 1995). There have been indications that temporal processing deficits occur frequently in dyslexics and might be an important consideration for investigating the underlying causes of dyslexia. Nevertheless, even if an association between temporal processing deficits and dyslexia is accepted and the plausibility of a causal path from the former to the latter recognised, the hypothesis that temporal processing deficits are the root cause of some cases of dyslexia may be far from established (Farmer & Klein, 1995).

The temporal processing deficit theory proposes that dyslexia might be caused by inefficiency in processing rapid sequences of very brief stimuli.

Do dyslexics have a temporal deficit in visual processing?

At one time, dyslexia was explained in terms of a visual deficit (Orton, 1937). This explanation imbued dyslexia with 'a certain exotic quality, manifested most prominently in the popular belief that children so afflicted literally perceive letters backward and frequently reverse them in their printing and writing' (Vellutino, 1979). Popular or not, this belief may be mistaken if it requires written reversals to be consistent, since observation shows that they are erratic. However, the implausibility of one kind of visual deficit does not exclude the possibility of a different kind of visual deficit in dyslexia. Because of the heterogeneity in reading disability, the validity of other explanations ought not to exclude the possibility of a valid visual-deficit explanation in some cases if not in all of them.

What, then, is the evidence for a visual deficit in dyslexia? Converging lines of evidence have shown that about three in four dyslexics have normal visual sustained system functioning but deficient visual transient system sensitivity (Lovegrove, 1994). Such a deficit might be only a correlate of dyslexia, but it raises the possibility of a more general deficit underlying systems processing temporal stimuli (Solan, 1999). Differences between groups may be attributable to a minority of dyslexics, but data from some tasks are consistent with deficits within the visual transient system (Everatt et al., 1999).

Against a visual transient system deficit, it has been argued that reading problems caused by a defect in the transient system would create most difficulty in reading prose and least difficulty in reading single, isolated words, whereas 'retarded' readers show a profound and intransigent impairment in word recognition skills (Hulme, 1988). If such an impairment were caused by neurological immaturity, there might be associated impairments on many tasks where deviation is unrelated to reading difficulty (Hulme, 1988); however, maturational impairments might not persist into adulthood (Bruck, 1998).

Alternatively, deficits in visual perception might result from inappropriate strategy decisions rather than any organic dysfunction (Geiger et al., 1992). Since normal reading ability appears to be compatible with the visual persistence across spatial frequency found in dyslexics (Slaghuis et al., 1993), it may be either that this problem is remediable or that a different pattern of impairment affects only a minority of dyslexics (Mattis et al., 1975). A further possibility is that the impairments originate not in the visual system but in the executive functions. However, with experimental control for attention and memory problems, visual deficits have not been observed (Bruck, 1998).

Yet again, it appears that only phonological dyslexics, not 'ordinary' poor readers (or 'surface dyslexics'), are impaired on some if not all visual tasks (Cestnick & Coltheart, 1999). Poor readers described as 'dyseidetic' or 'surface dyslexic' (who by definition have no phonological deficit) are unimpaired on contrast sensitivity tasks (Borsting et al., 1996; Spinelli et al., 1997), so these studies show no evidence of a visual deficit, either. Even where a visual deficit has been found, it is described as 'subtle' and rarely severe enough to cause symptomatic complaint (Solan, 1999).

It seems unlikely that dyslexia is characterised by impaired processing of rapidly-changing visual stimuli.

Do dyslexics have a temporal deficit in auditory processing?

Two hypotheses have been proposed for an auditory deficit in dyslexia (Studdert-Kennedy, 2002). On the evidence of low perceptual performance on speech (but not on non-speech), poor short-term memory for words (but not for non-verbal sounds) and similar error patterns in verbal short-term memory irrespective of whether words are read or heard, poor readers might have a speech-specific deficit (Studdert-Kennedy, 2002). Alternatively, on the evidence of impairments in temporal order judgments for rapidly presented non-verbal sounds, choice reaction times to pure tones differing in pitch, sensitivity to the rate and depth of acoustic frequency modulation and auditory localisation, poor readers might have a general auditory deficit (Studdert-Kennedy, 2002). In each hypothesis, the problem derives from a neurological impairment. Only the latter hypothesis, not the former, proposes that phonological deficits stem from impairments in *rapid* temporal processing (Studdert-Kennedy, 2002).

Atypical auditory anatomy has been found in a post-mortem study (Galaburda et al., 1994), but this finding may not be generalisable. However, there has been support for the hypothesis that dyslexic people have generally impaired development of neuronal systems responsible for rapid temporal processing in the auditory system, both from laboratory studies using non-verbal stimuli (McAnally & Stein, 1996; Stein & McAnally, 1995) and from an intervention study that used no linguistic material but nevertheless secured an improvement in reading skills (Kujala et al., 2001).

These issues are still unresolved. One complication is that, while a general auditory deficit could characterise a subset of children, such a deficit may be neither necessary nor sufficient to cause dyslexia (Rosen & Manganari, 2001). A further complication is the possibility that causality may be bidirectional between neuronal development and reading (Stein & Talcott, 1999). Using the Auditory Repetition Task, a measure of rapid auditory processing, one study found no evidence that phonological difficulties are secondary to impairments of rapid auditory processing, (Marshall et al., 2001). Other studies have interpreted their findings as precluding the conceptualisation of temporal language deficits as the unitary cause of phonological and language deficits in disabled readers (Heath et al., 1999), or as offering little support for the hypothesis that dyslexic listeners are impaired in their ability to process information in the temporal fine structure of auditory stimuli (Hill et al., 1999).

To date, it appears that no experimental study has yet supported either of the main assumptions of the rapid auditory processing hypothesis and no experimental study has yet demonstrated a mechanism by which an auditory deficit in people with reading impairments might disrupt either speech perception or phoneme awareness (Studdert-Kennedy, 2002). For example, one recent study found that although reading-disabled adults showed simple, across-the-board deficits at the level of reaction time, there was no evidence of the group-by-rate interaction that is central to the timing deficit hypothesis (Chiappe et al., 2002). It has also been argued that failure to find a single experimental timing measure contributing variance in continuous rapid automatised naming provides an unmistakable refutation of the temporal processing deficit hypothesis (Chiappe et al., 2002).

It seems unlikely that dyslexia is characterised by impaired processing of rapidly-changing auditory stimuli.

The magnocellular deficit hypothesis

It is only one of many paradoxes in this field of investigation that a wide-ranging explanatory hypothesis finds mixed support for its central observation of a temporal processing deficit in reading disability. Yet the magnocellular deficit hypothesis (Stein, 2001; Stein & Talcott, 1999; Stein et al., 2000; Stein, 1994; Stein & Walsh, 1997) is a comprehensive if not yet persuasive attempt to explain a wide range of behaviours associated with developmental dyslexia and to do so at every level in the three-level model (see *Appendix 4*).

The magnocellular deficit hypothesis starts from an observation that many dyslexic people find that the letters they are trying to read appear to move around and cross over each other (Stein, 2001). This phenomenon is explained in terms of impaired sensitivity to visual motion and unstable binocular fixation, caused by atypical development of the magnocellular layers of the lateral geniculate nucleus, a 'processing station' on the route from the eyes to other parts of the brain. The atypical development of the magnocells is ascribed to genetically-directed antibody attack during antenatal development, together with vulnerability resulting from diets low in essential fatty acids.

The magnocellular deficit hypothesis proposes a comprehensive account of dyslexia from biology to behaviour.

Limitations of the magnocellular deficit hypothesis

The hypothesis is highly speculative (Stein & Talcott, 1999) and most of the evidence is still circumstantial (Stein, 2001), so that further research is essential. The impairment in the dyslexic visual magnocellular system is slight and is not found in all dyslexics (Stein, 2001). It is not immediately obvious how the visual magnocellular system contributes to reading; it might even be an epiphenomenon connected with the dyslexic phenotype but playing no important causal role in dyslexic people's reading difficulties (Stein, 2001). Impaired contrast sensitivity is unlikely to be the *direct* cause of dyslexic reading difficulties, as print does not normally flicker and contrast is usually high (Stein & Talcott, 1999). Measures of visual motion sensitivity correlate with visual homophone test scores across the whole population (Stein, 2001), which implies that the differences between dyslexic and non-dyslexic are differences in degree rather than categorical distinctions. If this proves to be the case, then the best understanding of developmental disabilities may be achieved by investigating the causes of population variability (Gilger & Kaplan, 2001).

Although the evidence for an association between immune disorders and dyslexia is inconclusive (Flannery & Liederman, 1995; Galaburda, 1993; Gilger & Pennington, 1995; Gilger et al., 1998; Taylor et al., 2001; Tønnessen et al., 1993; Vincent et al., 2002), the question is one that merits further investigation. At the very least, the genetic evidence is suggestive; further research on the gene loci associated with myelination (Smith et al., 2001), for example, may or may not lead to effective interventions for enhancing information processing by addressing problems identified elsewhere as 'noisy neural networks' (Fawcett

& Nicolson, 1991), 'sluggish attentional shifting' (Renvall & Hari, 2002), or timing impairments in speech perception (Goswami et al., 2002; Helenius et al., 2002; Wolff, 2002).

The magnocellular deficit hypothesis itself may be a stage in progress towards a persuasive biological explanation of those cases of reading difficulty, possibly a minority, associated with multi-sensory perceptual deficits (Amitay et al., 2002). The hypothesis may not be best supported by findings from contrast sensitivity studies (Gross-Glenn et al., 1995; Skottun, 2000a, 2000b; Skottun & Parke, 1999). Alternatively, it may be that the information-processing deficit needs to be reconceptualised as an attentional rather than as a perceptual problem (Hari & Renvall, 2001; Hayduk et al., 1996; Saarelma et al., 2002; Stuart et al., 2001; Vidyasagar, 2001). Our present state of knowledge may not permit greater certainty than this.

> Although the magnocellular deficit hypothesis drives an active and wide-ranging research programme, it is too soon to expect any impact on practice in adult literacy teaching.

To conclude this Section, Table 1 summarises very briefly areas of difficulty that are or are not covered by four of the major theories discussed above.

Table 1. Four theories of dyslexia and their explanatory compass

	Reading		Beyond reading	
	Accuracy	Fluency	Cognition	Movement
Phonological deficit	•			
Double deficit	•	•		
Cerebellar deficit		•	•	•
Temporal Processing deficit	•	•	•	

Part three
The next generation of theories

Introduction

Part two discussed the 'four grand theories of dyslexia' at the time of writing (Richards et al., 2002). They are quite different from the theories of a generation ago. To a later generation, they may come to seem as unpersuasive as the theory of visual dysfunction (Orton, 1925, 1937) now seems to most scholars. What will the next generation of theories be like? Whatever form they take, it is probable that the three models described below will influence them.

A cognitive process model of reading disability

The concept of reading difficulty as an invariably biological problem is challenged by a model of reading difficulties based on 'stage' theories of normal reading development (Spear-Swerling, in press; Spear-Swerling & Sternberg, 1994, 1996, 1998). Although the proponents of this model do not rule out the possibility that genuine biological disorder impairs the development of a tiny proportion of poor readers, they argue that the assumption of biological abnormality is incorrect for most people who are identified as 'dyslexic'. Instead, they propose that while individual differences in specific cognitive abilities put some children at greater risk of school failure than others, whether or not those children actually fail may largely depend on their experiences in school. In this way, vulnerability to failure might be either ameliorated or never realised at all.

The model maps the route to highly proficient reading through cognitive processing stages of visual-cue word recognition, alphabetic insight, controlled word recognition, automatic word recognition and strategic reading (see *Appendix 7* for the figure in Spear-Swerling, in press). At each stage, the model shows how difficulty can lead to suboptimal reading and how that in turn may lead to lowered motivation, lowered levels of practice and lowered expectations. It is compatible with the three-level models of reading disability discussed earlier (Fletcher et al., 2002; Jackson & Coltheart, 2001; Morton & Frith, 1995) and also with the 'Matthew effects' model (Stanovich, 1986). In addition, it offers insights into the nature of reading difficulties and guidance as to the appropriate remedial intervention.

The model takes note of several difficulties with the application of the concept of dyslexia to large numbers of poor readers. These difficulties include lack of evidence for a distinctive defect in the biological domain, lack of evidence for a substantial difference between IQ-discrepant and non-discrepant poor readers, unresolved theoretical problems with IQ regression and lack of evidence that there is a group of students with dramatically different educational needs because of any discrepancy between 'potential' and achievement.

As an alternative to both intrinsic (or biological) and extrinsic (or environmental) perspectives on reading difficulties, the 'cognitive process' model takes an interactive perspective from which individual differences are understood in the context of a student's everyday life. In this way, the perspective implicit in the model is consistent with the current perspective on dyslexia in Britain (e.g. Herrington & Hunter-Carsch, 2001).

By stressing the importance of normal reading acquisition as a benchmark for reading difficulties, the model anticipates not one but several different patterns of cognitive and reading deficits. Whether the pattern is 'nonalphabetic', 'compensatory', 'nonautomatic', or 'delayed reading' will depend upon the point at which students go astray in reading acquisition. However, this is not to propose a new theory of causal 'subtypes'. The model illustrates not 'causes' but developmental outcomes. It holds that any individual instance of reading difficulty will involve multiple causes as an outcome of interaction between the environment and the student's individual characteristics.

The cognitive process model of reading disability differs from the explicitly biological theories of dyslexia reviewed in Part two by acknowledging that developmental outcomes are a consequence of complex interactions between the individual and the environment.

The model does not assume a biological abnormality as the default explanation for reading difficulties.

It details a sequence of stages in cognitive processing through which people pass when they learn to read.

At each stage, the model explains the conceptual nature of reading difficulties and it offers guidance on appropriate teaching strategies.

A self-organising systems model of reading disability

A challenge to the notion of specificity in dyslexia comes from a self-organising systems model of learning disability (Zera, 2001; Zera & Lucian, 2001), which derives from systems theory and nonlinear dynamics (see below). It has much in common with other concepts of developmental causality, whether they are general (Bronfenbrenner & Ceci, 1994; Cairns, 1996; Cicchetti & Cannon, 1999; Elman et al., 1996; Fischer & Bidell, 1998; Gottlieb & Halpern, 2002; Karmiloff-Smith, 1998; Sameroff, 1995; Sameroff & Chandler, 1975; Sroufe, 1997; Thelen & Smith, 1994; Thomas & Karmiloff-Smith, 2002) or specific to reading (Snowling, 2000). That is to say, the model is located within mainstream developmental psychology and its concept of 'epigenesis', in which both new structures and new functions are understood to arise in the course of individual development (Gottlieb, 1992).

The self-organising systems model states three main propositions about cognitive development.

First, the system is not modular but distributed. That is to say, complex behaviours like reading and writing are subserved by multifocal neural systems, not by specific anatomical sites within the brain, even though single-focus lesions may impair them. Whereas the specific learning disability concept suggests a more localised dysfunction, a self-organising systems model suggests widespread, diffuse outcomes. If this is really the case, then the notion of a 'specific' learning disability is mistaken.

Second, the system is not static but dynamic. Learning disabilities do not stay confined to specific brain areas. Dysfunction is not focal and constrained but far more pervasive, as a consequence of dynamic and recursive interactions within the neurological system. These interactions may take place in response to either biological or environmental stimuli. Taking the brain's plasticity (or capacity for reorganisation) into account, the model anticipates exponential effects from initial conditions. Once again, the concept of a 'specific' learning disability does not capture the dynamic interplay between the system's various components.

Third, the system is not linear but complex. Linear models of learning disability assume a closed-circuit relationship between brain functioning and behaviour, which in turn suggests direct causal links. We now know that this is not what happens in an open neurological system, where the components interact in a nonlinear, dynamic fashion. Although research into dyslexia has been dominated by linear causal models which then recursively advance the concept of 'specific' disability, it is clear that all disabilities become more pervasive over time, even those that appeared specific at the outset of development.

In this way, there are adverse developmental outcomes. At some point a specific deficit begins to have more generalised effects on processes that underlie a broader range of tasks than reading alone. There are both cognitive consequences and motivational side effects, so that the performance deficits are increasingly global (Stanovich, 1986). According to the self-organising systems model, an inefficiency in processing might begin as a specific deficit but then become global, as underutilisation of a dysfunctional part of the brain leads to overactivation of intact brain areas and to aggravation of any imbalance; repeatedly maladaptive patterns of mental activity may create constraints for future learning; and brain areas that are activated to compensate for the dysfunctional area may come to perform their original functions less efficiently, even though there might be no essential relationship between the two functions.

Tutors often encounter students whose reading problems overlap with impairments in the executive functions of attentional switching, selective attention, sustained attention and working memory. The self-organising systems model suggests that working memory and reading problems aggravate each other and that both might originate in phonological processing problems, in which case a working memory problem might be alleviated by an improvement in reading.

Few practitioners and diagnosticians of learning disabilities have a sufficiently comprehensive understanding of the neurological system to be able to interpret disabling conditions from this perspective (Zera, 2001). However, if they were to gain such an understanding, the model suggests that their remediation strategies might then take into account the ways in which a supposedly specific disability interacts with other parts of the neural system and strategies of this kind might lead to greater success in alleviating the related symptoms of dysfunction.

The self-organising systems model is compatible with the three-level model, although it entails a more complex view of causality than implied by that model. It does not challenge the idea of a developmental dysfunction resulting from an innate biological constraint, but it does challenge the notion that, regardless of how specific such a constraint might have been, the behavioural outcome itself could remain specific (see also Stanovich, 1986).

The self-organising systems model of reading disability contrasts with the essentially linear theories reviewed in Part two by drawing on non-linear concepts of the process of development.

The model challenges the assumption of specificity in dyslexia and in other learning disabilities.

It captures the dynamic nature of development and it explains why 'compensated' dyslexic students continue to experience difficulty.

It offers an explanation for the relationship between reading and memory problems.

The self-organising systems model alerts practitioners to ways in which teaching strategies might be made more effective.

An atypical brain development framework for the study of developmental learning disabilities

The primary causes of developmental disorders are complex, involving the interaction of genetic and environmental factors, prenatally or postnatally and primary consequences are seen in atypical brain development (Frith, 2001). The concept of atypical brain development may therefore offer a useful framework within which to develop theories, without being a theory in its own right (Gilger & Kaplan, 2001; Kaplan et al., 2001). It marks an increasing recognition that developmental disabilities are typically nonspecific and heterogeneous and that the scientific literature shows comorbidity of symptoms and syndromes to be the rule rather than the exception. The concept was prompted by the realisation that conventional diagnostic categories do not reflect the way that developmental disorders affect real people, that the co-occurrence of developmental disabilities is greater than chance and that it is difficult to find valid subtypes of developmental problems. The framework has been proposed in order to initiate dialogue and debate across a wide variety of disciplines. It reflects data-based theoretical developments not only in the field of learning disability but also in the wider area of developmental disorder.

Centrally, the framework addresses the unsubstantiated assumption of 'comorbidity', namely that any co-occurring symptoms have independent origins. While part of the apparent comorbidity between diagnostic categories happens in consequence of overlapping criteria, a greater part may be attributed to an underlying lack of specificity in the individual case. That is to say, discrete categories do not exist in real life. Because of this, the concept of atypical brain development has been introduced so that the data can be interpreted in a different way. The framework challenges both the practice of 'pigeonhole' diagnoses and also the notion of 'syndromes' in developmental disorders.

Like the earlier term 'minimal brain dysfunction', the concept of 'atypical brain development' links neurology with behavioural problems. However, unlike 'minimal brain dysfunction', it carries no implication of damage. Instead, it suggests that atypical development is the extreme of a continuous normal distribution. It takes into account the lack of empirical support for claims—prompted, possibly, by trauma studies—of simple brain localisation, contrasting with evidence that brain imaging studies of people with learning disabilities indicate multifocal dysfunction.

The framework accommodates multiple routes to the final common pathway of difficulty in acquiring a specific skill such as reading. It takes into account the unlikelihood that one common factor alone will explain a significant majority of nonsyndromic cases of developmental learning disability in the population. Similarly, it holds that no single gene is responsible for the majority of cases or deficit of any particular form of developmental learning disability and that, for example, genes putting individuals at risk do not necessarily correspond to specific cognitive aspects of reading ability. It thus contests the assumption that any genetic effect on reading ability will be focused, singular and direct.

With respect to theories associating dyslexia with abnormal neural migration, the concept of atypical brain development accommodates the possibility that such an effect could affect multiple brain areas, not just those associated with reading and that even a specific single-gene effect will show great variation between individuals. For this reason, it is suggested that the search for genes should be redirected towards those that cause brain variation in the population at large rather than towards those that might cause a specific defect. The concept of atypical brain development is not confined to gene effects, however; it embraces the effects of harmful substances in the environment, such as lead, drugs taken during pregnancy and impoverished postnatal environments.

It remains to be seen whether the concept of atypical brain dysfunction will lead to new strategies for research. At the very least, it provides an incentive to dispense with univariate contrasting-groups strategies. It also offers an opportunity to explore differential patterns of function and dysfunction across five large-scale neurocognitive networks: spatial awareness, language, memory and emotion, working memory and executive functions and face and object identification (Mesulam, 1998). It might also be an appropriate conceptual framework within which to explore (and perhaps also to rename) the concept of 'dyslexia' without literacy problems (Miles et al., 2003).

> The concept of atypical brain development provides a framework for the development of theory.

> The concept questions the validity of discrete categories and syndromes in the diagnosis of developmental disabilities.

> Atypical development may not have a single specific cause but may happen as the extreme of a continuously-distributed trait.

> Although the concept was formulated as a perspective for researchers, it might alert practitioners to student characteristics that would otherwise have escaped their notice.

Part four
Towards good practice for dyslexic students in adult literacy and numeracy education

'The development of appropriate and effective reading strategies is predicated upon a theoretical understanding of the causes of dyslexia' (*page* 160). Nicolson, R. I. and Fawcett, A. J. (1990). Automaticity: a new framework for dyslexia research? **Cognition,** 35, 159–182.

'Neurological approaches are inappropriate because they entail nothing about intervention. However true or valid neurological accounts of impairments are, one will never be able by neurological or physical means to either restore or donate the ability to read ... The reason is that reading is essentially an epistemological matter. It involves firstly the acquisition of concepts and secondly the translation of those concepts into skilled procedures or competences' (*page* 535). Marcel, A. J. (1978). Prerequisites for a more applicable psychology of reading. In M. M. Gruneberg & P. E. Morris & R. N. Sykes (Eds.), **Practical aspects of memory.** London: Academic Press.

'Pursuit of the goal of universal literacy has resulted in a field that has become the most fad-ridden of the social sciences, a crazy-quilt array of pedagogic tricks, half-baked theories, novel programs dead aborning, scores of assessment devices, unfulfilled hopes, frustrations, name-calling and nearly all of it unrelieved by clearly demonstrable progress, consensus, understanding, or even healthy humor' (*page* ix). Reber, A. S. and Scarborough, D. L. (Eds.). (1977). **Toward a Psychology of Reading: the proceedings of the CUNY conferences.** Hillsdale, NJ: Lawrence Erlbaum Associates.

'Earnest Wish expressed for a System of National Education established universally by Government. Glorious effects of this foretold. (Book Ninth. ARGUMENT)'
[*The Sage exclaimed*]
'O for the coming of that glorious time
When, prizing knowledge as her noblest wealth
And best protection, this imperial Realm,
While she exacts allegiance, shall admit
An obligation, on her part, to *teach*
Them who are born to serve her and obey;
Binding herself by statute* to secure
For all the children whom her soil maintains
The rudiments of letters, and inform
The mind with moral and religious truth
Both understood and practised, – so that none,
However destitute, be left to droop
By timely culture unsustained; or run
Into a wild disorder, or be forced
To drudge through a weary life without the help
Of intellectual implements and tools;
A savage horde among the civilised,

A servile band among the lordly free!'

* The discovery of Dr Bell affords marvellous facilities for carrying this into effect; and it is impossible to overrate the benefit which might accrue to humanity from the universal application of this simple engine under an enlightened government. – W.

William Wordsworth. *The Excursion*, IX, 291–310 (1814).

'Great advantages arise from teaching the alphabet [after the manner observed by Dr Bell, by forming the letters on a slate] ... it enables the pupil, at the very outset, to distinguish the letters of a similar cast or form, such as b, d, p, and q' (page 25). Colquhoun, P. (1806). A New and Appropriate System of Education for the Labouring People; elucidated and explained ... containing an exposition of the nature and importance of the design, as it respects the general interest of the community: with details, explanatory of the particular economy of the institution, and the methods prescribed for the purpose of securing and preserving a greater degree of moral rectitude, as means of preventing criminal offences by habits of temperance, industry, subordination, and loyalty, among that useful class of the community, comprising the labouring people of England ... *London: J. Hatchard.*

Introduction

What is to be done and why?
The main purpose of literacy instruction is to teach students how their writing system works, through knowledge of the sounds of the spoken language and their connection to print. Lack of phonological awareness is not a cause but a symptom of students' difficulties, which are likely to be both complex and varied. However, problems with phonological awareness in general and with phonemic awareness in particular, indicate what students most need to learn (Perfetti & Marron, 1995).

Once students have learned how their writing system works, they are in a position to continue by teaching themselves (Share, 1995). This step is essential, because no tutor can teach more than a small part of what learners need to know. Only through continuing exposure to print are adult literacy students likely to encounter written language both richer and more complex than the spoken language they typically experience in conversations or on television (Greenberg et al., 1997). This is important because, although they have lived longer, adult learners are not necessarily more likely to have greater knowledge of word meanings than children have; vocabulary growth after the age of ten or eleven years may be more heavily influenced by written language than by spoken language (Greenberg et al., 1997). So it is only through increasing exposure to print that new readers improve in automatic word recognition and gain the fluency needed to release their attentional capacity for understanding and enjoyment.

Adult learners need to understand how their writing system works for their language to develop sufficiently to meet their everyday needs.

How successful is intervention likely to be?
The success with which reading can be learned in adulthood varies from person to person. Nevertheless, the older the student, the more difficult any teaching and learning programme

is likely to prove (Fawcett, 2002). Many tutors but fewer researchers believe that successful learning can be achieved (Scarborough, 1984). Even after intensive tutoring in phonics, some learners continue to experience difficulty in reading regular new words (Felton et al., 1990). A developmentally dyslexic adult's decoding problem may be difficult to overcome, because the core phonological deficit is more severe in dyslexic readers than in 'ordinary' poor readers (Stanovich, 1988), so students with severe and profound difficulties will need a high allocation of resources (Fawcett, 2002). However, even one-to-one tuition may have no significant impact on the skills of the least able readers unless it contains very explicit and intensive instruction in phoneme awareness and phonemic decoding skills (Torgesen, Wagner, Rashotte, Rose, Lindamood, Conway, & Garvan, 1999).

That said, it could be misleading to apply a reading disability model to an adult learning to read who performs poorly on phonological awareness tests (Perfetti & Marron, 1995). These learners will not necessarily have serious difficulty in acquiring phonological awareness and, with it, an analytical approach to language. A more serious problem for them may be the need to abandon effortful but inefficient non-analytic strategies (such as trying to memorise all words by sight) prompted by their early difficulties (McGuinness, 1998; Perfetti, Georgi, & Beck, 1993), as those difficulties may have led to maladaptive self-beliefs (Chapman et al., 2001) and to other behavioural, motivational, and cognitive consequences (Pumfrey & Reason, 1991; Stanovich, 1986).

One of those consequences might be limited verbal working memory capacity. For adult dyslexics seeking help, difficulties with memory are typically the central problem (Fitzgibbon & O'Connor, 2002). The nature of the association between reading ability and working memory has been unclear (Kramer et al., 2000; Wadsworth et al., 1995); working memory difficulties may be symptoms of other problems rather than problems in themselves (Hulme & Roodenrys, 1995). These difficulties may appear to be specialised within the reading process (Caplan & Waters, 1999), or they may extend beyond reading into other domains (Swanson & Sachse-Lee, 2001). Recent evidence suggests, however, that the working memory deficits seen in dyslexia indicate constraints on a general capacity system which appear to be quite independent of reading skill and to be lifelong (Swanson, 2003). Whatever their origin, verbal working memory difficulties create a vicious cycle in which the laborious effort to decode a word reduces learning from successful trials; less efficient learning leads to reduced component skill automaticity; and this, in turn, limits both the quality of subsequent learning opportunities and efficiency at all levels of the reading process (Sabatini, 2002).

For intervention to be successful, adult students need to acquire analytic strategies in word-recognition and to abandon effortful but inefficient non-analytic strategies.

Even with explicit and intensive teaching, some students may make slow progress.

Students who make good progress are likely to have been wrongly identified as dyslexic.

Limitations in the intervention research

The intervention research, which is almost exclusively concerned with children, reveals a number of limitations (Abadzi, 1994; Lyon & Moats, 1997). These limitations make it very difficult to derive useful guidance for adult literacy tutors.

As in the investigative studies surveyed in Part one, the intervention research is characterised by inconsistent definitions and sampling techniques (Lyon & Moats, 1997). It may even happen that the criteria used for diagnosis are inconsistent between participants in a single study.

Poorly-defined interventions can also be a problem (Lyon & Moats, 1997). Even when one intervention is found to work better than another, it may not be obvious why this is the case. Because interventions tend to differ along many dimensions, it can be difficult to isolate the causal factors determining a specific pattern of outcome (Harm et al., 2003). Interventions are seldom described in sufficient detail. Information is not always provided about the extent to which explicit teaching of language structure is characterised by: deliberate organisation of lesson format and content; calibration of concept difficulty along both linguistic and developmental criteria; corrective feedback designed to foster linguistic insight and self-reliance; careful choice of reading material for practice; and conscious interplay between spoken and written language during teaching (Lyon & Moats, 1997).

Inadequate control groups present an additional difficulty (Lyon & Moats, 1997) and the use of no-treatment control groups can create both practical and ethical problems (Lyon & Moats, 1997). Inadequate instruction time and poor transfer effects are characteristic of some intervention studies (Lyon & Moats, 1997). Other studies may fail to take into account the effects of previous or concurrent tuition, the methods used by the tutor, the personal characteristics or attributes of the tutor (Lyon & Moats, 1997). Among further problems in the evaluation studies are a disregard of reading rate, or fluency (Lyon & Moats, 1997), which may nevertheless be the critical factor in the development of comprehension skill.

Meanwhile, there is little research which compares two types of adult newcomers to alphabetic literacy: 'normal' beginner-readers and those who are literate in other scripts (Abadzi, 1996). It may be that research of this kind would provide essential information on letter-processing, functional reading, the development of reading comprehension, relapse (that is, loss of literacy skills which have been learned), possible interference from different scripts and the cognitive benefits of adult literacy (Abadzi, 1996).

The value of the intervention research is compromised by a number of shortcomings in definitions and procedures.

It is not necessarily safe to apply findings from research with children to the problems of adult learners.

Intervention

Introduction

Although the evaluation studies offer little definitive guidance for adult literacy tutors, they offer some interesting ideas for consideration. For more detailed guidance on questions of day-to-day practice, tutors will need to refer to the forthcoming report by NIACE/LSDA. Meanwhile, it might be interesting for tutors to be reminded of some observations on Grace Fernald's kinaesthetic method (Fernald, 1943), which were made forty years ago (Morris, 1963). It was suggested that wide variations in the time taken to learn by the Fernald method might indicate other factors, among them the possibility that some who learnt by the method had no particular aptness for kinaesthetic impressions but made progress because the method suited them for other reasons. Among other things, the Fernald method gives learners an explanation for past failure and promotes morale-building. By leaving learners to decide the words to be learned, it avoids the danger that they will be confronted with boring or disturbing material. It thus ensures that symbols will be associated with vivid meanings. It employs the finger-tracing method to make a kinaesthetic impression ('the flux helps to bring about the fusion of ... orientation, visual pattern, auditory pattern'). Lastly, progress is self-paced by the learner.

Interventions should address both the cognitive and emotional needs of students.

Curriculum

The popular belief that developmental disorders are highly specific in their impact is not supported by systematic enquiry. There is thus no support for any idea that successful teaching for dyslexia, especially in the case of adults, can be accomplished by means of a 'silver bullet'; instead, programmes may need a 'grapeshot' approach (Ellis et al., 1997b). While it is clearly important for learners' morale that existing strengths should be acknowledged, it is recommended that a good teaching programme should focus on both the weak and the strong skills (Wolf et al., 2000b).

What are the curricular elements of the grapeshot? One element is phonology. This is particularly important for students who are not, for any reason, speakers of standard English and for whom the relationships between phonology and spelling might otherwise remain more mysterious than they need to be. Thus, while the most critical aspect of speech perception is organising the signal as appropriate for one's native language, rather than getting every detail (Nittrouer, 2002), this principle might equally apply to re-organising the signal for a non-native language or dialect (Cheung et al., 2001; Nathan et al., 1998). The process of reorganisation might be a particularly important task for adults who have had a specific language impairment as children (Nittrouer, 2002), although they are likely to be in a minority among adult literacy students. It might also be an important task for students whose childhood hearing was impaired by glue ear, even though the problem has long since been resolved (Bennett et al., 2001).

It may be helpful to repeat that phonological awareness is not a perceptual gift with which people may or may not be born, but rather conceptual knowledge which needs to be acquired. Although some students can induce the alphabetic principle by implicit learning from a sight-reading vocabulary, others may acquire a sight-reading vocabulary without developing a transferable skill (Byrne, 1998). For these students, especially if they are second-language speakers or come from disadvantaged backgrounds, the tuition needs to be both explicit and structured: 'It is unfair and unethical to withhold insider information until ... adults figure it out for themselves, as if they were insiders all along' (Purcell-Gates, 1995).

A second element is morphology. The importance of integrating phonological with morphological knowledge has been emphasised for work with adult college students with reading difficulties (Leong, 1999). Adult learners have been found to make a preponderance of misspellings that are rarely made by children, including omissions, substitutions and additions of derivational and inflectional morphemes and neglect of word endings in general (Worthy & Viise, 1996). These findings clearly indicate morphological difficulties, in addition to phonological coding problems (Worthy & Viise, 1996). Adult literacy students should benefit from specific direct teaching of linguistic analysis (Worthy & Viise, 1996), with particular attention to the morphological principles underlying inflections and derivations.

A third element is semantics, with which the study of morphology is necessarily linked. Semantics makes an important contribution to reading comprehension (Nation & Snowling, 1998; Rego & Bryant, 1993; Vellutino et al., 1995), so long as the semantically associated words have similarly close associations at the neurological level (Pulvermüller, 1999). Tutors can gain insight into this process when testing for verbal or semantic fluency—for example, while administering the Dyslexia Adult Screening Test (Fawcett & Nicolson, 1998). Normal performance may reveal systematic patterns of morphological association (such as 'swim', 'swimming', 'swimmingly' and 'swimmer') or semantic association (such as 'sieve', 'rolling pin', 'bowl' and 'blender'). This process, which is automatic, is called 'priming': a given stimulus activates mental pathways which enhance the ability to process subsequent stimuli if they are connected to the original stimulus in some way. When complex networks of semantic and morphological associations are established in the brain, priming takes place more easily and assists comprehension.

A fourth element is the structure of language and especially its syntax—'the capacity to integrate different content-bearing items into a single thought' (Carruthers, 2002). Speech is usually accompanied by non-verbal signs and non-semantic meanings that are part of the speaker's intention (Levinson, 1983) and so a simple transcription of speech is likely to under-represent the speaker's intentions (Olson, 1994). Every reader needs an understanding of the different ways in which written words can be combined in phrases, sentences and paragraphs in order to convey different meanings or shades of meaning. Where there might be ambiguity, a knowledge of syntax can help writers to avoid it and readers to resolve it (Rego & Bryant, 1993).

There is no 'silver bullet' for adult literacy teachers to fire.

Students may need help to develop phonological awareness in a way that informs their understanding of the spelling system.

Students may need help in understanding the principles that underlie the inflections and derivations in the English language, with additional help in understanding the morpho-phonemic basis of English spelling.

Students may need help in understanding the ways in which the meanings of words are conveyed through roots and affixes.

Even for single-word reading, students will need a knowledge of syntax in order to be able to detect and resolve ambiguity.

The tutor therefore needs a knowledge of linguistics.

Methods
How should the grapeshot be fired?

It is one thing to know *that*—to possess declarative knowledge that, for example, a word is spelled with a certain sequence of letters. It is quite a different thing to know *how*—to have the procedural knowledge which enables people to write the word on paper or (by using procedural knowledge of a different kind) to type the word on a keyboard and to do so automatically when the idea of the word enters their heads. Procedural knowledge relies on sensorimotor protocols. By definition, these protocols are not established in people who do not write; they must be put in place and it is 'never too late to do so' (McGuinness, 1998). There is no novelty in the use of multisensory methods with adult newcomers to literacy; tactile methods were used in the mass education movement of the early nineteenth century (Dickson, 1986). Nor should there be any mystique about this, for although reading and writing draw on shared knowledge they are separate skills and writing needs to be learned by—as well as with—the hands (Berninger et al., 2002).

Simple component skills also need to become fluent, if they are to be successfully combined in more complex cognitive operations (Johnson & Layng, 1992). In fluent spelling, for example, the learner will be able to spell words swiftly enough not to lose momentum, remember how to spell words after a significant period of no practice and spell them correctly when concentrating on the subject of a composition in which they are used (Johnson & Layng, 1992). The components of mathematical problem-solving procedures can be similarly modelled. All procedural learning needs to be thoroughly assimilated by drill, or overlearning (Kohl, 1988; Oakland et al., 1998), in order to establish new and active networks of neural connectivity; the more extensive these networks become, the more easily the new learning can be applied. Dysfluent component skills make progress impossible at worst and tedious at best (Johnson & Layng, 1992), but there is evidence that computer-supported teaching can make drill acceptable to literacy learners (Cromley, 2000; Singleton & Simmons, 2001).

Then, since critical developmental changes result from adequate language experience in naturalistic contexts, it has been suggested that intervention strategies for learners with language learning problems should focus on enhancing language experience in natural contexts (Nittrouer, 2002). One way of doing so with adult students might be to base teaching on directly relevant materials such as small advertisements in the local newspaper or work-related vocabulary; building up a sight vocabulary related to life-experiences and interests might be a useful first step toward functional literacy (Gottesman et al., 1996).

The tutor's aim must be to impart declarative knowledge (knowledge that) and to ensure that the student then transforms it into procedural knowledge (knowledge how) that can be drawn upon without conscious attention.

Students will not become proficient without repetitive practice.

Computer-supported instruction can make repetitive practice acceptable to adult students.

Agents

Who should be entrusted to fire this grapeshot? It is sometimes argued that this role should be undertaken by specialists in dyslexia, which is a critically important safeguard if the alternative is to assign the task to untrained volunteers. But it does not follow that expertise in the teaching of reading should be the monopoly of specialists who are called in when things go wrong. From nursery school onwards, everyone who teaches literacy needs to be knowledgeable about language and language learning (Brooks et al., 2001a; Brooks et al., 1992; Locke et al., 2002; Mather et al., 2001; Moats, 1994; Moats & Lyon, 1996). The professional development of adult literacy teachers might helpfully be understood by analogy as a training not in first aid but in reconstructive surgery.

Appendix 9 lists some useful books for teachers of reading.

Teachers of both initial reading and adult literacy need to be well-informed about language and its acquisition.

Adult literacy tutors need skills that are analogous with those of reconstructive surgeons, not first-aiders (see above).

Evaluation studies

Introduction

An evaluation of a single intervention may ask only one question: 'Is the intervention effective?' A comparative evaluation will ask two questions: 'Is either intervention effective?' and 'Is one intervention more effective than the other one?'

The appearance of effectiveness is no guarantee that the intervention is effective in reality. In naturalistic situations, where conditions likely to influence the outcome can not be standardised or even in some cases, identified, evaluation research is difficult. Often, there are a number of possible alternative explanations. The conscientious researcher will seek to rule them out before claiming effectiveness for an intervention. However, it is not uncommon for studies in this field to be undertaken by untrained researchers who have not been alerted to the pitfalls in their procedures and whose claims, in consequence, are flawed (although the flaws are seldom, if ever, a bar to media coverage).

The validity of evaluation studies may be subject to a number of challenges (Gliner & Morgan, 2000; Harrington et al., 2002; Pawson & Tilley, 1997; Torgerson et al., 2002; Troia, 1999). One such challenge comes from illusory change. Simply by statistical 'regression', or the test-retest effect, an extreme score on initial testing may be followed by a more normal score on subsequent testing for reasons unrelated to anything that has happened in the interim. If the initial score is untypically low, possibly because of the unfamiliarity of the testing situation, the later score may be a more accurate reflection of the participant's normal performance.

A second group of challenges is associated with genuine changes which bear no specific relation to the intervention. Normal maturation will occur over time, irrespective of any intervention. A placebo (or expectation) effect may occur when the intervention gives participants the motivation to make their own adjustments (perhaps by reading more than they would otherwise have done) while a similar but temporary distortion may occur when unusual care and attention are lavished on the participants (so that they feel happier and become more receptive to ideas).

The validity of evaluation studies can be challenged in a third way by shortcomings on the part of the experimenter. It may happen that conditions for inclusion in either the participant or control group are poorly specified, so that either or both groups are heterogeneous in ways that could affect the outcome of any comparison in their final test scores. There is a particular hazard from experimenter bias, no matter how innocent researchers' intentions are, when they stand to make financial gains from an intervention programme of their own devising. There might be assignment bias, which can occur when members of the intervention group differ from controls in ways that predict a better response to the intervention, perhaps by having higher motivation or greater ability. Although there are procedures to avoid these kinds of bias, they are not always followed in intervention studies.

A fourth group of challenges is associated with shortcomings in the administration of the intervention, such as insufficient treatment duration, differential withdrawal from the programme on the part of successful and unsuccessful participants, or lack of follow-up to determine whether the intervention has had a lasting effect. Inappropriate statistical analyses, especially those which violate the assumptions of the tests used, are not uncommon. These violations can suggest that differences in outcome are statistically significant when they could have occurred by chance. Alternatively, differences in outcome might be statistically significant but trivial to the policy-maker.

A further question can be asked of any apparently-effective intervention, namely: 'Will it be effective for others?' This is an especially pertinent question to ask of the lateral visual masking study of 'four severe adult dyslexics' by Geiger et al. (1992). Even if the initial diagnosis was accurate (and if the intervention addressed the participants' problem successfully), no finding from such a small-scale study can be generalised with confidence to a larger population. For future researchers, studies like this one can be important, but for policy-makers they offer little guidance.

A different question can be asked of the study of thirty college students (Guyer, Banks, & Guyer, 1993): 'Is the superior intervention the most effective one available?' One of the two interventions in the comparison was an explicit, structured remedial spelling programme using analytic and synthetic phonics. The comparison programme 'taught spelling using a non-phonetic approach'. In effect, the programmes were horses for different courses, one for regularly-spelled words and one for irregular words. The outcome was that the 'regular' horse ran faster than the 'irregular' horse, since most spellings are regular. Readers of a specialist dyslexia journal might be disposed to believe that the 'regular' horse (in the form of an Orton-Gillingham programme) would have won the gold cup in any comparison, but in this comparison the race was fixed and the finding offers no answer to the question.

There are many pitfalls in evaluation research.

How can we know what really works?
What kinds of intervention study are likely to offer reliable guidance to tutors? This is not an idle question. The design of intervention studies is exacting in any circumstances; it is especially so when the participants are hard to reach. Perhaps for these reasons, there are many design limitations in existing reading intervention research (Abadzi, 1994; Beder, 1999; Lyon & Moats, 1997; Simmerman & Swanson, 2001; Torgerson et al., 2002).

Nevertheless, a good intervention study should satisfy a number of criteria. They include:

- a focused research question, specifying a theoretically plausible mechanism of change;
- a design that permits investigators to minimise the effects of extraneous variables, such as teacher effects and differences in motivation;
- a large enough sample to reduce the possibility that the outcomes of the intervention might have occurred by chance;

- a stable enough sample for attrition not to call the findings into question;
- a sample described in sufficient detail for researchers to determine whether the intervention is differentially effective on demographic and psychometric criteria;
- an intervention curriculum specified as to content, teaching method and duration;
- appropriate, reliable and validated tests, with different forms at pre- and post-testing and test administration that scrupulously follows the test protocols;
- assessment of whether the new knowledge and skills are then applied to materials not originally part of the intervention; and
- assessment of whether new knowledge and skills are retained in the long term.

One suggested hierarchy of intervention research methods has listed, in descending order of reliability:

- experimental designs employing two identical groups of participants assigned randomly to treatment and control groups;
- quasi-experimental designs, employing apparently identical (matched) but non-randomly assigned treatment and control groups;
- correlational designs, employing non-identical treatment and control groups but with statistical controls for differences that may be important;
- correlational designs with non-identical treatment and control groups, on an assumption that the differences between them are unimportant; and
- case studies, with a treatment group only and an assumption that differences among participants are either obvious or not important.

It would be difficult to justify a nationally advocated intervention policy except by reference to designs at the head of this hierarchy.

No studies were found that evaluated specific interventions with the mathematical difficulties of adults with dyslexia.

No studies were found that evaluated specific interventions with adult dyslexic speakers of English as a second or other language.

No studies were found that evaluated reading interventions addressing dyslexics' difficulties with verbal working memory.

No studies were found that evaluated reading interventions addressing dyslexics' attentional difficulties of any kind (i.e. difficulty in sustaining attention, difficulty in switching attention, or difficulty in selective attention).

No studies were found that evaluated reading interventions addressing dyslexics' difficulties in inferring intention or mood.

No studies were found that evaluated reading interventions addressing specific language impairment in dyslexics.

No studies were found that evaluated interventions addressing dyslexics' difficulties with the organisation of thought in writing.

Only seven research publications were found which evaluated specific interventions with adult dyslexic speakers of English as a first language. All took place in the USA. They are listed in Table 2 below. It will be seen that most cells in the table are empty and that only three papers report findings from studies in which the participants were not university students. Part of the explanation for this is NRDC's decision to include only studies published in peer-reviewed journals (because these are likely to be the best-conducted studies); part is the decision to include only studies that are explicitly and unquestionably concerned with developmentally dyslexic adults (as opposed to 'ordinary' poor readers whose problems are largely if not exclusively attributable to environmental circumstances) and part is the very great difficulty, already noted, of designing robust evaluations in adult literacy acquisition.

Table 2. Selected intervention studies with adult dyslexics

Type of Study	Adult Dyslexics in Higher Education	Adult Dyslexics in Further Education and the Community
Randomised controlled trial	—	—
Matched groups	—	—
Single-group, pre/post-test	Kitz & Nash (1992) Elkind et al., (1996), Studies 1 and 2	Elkind et al. (1996), Studies 1,2, 3 and 4
Single group, post-test only	—	—
Multiple-baseline, unmatched groups	Guyer & Sabatino (1989) Guyer et al. (1993) Higgins & Zvi (1995)	Geiger et al. (1992)
Non multiple-baseline, single-case studies	—	—
Observational single-case studies	—	Migden (1990)

The decision not to review intervention studies from the informally-published 'grey literature' was carefully considered. Such studies are typically the work of zealous but naïve investigators; their methods are often flawed and their findings may be unsafe. While the peer review process itself is not perfect, since seriously-flawed studies appear from time to time in peer-reviewed journals, it is a reasonable assumption that papers published in this way are the most appropriate to analyse. The converse assumption holds for the grey literature.

Evaluation studies need to satisfy demanding criteria in order to meet the needs of policy-makers.

There appear to be no studies in this field with specifications that would justify the use of their findings as a basis for national policy.

Intervention studies on adults with dyslexia

A multisensory alphabetic phonetic approach with college students (Guyer & Sabatino, 1989). This study sought to determine whether learners would make more progress with an adaptation of the Orton-Gillingham approach than if they were taught by a 'nonphonetic' approach or not taught at all. The participants were thirty students aged between 17 and 24 years. Their measured IQs ranged from 94 to 135, with a mean of 106. They had been diagnosed as 'learning disabled' by means of various ability-achievement discrepancy criteria.

In a summer school programme lasting for five weeks, ten of the students were taught by an 'alphabetic synthetic multisensory phonetic' method incorporating alphabetic knowledge, letter sounds and blends, syllable division, directionality and simultaneous reading, spelling and handwriting.

A comparison group of ten students was taught by a method which did not attempt to teach individual letter sounds or to integrate the teaching of spelling, reading and handwriting. A further group of ten students did not attend the summer school.

Data analyses showed that the reading scores of the Orton-Gillingham group improved more over the programme period than those of the other two groups, with a mean improvement of approximately one and a half grades (or academic years).

Dyslexia and psychodynamics: a case study of a dyslexic adult (Migden, 1990)

The subject of this study was a 33 year-old with an IQ in the normal range. He had a history of alcoholism, emotional outbursts and difficulty in sustaining relationships with other people. He was dependent on his parents, with whom he lived, for help with literacy tasks. Previous interventions (including private tutors, optometric training, child psychotherapy and medical consultations) had been ineffective in helping him develop his literacy skills.

Weekly psychotherapy ran concurrently with a twice-weekly literacy programme that involved use of a 'speak and spell' machine. To help the student to sublimate his aggressive impulses, his psychotherapist encouraged him to read books of two kinds: books on the problems of growing up with a disability, books about guns, rifles and weapons of war. Just as psychotherapy helped the student's learning, it appeared that learning was helping his psychotherapy.

The literacy programme ended after two years, when the student had attained his goals. He later earned a high school diploma and started a family of his own. The study endorses what might be intuitive: that students with multiple problems are most likely to make progress when all of those problems are being addressed. However, it also suggests that, no matter how understanding a basic skills tutor might be, she or he may need to collaborate with other professionals in helping students whose learning difficulties have caused problems in other aspects of their lives.

Task-determined strategies of visual process (Geiger et al., 1992)

These studies took place following the discovery that an atypical subgroup in a study of visual lateral masking had previous diagnoses of dyslexia. The purpose was to determine whether the information necessary for reading could be blunted by misuse of a normal visual process and whether any blunting could be relieved by suitably-designed practice in normal lateral masking strategies.

The participants in the first study were ten 'ordinary' readers and ten with severe dyslexia. The 'ordinary readers' were university students, while the dyslexics were volunteers from various backgrounds. After this study had confirmed that ordinary readers recognise letters best in and near the centre of gaze, whereas severe dyslexics recognise letters farther in the periphery in the direction of reading, an intervention study took place. An intervention case-study of a severely dyslexic male participant in his mid-20s was supplemented when three more dyslexic participants from the first study volunteered for the intervention.

The intervention regime, which was unsupervised, was followed for periods of four or five months. It had two parts. For the first part, volunteers were advised to spend two hours a day in novel, direct, small-scale hand-eye coordination tasks such as drawing, painting, or model-building. For the second part, volunteers were ask to read by placing over their chosen text a transparent (or translucent, or opaque) sheet on which there was a fixation mark and, to the right of it, a window large enough for a long word to be visible.

The investigators concluded that, when people with severe dyslexia are taught to read by a regimen of practice that does not challenge their existing visual strategies, their acquired ability to read is accompanied by a shift of visual strategy to that of the ordinary reader, which suggests that visual strategies can be learned and that the distribution of lateral masking found in the ordinary reader is what makes ordinary reading possible.

The first volunteer was reported to have made seven years' reading progress in the space of four months. There were various outcomes for the other three volunteers. After they had stopped practising, however, three of the four volunteers quickly regressed in their ability to read.

It is unclear how the participants acquired the word-recognition skills implicit in these claims. However, the investigators subsequently replicated their intervention in two studies of children (Geiger & Lettvin, 1997), from which comparably rapid improvement was reported.

Simultaneous multi-sensory instructional procedure (Kitz & Nash, 1992)
This study sought to determine whether the intervention programme would improve poor readers' word-level decoding, comprehension, spelling, reading rate and which measures are the best predictors of reading comprehension among adult poor readers. The programme consisted of seven weeks of formal reading and spelling instruction, using a simultaneous multi-sensory instructional procedure paradigm teaching sound-symbol associations and synthetic phonics with morphological analyses of prefixes, suffixes and word roots.

The participants were 63 college students attending a summer programme. Their mean age was 20 years and they had previously been identified by various criteria as learning-disabled.

There were significant differences between pre- and post-test scores on spelling, reading rate, reading comprehension and phoneme deletion.

The investigators drew attention to the fact that this intervention was generally provided in large group settings of seven to 18 students, contrasting it with a reading-remediation literature consisting mainly of case studies or small-sample studies. However, they noted that the contribution of the multisensory component of the strategy is insufficiently understood.

Spelling improvement for college students who are dyslexic (Guyer et al., 1993)
The purpose of this study was to determine if college students with dyslexia would make more progress when taught with an 'alphabetic-synthetic and multisensory phonetic' method, or an analytic 'nonphonetic' approach which taught repeated copying and visual memory, or with no intervention at all. The methods appear to differ in that the synthetic method taught syllable division according to morphological criteria whereas the analytic method did not. The intervention

consisted of two one-hour sessions per week for 16 weeks. No attrition was reported.

The participants were three groups of ten university students, mostly white males, with IQ-discrepancy diagnoses of dyslexia who had enrolled on a learning support programme. Full-scale IQs ranged from 91 to 130, with a mean of 110. Two intervention groups had been randomly selected from approximately 100 students currently taking part in the programme. A third group had been randomly selected from a group of 70 students who were not currently taking part in the programme. There is no indication that the groups were matched on either psychometric or demographic criteria.

The 'multisensory phonetic' group was the only one with significantly higher pre- and post-test mean scores. There were reported transfer effects to essay-writing for members of this group. The investigators conclude that their findings 'seem to point to benefits from the multisensory synthetic phonetic [sic] approach for dyslexic students even at college age'. However, it is unclear whether the multisensory method, the synthetic phonics, or the two in combination conferred the benefit.

Assistive technology for postsecondary students with learning disabilities: from research to practice (Higgins & Zvi, 1995)

The investigators set out to assess the usefulness of optical character recognition technology with speech synthesis. In each of three formal studies, participants completed a task with computer assistance, or with human help, or without any help.

The participants were 80 young adults of average intelligence, most of whom were white and middle class. All had been assessed as learning-disabled according to discrepancy criteria. Not every one of them took part in all three studies.

In reading comprehension, both assistive technology and human assistance helped students with below-average scores in silent reading but impeded students with above-average scores. In proof-reading, however, the assistive technology was significantly more helpful than human assistance. In essay-writing, there was no clear advantage in either assistive technology or the use of an amanuensis. Extra time for essay-writing did not help students who were short of ideas or who lacked the vocabulary with which to express their ideas adequately. Nevertheless, in the longer term, both success rates and retention rates improved in relation to those of learning-disabled students who had not used assistive technology.

The investigators make eight recommendations based on their research and teaching experience. First, they emphasise the assistive (rather than the remedial or instructional) use of technology. Next, they encourage fluency and vocabulary expansion. Third, they suggest that tutors should focus on strengths in the students' work, leaving technology to contend with weaknesses such as spelling and punctuation. Fourth, they recommend focusing on process and content rather than on the mechanics of writing. Fifth, they advocate one-to-one teaching. Sixth, they stipulate enthusiastic tutors. Seventh, they warn against the 'heavy editing' of students' work. Eighth, they limit the provision of remedial instruction to essential information.

Computer-based compensation of adult reading difficulties (Elkind et al., 1996)

This paper reports four studies. The first study sought to determine the effect of a computer-reader speech-synthesiser component upon the reading ability of dyslexic adults. The second study sought to find a way of predicting how individuals would respond to this technology. The third study sought to identify the practical benefits and problems associated with the use of assistive technology in the workplace. The fourth study investigated the use of assistive technology to supplement adult remediation.

There were different participants in each study. Those in the first study were a diverse group of fifty Ivy League and community college students; three had acquired learning disabilities through brain injury, while the others had been diagnosed as learning-disabled by criteria which varied from group to group. Those in the second study were a subgroup of 29 student participants from the first study. A research sample of eight learning-disabled participants in the third study, an intervention lasting for three months, was identified 'with considerable effort' through a variety of community agencies. A research sample of eight participants in the fourth study consisted of dyslexic adults in a remedial language arts tutorial programme.

Outcomes were mixed. In summary, the investigators found that students for whom computer reader technology is helpful tend to be slow readers with poor comprehension and limited ability to sustain their concentration. However, they need good ability to integrate auditory and visual stimuli. With much ground to make up, these users have a high potential gain from the intervention. They nevertheless need to experience success when they first use the technology. They also need to be strongly motivated, with a substantial reading workload. Although they need sufficient time to use the system in a supportive environment, the time needed to scan reading matter must not be so great as to offset any benefits.

Summary

It will be clear that the studies in the preceding section bear no relationship to two of the theories described in Part two and none to any of the theoretical developments outlined in Part three, although there is no necessity for such a relationship (Sroufe, 1997). The first two theories in Part two and the first theory in Part three, are concerned with what students need to learn, whereas the other theories seek to explain why students experience difficulty in learning. Insofar as the evaluation studies have little to say to teachers of adults with learning difficulties, good practice in this field rests almost entirely on professional judgement informed by a background in linguistics and knowledge of the developmental course of normal reading acquisition.

Interestingly, there appears to be no experimental evidence comparing group outcomes between adult dyslexics and 'ordinary' adult literacy learners. As earlier studies have concluded (e.g. Fowler & Scarborough, 1993), much of what has been learned from research on reading disabilities may be pertinent to the identification and the literacy development of adult learners generally—that is to say, to people who need to acquire knowledge and skills, but who have no specific difficulty in learning. However, the applicability of that research may itself be partly or largely a consequence of an over-extended reading disability concept. There is evidence from intervention studies with children that systematic and explicit teaching of phonics and exception words, with multisensory learning and intensive reinforcement, is generally effective, but that there is a minority of students whom it does not appear to help (Rack & Hatcher, 2002; Vellutino et al., 1996).

Are these 'treatment-resisters' the true 'dyslexics'? The logic of this interpretation is compelling and it is certainly easier to argue that 'treatment-resisters' are different from 'normal' readers in a way that 'treatment-responders' are not. Do 'treatment-resisters' have anything in common with one another, apart from their difficulty in learning to read? The research does not directly address this question, but it is unlikely that 'treatment-resisters' are a homogeneous group; for this reason, perhaps, the illusion of homogeneity should not be created by including them in the same classification. The best guidance for tutors might then be expected to come not from group studies but from a range of well-designed single-case studies, which might address various kinds of attentional difficulty and difficulties in drawing inferences. These studies have yet to be undertaken.

General conclusions

For the writer as well as for the reader, this has been a long and arduous review. It could easily have been more so. The scientific literature on reading and reading difficulties is vast and complex; the non-scientific literature is also extensive and highly problematic in its own way. When scientists of international distinction describe the situation in terms like those quoted in the opening paragraphs, they are not being alarmist. Although this review has tried to clarify the points at issue, the writer is painfully conscious of the loose ends and inconsistencies that remain; complexity can be simplified, but chaos remains chaos.

Among members of the general public, there are several myths and misconceptions about dyslexia—namely that dyslexics are brighter than ordinary people, that they are especially gifted, that they are especially anti-social, that there is at least 'one in every classroom' and that, although there is 'a gene for dyslexia', its adverse effects can be dispelled by a course of literacy teaching which addresses their needs. Scientific support for these beliefs is lacking. But even systematic researchers can only stumble towards the truth. In what we thought we knew about dyslexia a generation ago, we now seem to have been largely mistaken. Month by month, new research findings make it necessary for us to update and perhaps modify our understanding of reading and reading difficulties. We are all revisionists now.

The most urgent topic for revision is the concept of dyslexia itself, not least because it has in effect been commandeered in order to invest unsuccessful learners with responsibility for the shortcomings of their teachers. Worse even than that, it has led to an assumption that the skills essential for mainstream teaching are needed only by remedial specialists—an assumption which is guaranteed to put greater numbers of learners at risk.

Every method of reading instruction appears to succeed with some learners (although success occurs with some methods only when the poverty of the stimulus is compensated by the ingenuity of the response). All methods fail with some learners (and possibly with some teachers, too). The lowest failure rate is achieved with systematic and explicit instruction in the alphabetic principle. However, even with this method, a few learners experience intractable difficulty. These are the learners whom it is appropriate to call 'dyslexic'. It is not appropriate to think of them as the casualties of system failure. At the time of writing, they may find it more liberating to use alternative strategies than to persist in a struggle for literacy that can end only in a further experience of failure.

However, describing all these learners as 'dyslexic' may suggest that they have more in common than is actually the case. It might also come, in time, to stigmatise them. After the first awareness campaign, over ten years ago, dyslexics appeared to become the butt of a spate of cruel jokes. We should not be surprised if the word 'dyslexic' eventually goes the way of 'spastic' and for much the same reason. Science and the world of literacy teaching and learning might be no poorer if it did.

We end with answers to the questions with which we began. It appears that:

There are many reasons why people find it difficult to learn how to read, write and spell.

With some learners, we identify the causes of their difficulty as predominantly a matter of experience.

With other learners, we conjecture that the causes of their difficulty are predominantly a question of biology.

Either way, we acknowledge that developmental outcomes reflect interactions between experience and the human organism.

The research on 'developmental dyslexia' in children can help adult literacy tutors to respond to the needs of adult students, insofar as the research addresses fundamental issues in language acquisition.

It is by no means certain that the categorical distinctions embodied in terms such as 'dyslexic' and 'non-dyslexic' correspond to distinct realities when the individual person (rather than the behaviour) is the unit of analysis.

In our present state of knowledge, it does not appear to be helpful for tutors to think of some of their students as 'dyslexics' and of others as 'ordinary poor readers'.

The screening of adult literacy students for 'dyslexia' is difficult to justify on either theoretical or practical grounds.

By contrast, the psychometric assessment of reading-related skills is essential and every adult literacy teacher should be competent in it.

Even if dyslexia were to prove categorically rather than dimensionally different from ordinary poor reading, tutors are not resourced to determine the issue and screening tests yield high rates of false positives.

Telling a tutor that a student is 'dyslexic' may elicit a number of inappropriate assumptions about the student's problems and abilities.

The research does not indicate that a different curriculum should be followed for 'dyslexics'; the curriculum will depend very much on the needs of each individual student.

The research does not indicate that 'dyslexics' and 'ordinary poor readers' should be taught by different methods; however, the methods promoted as specialist interventions for dyslexics are well-suited to be mainstream methods of reading instruction, which is how they originated.

'Dyslexia' is not one thing but many, to the extent that it may be a conceptual clearing-house for a variety of difficulties with a variety of causes.

Different explanations of 'dyslexia' indicate different responses to the difficulties of different 'dyslexic' students, but the evaluation research on these responses is very limited.

References

Aaron, P. G. (1997). 'The impending demise of the discrepancy formula.' **Review of Educational Research,** 67(4), 461–502.

Abadzi, H. (1994). **What We Know about Acquisition of Adult Literacy: Is There Hope? (World Bank Discussion Papers No. 245)**. Washington, DC: World Bank.

Abadzi, H. (1996). 'Does age diminish the ability to learn fluent reading?' **Educational Psychology Review,** 8(4), 373–395.

Abelson, R. P. (1995). **Statistics as Principled Argument**. Hillsdale, NJ: Lawrence Erlbaum Associates.

Ables, B. S., Aug, R. G. and Looff, D. H. (1971). 'Problems in the diagnosis of dyslexia: a case study.' **Journal of Learning Disabilities,** 4(8), 409–417.

Ackermann, H., Gräber, S., Hertrich, I. and Daum, I. (1997). 'Categorical speech perception in cerebellar disorders.' **Brain and Language,** 60(2), 323–331.

Adams, M. J. (1990). **Beginning to Read: Thinking and Learning about Print.** Cambridge, MA: The MIT Press.

Adelman, K. A. and Adelman, H. S. (1987). 'Rodin, Patton, Edison, Wilson, Einstein: were they really learning disabled?' **Journal of Learning Disabilities,** 20(5), 270–279.

Adrián, J. A., Alegria, J. and Morais, J. (1995). 'Metaphonological abilities of Spanish illiterate adults.' **International Journal of Psychology,** 30(3), 329–353.

Ahn, J., Won, T. W., Kaplan, D. E., Londin, E. R., Kuzmic, P., Gelernter, J. and Gruen, J. R. (2002). 'A detailed physical map of the 6p reading disability locus, including new markers and confirmation of recombination suppression.' **Human Genetics,** 111(4–5), 339–349.

Alarcón, M., Plomin, R., Fulker, D. W., Corley, R. and DeFries, J. C. (1999). 'Molarity not modularity: multivariate genetic analysis of specific cognitive abilities in parents and their 16–year-old children in the Colorado Adoption Project.' **Cognitive Development,** 14(1), 175–193.

ALBSU. (1994). **Basic Skills in Prisons: assessing the need.** London: Adult Literacy & Basic Skills Unit.

Alegria, J., Pignot, E. and Morais, J. (1982). 'Phonetic analysis of speech and memory codes in beginning readers.' **Memory & Cognition,** 10(5), 451–456.

Alexander, J. R. M. and Martin, F. (2000). 'Norming tests of basic reading skills.' **Australian Journal of Psychology,** 52(3), 139–148.

Alm, J. and Andersson, J. (1997). 'A study of literacy in prison in Uppsala.' **Dyslexia,** 3, 245–246.

American Psychiatric Association. (1994). **Diagnostic and Statistical Manual of Mental Disorders – DSM-IV**. Washington, DC: APA.

Amitay, S., Ben-Yehudah, G., Banai, K. and Ahissar, M. (2002). 'Disabled readers suffer from visual and auditory impairments but not from a specific magnocellular deficit.' **Brain,** 125, 2272–2285.

Anderson, P. L. and Meier-Hedde, R. (2001). 'Early case reports of dyslexia in the United States and Europe.' **Journal of Learning Disabilities,** 34(1), 9–21.

Annett, M. (1985). **Left, Right, Hand and Brain: the right shift theory**. London: Lawrence Erlbaum Associates.

Anthony, J. L., Lonigan, C. J., Burgess, S. R., Driscoll, K., Phillips, B. M. and Cantor, B. G. (2002). 'Structure of preschool phonological sensitivity: overlapping sensitivity to rhyme, words, syllables, and phonemes.' **Journal of Experimental Child Psychology,** 82(1), 65–92.

Archer, N. and Bryant, P. (2001). 'Investigating the role of context in learning to read: a direct test of Goodman's model.' **British Journal of Psychology,** 92, 579–591.

Asherson, P. J. and Curran, S. (2001). 'Approaches to gene mapping in complex disorders and their application in child psychiatry and psychology.' **British Journal of Psychiatry,** 179, 122–128.

Atran, S. (1998). 'Folk biology and the anthropology of science: cognitive universals and cultural particulars.' **Behavioral and Brain Sciences,** 21(4), 547–609.

August, G. J. and Garfinkel, B. D. (1990). 'Comorbidity of ADHD and reading disability among clinic-referred children.' **Journal of Abnormal Child Psychology,** 18(1), 29–45.

Baddeley, A. D., Ellis, N. C., Miles, T. R. and Lewis, V. J. (1982). 'Developmental and acquired dyslexia: a comparison.' **Cognition,** 11, 185–199.

Badian, N. A. (1999). 'Reading disability defined as a discrepancy between listening and reading comprehension: a longitudinal study of stability, gender differences, and prevalence.' **Journal of Learning Disabilities,** 32(2), 138–148.

Bailey, K. D. (1973). 'Monothetic and polythetic typologies and their relation to conceptualization, measurement and scaling.' **American Sociological Review,** 38(February), 18–33.

Baraitser, M. (1997). **The Genetics of Neurological Disorders** (Third ed.). Oxford: Oxford University Press.

Barker, D. J. P., Cooper, C. and Rose, G. (1998). **Epidemiology in Medical Practice** (Fifth ed.). Edinburgh: Churchill Livingstone.

Baron, J. (1979). 'Orthographic and word specific mechanisms in children's reading of words.' **Child Development,** 50, 60–72.

Baron, J. and Strawson, C. (1976). 'Use of orthographic and word-specific knowledge in reading words aloud.' **Journal of Experimental Psychology: Human Perception and Performance,** 2(3), 386–393.

Bates, E. (1999). 'Plasticity, localization, and language development.' In S. H. Broman & J. M. Fletcher (Eds.), **The Changing Nervous System** (pp. 214–253). New York, NY: Oxford University Press.

Bates, E. and Appelbaum, M. (1994). 'Methods of studying small samples: issues and examples.' In S. H. Broman & J. Grafman (Eds.), **Atypical Cognitive Deficits in Developmental Disorders: implications for brain function.** (pp. 245–280). Hillsdale, NJ: Lawrence Erlbaum Associates.

Bateson, P. and Martin, P. (1999). **Design for a Life: how behaviour develops**. London: Jonathan Cape.

Baudouin de Courtenay, J. I. N. (1895). **Versuch einer Theorie phonetischer Alternationen; ein Kapitel aus der Psychophonetik.** Strassburg: Trübner.

Beard, R. and McKay, M. (1998). 'An unfortunate distraction: the real books debate, 10 years on.' **Educational Studies,** 24(1), 69–81.

Beaton, A. A. (2002). 'Dyslexia and the cerebellar deficit hypothesis.' **Cortex,** 38, 479–490.

Beder, H. (1999). **The Outcomes and Impacts of Adult Literacy Education in the United States**. Cambridge, MA: National Center for the Study of Adult Learning and Literacy.

Bennett, K. E., Haggard, M. P., Silva, P. A. and Stewart, I. A. (2001). 'Behaviour and developmental effects of otitis media with effusion into the teens.' **Archives of Disease in Childhood,** 85(2), 91–95.

Berninger, V. W., Abbott, R. D., Abbott, S. P., Graham, S. and Richards, T. (2002). 'Writing and reading: connections between language by hand and language by eye.' **Journal of Learning Disabilities,** 35(1), 39–56.

Bernstein, B. (1971). **Class, Codes and Controls**. London: Routledge & Kegan Paul.

Binder, J. R., Frost, J. A., Hammeke, T. A., Cox, R. W., Rao, S. M. and Prieto, T. (1997). 'Human brain language areas identified by functional magnetic resonance imaging.' **Journal of Neuroscience,** 17(1), 353–362.

Bird, J. and Bishop, D. V. M. (1992). 'Perception and awareness of phonemes in phonologically impaired children.' **European Journal of Disorders of Communication,** 27, 289–311.

Bishop, D. V. M. (1997). 'Cognitive neuropsychology and developmental disorders: uncomfortable bedfellows.' **Quarterly Journal of Experimental Psychology,** 50A(4), 899–923.

Bishop, D. V. M. (2001). 'Genetic influences on language impairment and literacy problems in children: same or different?' **Journal of Child Psychology and Psychiatry,** 42(2), 189–198.

Bishop, D. V. M. (2002). 'Cerebellar abnormalities in developmental dyslexia: cause, correlate or consequence?' **Cortex,** 38, 491–498.

Bishop, D. V. M. and Butterworth, G. E. (1980). 'Verbal-performance discrepancies: relationship to birth risk and specific reading retardation.' **Cortex,** 16, 375–389.

Blachman, B. A., Ball, E. W., Black, R. S. and Tangel, D. M. (1994). 'Kindergarten teachers develop phoneme awareness in low-income, inner-city classrooms: does it make a difference?' **Reading and Writing,** 6(1), 1–18.

Black, S., Rouse, R. and Wickert, R. (1990). **The Illiteracy Myth: A Comparative Study of Prisoner Literacy Abilities**. Canberra: Australian Department of Employment, Education and Training.

Boder, E. (1973). 'Developmental dyslexia: a diagnostic approach based on three atypical reading-spelling patterns.' **Developmental Medicine and Child Neurology,** 15, 663–687.

Booth, J. R., Burman, D. D., Van Santen, F. W., Harasaki, Y., Gitelman, D. R., Parrish, T. B. and Mesulam, M.-M. (2001). 'The development of specialized brain systems in reading and oral language.' **Child Neuropsychology,** 7(3), 19–141.

Borges, J. L. (2000). **The Total Library: non-fiction 1922–1986** (E. Weinberger, Trans.). London: Allen Lane.

Borsting, E., Ridder, W. H., Dudeck, K., Kelley, C., Matsui, L. and Motoyama, J. (1996). 'The presence of a magnocellular deficit depends on the type of dyslexia.' **Vision Research,** 36(7), 1047–1053.

Bourassa, D. and Treiman, R. (2001). 'Spelling development and disability: the importance of linguistic factors.' **Language, Speech and Hearing Services in Schools,** 32(3), 172–181.

Bourassa, D. and Treiman, R. (2003). 'Spelling in dyslexic children with dyslexia: analyses from the Treiman-Bourassa early spelling test.' **Scientific Studies of Reading**, 7(4), 309–333.

Bowers, P. G. and Wolf, M. (1993). 'Theoretical links among naming speed, precise timing mechanisms and orthographic skill in dyslexia.' **Reading and Writing,** 5(1), 69–85.

Bowey, J. A. (1995). 'Socioeconomic status differences in preschool phonological sensitivity and first-grade reading achievement.' **Journal of Educational Psychology,** 87(3), 476–487.

Bradley, L. and Bryant, P. E. (1978). 'Difficulties in auditory organisation as a possible cause of reading backwardness.' **Nature,** 271, 746–747.

Bradshaw, J., Sewell, J., Adams, E. and Page, N. (2002). **Skills for Life diagnostic assessments in literacy (dyslexia): trial report**. Slough: National Foundation for Educational Research (unpublished).

Briscoe, J., Bishop, D. V. M. and Norbury, C. F. (2001). 'Phonological processing, language, and literacy: a comparison of children with mild-to-moderate sensorineural hearing loss and those with specific language impairment.' **Journal of Child Psychology and Psychiatry,** 42(3), 329–340.

British Psychological Society. (1999). **Dyslexia, Literacy and Psychological Assessment (Report of a Working Party of the Division of Educational and Child Psychology)**. Leicester: Author.

Bronfenbrenner, U. and Ceci, S. J. (1994). 'Nature-nurture reconceptualized in developmental perspective: a bioecological model.' **Psychological Review,** 101(4), 568–586.

Brooks, G., Davies, R., Duckett, L., Hutchison, D., Kendall, S. and Wilkin, A. (2001a). **Progress in Adult Literacy: do learners learn?** London: The Basic Skills Agency.

Brooks, G., Giles, K., Harman, J., Kendall, S., Rees, F. and Whittaker, S. (2001b). **Assembling the Fragments: a review of research in adult basic skills**. London: Department for Education and Employment.

Brooks, G., Gorman, T., Kendall, L. and Tate, A. (1992). **What Teachers in Training are Taught about Reading: the working papers**. Slough: National Foundation for Educational Research.

Bruck, M. (1998). **Outcomes of adults with childhood histories of dyslexia.** In C. Hulme & R. M. Joshi (Eds.) (pp. 179–200). Mahwah, NJ: Lawrence Erlbaum Associates.

Brunswick, N., McCrory, E., Price, C. J., Frith, C. D. and Frith, U. (1999). 'Explicit and implicit processing of words and pseudowords by adult developmental dyslexics – a search for Wernicke's Wortschatz?' **Brain,** 122, 1901–1917.

Bryant, P. (2002). 'Children's thoughts about reading and spelling.' **Scientific Studies of Reading,** 6(2), 199–216.

Bryant, P. and Bradley, L. (1985). **Children's Reading Problems: psychology and education**. Oxford: Basil Blackwell.

Bryant, P. and Impey, L. (1986). 'The similarities between normal readers and developmental and acquired dyslexics.' **Cognition,** 24(1–2), 121–137.

Bus, A. G. and van IJzendoorn, M. H. (1999). 'Phonological awareness and early reading: a meta-analysis of experimental training studies.' **Journal of Educational Psychology,** 91(3), 403–414.

Byrne, B. (1998). **The Foundation of Literacy: the child's acquisition of the alphabetic principle**. Hove: Psychology Press.

Cabeza, R. and Nyberg, L. (1997). 'Imaging Cognition: an empirical review of PET studies with normal subjects.' **Journal of Cognitive Neurosciences,** 9(1), 1–26.

Cairns, R. B. (1996). Socialization and sociogenesis. In D. Magnusson (Ed.), **The lifespan development of individuals: behavioral, neurobiological, and psychosocial perspectives: a synthesis.** (pp. 277–295). Cambridge: Cambridge University Press.

Caplan, D. and Waters, G. S. (1999). 'Verbal working memory and sentence comprehension.' **Behavioral and Brain Sciences,** 22(1), 77–126.

Caramazza, A. and McCloskey, M. (1988). 'The case for single-patient studies.' **Cognitive Neuropsychology,** 5(5), 517–528.

Caravolas, M., Hulme, C. and Snowling, M. J. (2001). 'The foundations of spelling ability: evidence from a three-year longitudinal study.' **Journal of Memory and Language,** 45(4), 751–774.

Cardon, L. R., Smith, S. D., Fulker, D. W., Kimberling, W. J., Pennington, B. F. and DeFries, J. C. (1994). 'Quantitative trait locus for reading disability on chromosome 6.' **Science,** 266(14 October 1994), 276–279.

Cardoso-Martins, C. (2001). 'The reading abilities of beginning readers of Brazilian Portuguese: implications for a theory of reading acquisition.' **Scientific Studies of Reading,** 5(4), 289–317.

Carr, T. H., Brown, T. L., Varus, L. G. and Evans, M. A. (1990). 'Cognitive skill maps and cognitive skill profiles: componential analysis of individual differences in children's reading efficiency.' In T. H. Carr & B. A. Levy (Eds.), **Reading and its Development: component skills approaches.** (pp. 1–55). San Diego: Academic Press.

Carr, T. H. and Posner, M. I. (1995). 'The impact of learning to read on the functional anatomy of language processing.' In B. de Gelder & J. Morais (Eds.), **Speech and Reading: a comparative approach**. Hove: Erlbaum (UK) Taylor & Francis.

Carrier, J. G. (1983). 'Masking the social in educational knowledge: the case of learning disability theory.' **American Journal of Sociology,** 88(5), 948–974.

Carruthers, P. (2002). 'The cognitive functions of language.' **Behavioral and Brain Sciences,** 25(6), 657–725.

Cashdan, A. (1969). 'Handicaps in Learning.' In J. F. Morris & E. A. Lunzer (Eds.), **Contexts of Education** (pp. 165–194). London: Staples Press.

Castles, A. and Coltheart, M. (1993). 'Varieties of developmental dyslexia.' **Cognition,** 47, 149–180.

Castles, A., Datta, H., Gayán, J. and Olson, R. K. (1999). 'Varieties of developmental reading disorder: genetic and environmental influences.' **Journal of Experimental Child Psychology,** 72(2), 73–94.

Castro-Caldas, A., Petersson, K. M., Reis, A., Stone-Elander, S. and Ingvar, M. (1998). 'The illiterate brain: learning to read and write during childhood influences the functional organisation of the adult brain.' **Brain,** 121(6), 1053–1063.

Castro-Caldas, A. and Reis, A. (2003). 'The knowledge of orthography is a revolution in the brain.' **Reading and Writing,** 16(1), 81–97.

Catts, H. W., Gillispie, M., Leonard, L. B., Kail, R. V. and Miller, C. A. (2002). 'The role of speed of processing, rapid naming, and phonological awareness in reading achievement.' **Journal of Learning Disabilities,** 35(6), 509–524.

Ceci, S. J. (1991). 'How much does schooling influence general intelligence and its cognitive components? A reassessment of the evidence.' **Developmental Psychology,** 27(5), 703–722.

Cestnick, L. and Coltheart, M. (1999). 'The relationship between language-processing and visual-processing deficits in developmental dyslexia.' **Cognition,** 71(3), 231–255.

Chall, J. S. (1967). **Learning to Read: The Great Debate**. New York, NY: McGraw-Hill.

Chall, J. S., Jacobs, V. A. and Baldwin, L. E. (1990). **The Reading Crisis: why poor children fall behind**. Cambridge, MA: Harvard University Press.

Chapman, J. W., Tunmer, W. E. and Prochnow, J. E. (2001). 'Does success in the Reading Recovery program depend on developing proficiency in phonological-processing skills? A longitudinal study in a whole-language context.' **Scientific Studies of Reading,** 5(2), 141–176.

Cheung, H. (1999). 'Improving phonological awareness and word reading in a later learned alphabetic script.' **Cognition,** 70(1), 1–26.

Cheung, H., Chen, H. C., Lai, C. Y., Wong, O. C. and Hills, M. (2001). 'The development of phonological awareness: effects of spoken language experience and orthography.' **Cognition,** 81(3), 227–241.

Chiappe, P., Chiappe, D. L. and Siegel, L. S. (2001). 'Speech perception, lexicality, and reading skill.' **Journal of Experimental Child Psychology,** 80(1), 58–74.

Chiappe, P., Stringer, R., Siegel, L. S. and Stanovich, K. E. (2002). 'Why the timing deficit hypothesis does not explain reading disability in adults.' **Reading and Writing,** 15, 73–107.

Chomsky, N. (1957). **Syntactic Structures**. The Hague: Mouton.

Cicchetti, D. and Cannon, T. D. (1999). 'Neurodevelopmental processes in the ontogenesis and epigenesis of psychopathology.' **Development and Psychopathology,** 11, 375–393.

Clay, M. M. (1987). 'Learning to be learning disabled.' **New Zealand Journal of Educational Studies,** 22, 155–173.

Cloninger, C. R. (2000). 'A practical way to diagnose personality disorder: a proposal.' **Journal of Personality Disorders,** 14(2), 99–108.

Cloninger, C. R., Svrakic, N. M. and Svrakic, D. M. (1997). 'Role of personality self-organisation in development of mental order and disorder.' **Development and Psychopathology,** 9(4), 881–906.

Cole, P. and Sprenger-Charolles, L. (1999). 'Syllabic processing in visual word identification by dyslexic children, late readers and normal readers at age 11.' **Revue de Neuropsychologie,** 9(4), 323–360.

Coles, G. (2000). **Misreading Reading: the bad science that hurts children**. Portsmouth, NH: Heinemann.

Coltheart, M. and Davies, M. (2003). 'Inference and explanation in cognitive psychology.' **Cortex,** 39(1), 188–191.

Corballis, M. C. (in press). 'From mouth to hand: gesture, speech, and the evolution of right-handedness.' **Behavioral and Brain Sciences**.

Cornoldi, C. and Oakhill, J. (Eds.). (1996). **Reading Comprehension Difficulties: processes and intervention**. Mahwah, NJ: Lawrence Erlbaum Associates.

Cossu, G. (1999). 'Biological constraints on literacy acquisition.' **Reading and Writing,** 11, 213–237.

Cox, T. and Jones, G. (1983). **Disadvantaged 11-Year-Olds: Book Supplement to the Journal of Child Psychology and Psychiatry No. 3**. Oxford: Pergamon Press.

Cromley, J. G. (2000). 'Learning with computers: the theory behind the practice.' **Focus on Basics,** 4(C).

Curtin, S., Manis, F. R. and Seidenberg, M. S. (2001). 'Parallels between the reading and spelling deficits of two subgroups of developmental dyslexics.' **Reading and Writing,** 14(5–6), 515–547.

Cutting, L. E. and Denckla, M. B. (2001). 'The relationship of rapid serial naming and word reading in normally developing readers: an exploratory model.' **Reading and Writing,** 14(7–8), 673–705.

Davie, R., Butler, N. and Goldstein, H. (1972). **From Birth to Seven: the Second Report of the National Child Development Study (1958 cohort), with full statistical appendix.** London: Longman.

Davies, K. and Byatt, J. (1998). **Something can be done! (Final Report 1998: Executive Summary)**. Shrewsbury: Shropshire STOP Project: Specific Training for Offenders on Probation.

Davis, C. J., Knopik, V. S., Olson, R. K., Wadsworth, S. J. and DeFries, J. C. (2001). 'Genetic and environmental influences on rapid naming and reading ability: a twin study.' **Annals of Dyslexia,** 51, 231–247.

Davis, D. R. and Cashdan, A. (1963). 'Specific dyslexia.' **British Journal of Educational Psychology,** 33, 80–82.

Davis, R. D. (1994). **The Gift of Dyslexia: why some of the smartest people can't read, and how they can learn.** San Capistrano, CA: Ability Workshop Press.

De Bellis, M. D. (2001). 'Developmental traumatology: the psychobiological development of maltreated children and its implications for research, treatment, and policy.' **Development and Psychopathology,** 13, 539–564.

de Jong, P. F. and van der Leij, A. (1999). 'Specific contributions of phonological abilities to early reading acquisition: results from a Dutch latent variable longitudinal study.' **Journal of Educational Psychology,** 91(3), 450–476.

Denckla, M. B. and Cutting, L. E. (1999). 'History and significance of rapid automatized naming.' **Annals of Dyslexia,** 49, 29–42.

Department for Education and Employment. (1998). **The National Literacy Strategy: framework for teaching**. London: Author.

Desmond, J. E. and Fiez, J. A. (1998). 'Neuroimaging studies of the cerebellum: language, learning and memory.' **Trends in Cognitive Sciences,** 2(9), 355–362.

DfES. (2001). **Skills for Life: the National Literacy Strategy for improving adult literacy and numeracy skills.** London: Department for Education and Skills.

Dickson, M. (1986). **Teacher Extraordinary: Joseph Lancaster,** 1778–1838. Lewes: The Book Guild Limited.

Doctor, E. A. and Coltheart, M. (1980). 'Children's use of phonological encoding when reading for meaning.' **Memory & Cognition,** 8, 195–209.

Dodd, T. and Hunter, P. (1992). **The national prison survey 1991: A report to the Home Office of a study of prisoners in England and Wales carried out by the Social Survey Division of OPCS**. London: HMSO.

Dogil, G., Ackermann, H., Grodd, W., Haider, H., Kamp, H., Mayer, J., Riecker, A. and Wildgruber, D. (2002). 'The speaking brain: a tutorial introduction to fMRI experiments in the production of speech, prosody and syntax. '**Journal of Neurolinguistics,** 15(1), 59–90.

Dollaghan, C. A., Biber, M. E. and Campbell, T. F. (1995). 'Lexical influences on nonword repetition.' **Applied Psycholinguistics,** 16(2), 211–222.

Dudley-Marling, C. and Murphy, S. (1997). 'A political critique of remedial reading programs: the example of Reading Recovery.' **Reading Teacher,** 50(6), 460–468.

Duncan, L. G. and Seymour, P. H. K. (2000). 'Socio-economic differences in foundation-level literacy.' **British Journal of Psychology,** 91, 145–166.

Durgunoglu, A. Y. and Öney, B. (2002). 'Phonological awareness in literacy acquisition: it's not only for children.' **Scientific Studies of Reading,** 6(3), 245–266.

Eckert, M. A., Leonard, C. M., Molloy, E. A., Blumenthal, J., Zijdenbos, A. and Giedd, J. N. (2002). 'The epigenesis of planum temporale symmetry in twins.' **Cerebral Cortex,** 12(7), 749–755.

Eckert, M. A., Lombardino, L. J. and Leonard, C. M. (2001). 'Planar asymmetry tips the phonological playground and environment raises the bar.' **Child Development,** 72(4), 988–1002.

Ehri, L. C., Nunes, S. R., Willows, D. M., Schuster, B. V., Yaghoub-Zadeh, Z. and Shanahan, T. (2001). 'Phonemic awareness instruction helps children learn to read: evidence from the National Reading Panel's meta-analysis.' **Reading Research Quarterly,** 36(3), 250–287.

Elkind, J., Black, M. S. and Murray, C. (1996). 'Computer-based compensation of adult reading disabilities.' **Annals of Dyslexia,** 46, 159–186.

Elley, W. B. (Ed.). (1994). **The IEA Study of Reading Literacy: achievement and instruction in thirty-two school systems**. Oxford: Pergamon.

Ellis, A. W. (1985). 'The cognitive neuropsychology of developmental (and acquired) dyslexia: a critical survey.' **Cognitive Neuropsychology,** 2(2), 169–205.

Ellis, A. W., McDougall, S. J. P. and Monk, A. F. (1996). 'Are dyslexics different? II. Individual differences among dyslexics, reading age controls, poor readers and precocious readers.' **Dyslexia,** 2, 59–68.

Ellis, A. W., McDougall, S. J. P. and Monk, A. F. (1997a). 'Are dyslexics different? III. Of course they are!' **Dyslexia,** 3(1), 2–8.

Ellis, A. W., McDougall, S. J. P. and Monk, A. F. (1997b). 'Are dyslexics different? IV. In defence of uncertainty.' **Dyslexia,** 3(1), 12–14.

Ellis, N. and Large, B. (1987). 'The development of reading: as you seek so shall you find.' **British Journal of Psychology,** 78(1), 1–28.

Ellis, N. C. and Hooper, A. M. (2001). 'Why learning to read is easier in Welsh than English: orthographic transparency effects evinced with frequency-matched tests.' **Applied Psycholinguistics,** 22(5), 571–599.

Ellis, N. C. and Miles, T. R. (1981). 'A lexical encoding deficiency I: experimental evidence.' In G. T. Pavlidis & T. R. Miles (Eds.), **Dyslexia Research and its Applications to Education** (pp. 177–215). Chichester: John Wiley & Sons.

Elman, J. L., Bates, E. A., Johnson, M. H., Karmiloff-Smith, A., Parisi, D. and Plunkett, K. (1996). **Rethinking Innateness: a connectionist perspective on development**. Cambridge, MA: MIT Press.

Everatt, J. (1997). 'The abilities and disabilities associated with adult developmental dyslexia.' **Journal of Research in Reading,** 20(1), 13–21.

Everatt, J., Bradshaw, M. F. and Hibbard, P. B. (1999). 'Visual processing and dyslexia.' **Perception,** 28(2), 243–254.

Everitt, B. S. and Wykes, T. (1999). **Dictionary of Statistics for Psychologists**. London: Arnold.

Fagerheim, T., Raeymaekers, P., Tønnessen, F. E., Pedersen, M., Tranebjærg, L. and Lubs, H. A. (1999). 'A new gene (DYX3) for dyslexia is located on chromosome 2.' **Journal of Medical Genetics,** 36, 664–669.

Farmer, M. E. and Klein, R. M. (1995). 'The evidence for a temporal processing deficit linked to dyslexia: a review.' **Psychonomic Bulletin & Review,** 2(4), 460–493.

Farrington, D. P. (1998). 'Predictors, Causes, and Correlates of Male Youth Violence.' In M. Tonry & M. H. Moore (Eds.), **Youth Violence** (pp. 421–475). Chicago: The University of Chicago Press.

Fawcett, A. (2002). **Reading Remediation: an evaluation of traditional phonologically based interventions. A review for the Department for Education and Skills, British Dyslexia Association and the Dyslexia Institute. Review 3, March 2002. [Accessed at www.dfes.gov.uk/sen/documents/Dyslexia_3rd_review.htm on 2 December 2002].**

Fawcett, A. and Nicolson, R. (Eds.). (1994). **Dyslexia in Children: multidisciplinary perspectives**. Hemel Hempstead: Harvester Wheatsheaf.

Fawcett, A. J. and Nicolson, R. I. (1991). **Dyslexia and Automatisation: tests of a hypothesis.** Paper presented at the British Dyslexia Association International Conference, Oxford.

Fawcett, A. J. and Nicolson, R. I. (1998). **The Dyslexia Adult Screening Test**. London: The Psychological Corporation.

Fawcett, A. J., Nicolson, R. I. and Dean, P. (1996). 'Impaired performance of children with dyslexia on a range of cerebellar tasks.' **Annals of Dyslexia,** 46, 259–283.

Fawcett, A. J., Nicolson, R. I. and Maclagan, F. (2001). 'Cerebellar tests differentiate between groups of poor readers with and without IQ discrepancy.' **Journal of Learning Disabilities,** 34(2), 119–135.

Feagans, L. and Farran, D. C. (Eds.). (1982). **The Language of Children Reared in Poverty: Implications for evaluation and intervention.** New York: Academic Press.

Felton, R. H., Naylor, C. E. and Wood, F. B. (1990). 'Neuropsychological profile of adult dyslexics.' **Brain and Language,** 39, 485–497.

Fergusson, D. M., Horwood, L. J., Caspi, A., Moffitt, T. E. and Silva, P. A. (1996). 'The (artefactual) remission of reading disability: psychometric lessons in the study of stability and change in behavioral development.' **Developmental Psychology,** 32(1), 132–140.

Fergusson, D. M. and Lynskey, M. T. (1997). 'Early reading difficulties and later conduct problems.' **Journal of Child Psychology and Psychiatry,** 38(8), 899–907.

Fernald, G. M. (1943). **Remedial Techniques in Basic School Subjects**. New York, NY: McGraw-Hill.

Filipek, P. A. (1995). 'Neurobiologic correlates of developmental dyslexia: how do dyslexics' brains differ from those of normal readers?' **Journal of Child Neurology,** 10(Supplement Number 1), S62–S68.

Filipek, P. A. (1999). 'Neuroimaging in the developmental disorders: the state of the science.' **Journal of Child Psychology and Psychiatry,** 40(1), 113–128.

Fischer, K. W. and Bidell, T. R. (1998). 'Dynamic development of psychological structures in action and thought.' In W. Damon & R. M. Lerner (Eds.), **Handbook of Child Psychology** (Vol. 1 Theoretical Models of Human Development., pp. 467–561). New York, NY: John Wiley & Sons, Inc.

Fisher, S. E., Francks, C., Marlow, A. J., MacPhie, I. L., Newbury, D. F., Cardon, L. R., Ishikawa-Brush, Y., Richardson, A. J., Talcott, J. B., Gayán, J., Olson, R. K., Pennington, B. F., Smith, S. D., DeFries, J. C., Stein, J. F. and Monaco, A. P. (2002). 'Independent genome-wide scans identify a chromosome 18 quantitative-trait locus influencing dyslexia.' **Nature Genetics,** 30(1), 86–91.

Fisher, S. E., Marlow, A. J., Lamb, J., Maestrini, E., Williams, D. F., Richardson, A. J., Weeks, D. E., Stein, J. F. and Monaco, A. P. (1999). 'A quantitative trait locus on chromosome 6p influences different aspects of developmental dyslexia.' **American Journal of Human Genetics,** 64(1), 146–156.

Fitzgibbon, G. and O'Connor, B. (2002). **Adult Dyslexia: a guide for the workplace**. Chichester: John Wiley & Sons.

Flannery, K. A. and Liederman, J. (1995). 'Is there really a syndrome involving the co-occurrence of neurodevelopmental disorder, talent, non-right handedness and immune disorder among children?' **Cortex,** 31, 503–515.

Fletcher, J. M., Foorman, B. R., Boudousquie, A., Barnes, M. A., Schatschneider, C. and Francis, D. J. (2002). 'Assessment of reading and learning disabilities: a research-based intervention-oriented approach.' **Journal of School Psychology,** 40(1), 27–63.

Fletcher, J. M., Francis, D. J., Rourke, B. P., Shaywitz, S. E. and Shaywitz, B. A. (1992). 'The validity of discrepancy-based definitions of reading disabilities.' **Journal of Learning Disabilities,** 25(9), 555–561, 573.

Fletcher, J. M. and Satz, P. (1985). 'Cluster analysis and the search for learning disability subtypes.' In B. P. Rourke (Ed.), **Neuropsychology of Learning Disabilities: essentials of subtype analysis.** (pp. 40–64). New York: The Guilford Press.

Fletcher, J. M., Shaywitz, S. E., Shankweiler, D. P., Katz, L., Liberman, I. Y., Stuebing, K. K., Francis, D. F., Fowler, A. E. and Shaywitz, B. A. (1994). 'Cognitive profiles of reading disability: comparisons of discrepancy and low achievement definitions.' **Journal of Educational Psychology,** 86(1), 6–23.

Fletcher, J. M., Taylor, H. G., Levin, H. S. and Satz, P. (1995). 'Neuropsychological and intellectual assessment of children.' In H. Kaplan & B. Sadock (Eds.), **Comprehensive Textbook of Psychiatry** (Sixth ed., pp. 581–601). Baltimore, MD: Williams & Wilkens.

Flood-Page, C., Campbell, S., Harrington, V. and Miller, J. (2000). **Youth Crime: findings from the 1998/99 Youth Lifestyles Survey. Home Office Research Study 209**. London: The Stationery Office.

Fowler, A. E. and Scarborough, H. S. (1993). **Should Reading-Disabled Adults Be Distinguished From Other Adults Seeking Literacy Instruction? A Review Of Theory And Research**. Philadelphia, PA: National Center on Adult Literacy.

Fowler, C., Liberman, I. Y. and Shankweiler, D. (1977). 'On interpreting the error pattern in beginning reading.' **Language and Speech,** 20, 162–173.

Francks, C., Fisher, S. E., Olson, R. K., Pennington, B. F., Smith, S. D., DeFries, J. C. and Monaco, A. P. (2002). 'Fine mapping of the chromosome 2p12–16 dyslexia susceptibility locus: quantitative association analysis and positional candidate genes SEMA4F and OTX1.' **Psychiatric Genetics,** 12(1), 35–41.

Frank, J. and Levinson, H. (1973). 'Dysmetric dyslexia and dyspraxia.' **Journal of the American Academy of Child Psychiatry,** 12, 690–701.

Fredman, G. and Stevenson, J. (1988). 'Reading processes in specific reading retarded and reading backward 13-year-olds.' **British Journal of Developmental Psychology,** 6, 97–108.

Frith, U. (1995). 'Dyslexia: can we have a shared theoretical framework?' **Educational and Child Psychology,** 12(1), 6–17.

Frith, U. (1999). 'Paradoxes in the definition of dyslexia.' **Dyslexia,** 5, 192–214.

Frith, U. (2001). 'What framework should we use for understanding developmental disorders?' **Developmental Neuropsychology,** 20(2), 555–563.

Fuchs, L. S., Fuchs, D., Hosp, M. K. and Jenkins, J. R. (2001). 'Oral reading fluency as an indicator of reading competence: a theoretical, empirical, and historical analysis.' **Scientific Studies of Reading,** 5(3), 241–258.

Fulbright, R. K., Jenner, A. R., Mencl, W. E., Pugh, K. R., Shaywitz, B. A., Shaywitz, S. E., Frost, S. J., Skudlarski, P., Constable, R. T., Lacadie, C. M., Marchione, K. E. and Gore, J. C. (1999). 'The cerebellum's role in reading: a functional MR imaging study.' **American Journal of Neuroradiology,** 20(10), 1925–1930.

Gabel, L. A. and Turco, J. J. L. (2002). 'Layer 1 ectopias and increased excitability in murine neocortex.' **Journal of Neurophysiology,** 87(5), 2471–2479.

Galaburda, A. (Ed.). (1993). **Dyslexia and Development: neurobiological aspects of extra-ordinary brains**. Cambridge, MA: Harvard University Press.

Galaburda, A. M., Menard, M. T. and Rosen, G. D. (1994). 'Evidence for aberrant auditory anatomy in developmental dyslexia.' **Proceedings of the National Academy of Sciences,** 91, 8010–8013.

Galaburda, A. M., Rosen, G. D., Denenberg, V. H., Fitch, R. H., LoTurco, J. J. and Sherman, G. F. (2001). 'Models of temporal processing and language development.' **Clinical Neuroscience Research,** 1(3), 230–237.

Galaburda, A. M., Rosen, G. D. and Sherman, G. F. (1989). 'The neural origin of developmental dyslexia: implications for medicine, neurology, and cognition.' In A. M. Galaburda (Ed.), **From Reading to Neurons** (pp. 377–388). Cambridge, MA: MIT Press.

Gayán, J. and Olson, R. K. (2003). 'Genetic and environmental influences on individual differences in printed word recognition.' **Journal of Experimental Child Psychology,** 84(2), 97–123.

Geiger, G. and Lettvin, J. Y. (1997). **A view on dyslexia (A.I. Memo No. 1608/C.B.C.L. Paper No. 148)**. Cambridge, MA: Massachusetts Institute of Technology Artificial Intelligence Laboratory and Center for Biological and Computational Learning Department of Brain and Cognitive Sciences.

Geiger, G., Lettvin, J. Y. and Zegarra-Moran, O. (1992). 'Task-determined strategies of visual process.' **Cognitive Brain Research,** 1(1), 39–52.

Gersons-Wolfensberger, D. C. M. and Ruijssenaars, W. A. J. J. M. (1997). 'Definition and treatment of dyslexia: a report by the Committee of Dyslexia of the Health Council of the Netherlands.' **Journal of Learning Disabilities,** 30(2), 209–213.

Geschwind, N. (1984). 'The biology of cerebral dominance: implications for cognition.' **Cognition,** 17, 193–208.

Geschwind, N. and Galaburda, A. M. (1985). 'Cerebral lateralization: biological mechanisms, associations, and pathology: 1. A hypothesis and a program for research.' **Archives of Neurology,** 42, 428–459.

Gilger, J. W., Ho, H.-Z., Whipple, A. D. and Spitz, R. (2001). 'Genotype-environment correlations for language-related abilities: implications for typical and atypical learners.' **Journal of Learning Disabilities,** 34(6), 492–502.

Gilger, J. W. and Kaplan, B. J. (2001). 'Atypical brain development: a conceptual framework for understanding developmental learning disabilities.' **Developmental Neuropsychology,** 20(2), 465–481.

Gilger, J. W. and Pennington, B. F. (1995). 'Why associations among traits do not necessarily indicate their common etiology: a comment on the Geschwind-Behan-Galaburda model.' **Brain and Cognition,** 27, 89–93.

Gilger, J. W., Pennington, B. F., Harbeck, R. J., DeFries, J. C., Kotzin, B., Green, P. and Smith, S. (1998). 'A twin and family study of the association between immune system dysfunction and dyslexia using blood serum immunoassay and survey data.' **Brain and Cognition,** 36(3), 310–333.

Gleitman, L. R. and Rozin, P. (1977). 'The structure and acquisition of reading I: relation between orthography and the structured language.' In A. S. Reber & D. L. Scarborough (Eds.), **Toward a Psychology of Reading: the proceedings of the CUNY conferences** (pp. 1–53). Hillsdale, NJ: Lawrence Erlbaum Associates.

Gliner, J. A. and Morgan, G. A. (2000). **Research Methods in Applied Settings: an integrated approach to design and analysis**. Mahwah, NJ: Lawrence Erlbaum Associates.

Goodman, K. S. (1970). 'Reading: a psycholinguistic guessing game.' In H. Singer & R. B. Ruddell (Eds.), **Theoretical Models and Processes of Reading** (pp. 259–271). Newark, DE: International Reading Association.

Goodman, K. S. (Ed.). (1978). **The Psycholinguistic Nature of the Reading Process**. Detroit, MI: Wayne State University Press.

Goswami, U. and Bryant, P. (1990). **Phonological Skills and Learning to Read.** Hove: Lawrence Erlbaum Associates.

Goswami, U., Porpodas, C. and Wheelwright, S. (1997). 'Children's orthographic representations in English and Greek.' **European Journal of Psychology of Education,** 12(3), 273–292.

Goswami, U., Thomson, J., Richardson, U., Stainthorp, R., Hughes, D., Rosen, S. and Scott, S. K. (2002). 'Amplitude envelope onsets and developmental dyslexia: a new hypothesis.' **Proceedings of the National Academy of Sciences of the United States of America,** 99(16), 10911–10916.

Gottesman, R. L., Bennett, R. E., Nathan, R. G. and Kelly, M. S. (1996). 'Inner-city adults with severe reading difficulties: a closer look.' **Journal of Learning Disabilities,** 29(6), 589–597.

Gottfredson, D. C. (2001). **Schools and Delinquency**. Cambridge: Cambridge University Press.

Gottlieb, G. (1992). **Individual Development and Evolution: the genesis of novel behaviour**. New York: Oxford University Press.

Gottlieb, G. and Halpern, C. T. (2002). 'A relational view of causality in normal and abnormal development.' **Development and Psychopathology,** 14, 421–435.

Gottlieb, G., Wahlstein, D. and Lickliter, R. (1998). 'The Significance of Biology for Human Development: a developmental psychobiological systems view.' In W. Damon & R. M. Lerner (Eds.), **Handbook of Child Psychology, Volume 1: Theoretical Models of Human Development** (Fifth ed., pp. 233–273). New York: John Wiley & Sons.

Gough, P. B. and Tunmer, W. E. (1986). 'Decoding, reading, and reading disability.' **Remedial and Special Education,** 7(1), 6–10.

Gough, P. B. and Wren, S. (1999). 'Constructing meaning: the role of decoding.' In J. Oakhill & R. Beard (Eds.), **Reading Development and the Teaching of Reading: a psychological perspective** (pp. 59–78). Oxford: Blackwell.

Greenberg, D., Ehri, L. C. and Perin, D. (1997). 'Are word-reading processes the same or different in adult literacy students and third-fifth graders matched for reading level?' **Journal of Educational Psychology,** 89(2), 262–275.

Griffiths, Y. M. and Snowling, M. J. (2002). 'Predictors of exception word and nonword reading in dyslexic children: the severity hypothesis.' **Journal of Educational Psychology,** 94(1), 34–43.

Grigorenko, E. L. (2001). 'Developmental dyslexia: an update on genes, brains, and environments.' **Journal of Child Psychology and Psychiatry,** 42(1), 91–125.

Grigorenko, E. L., Wood, F. B., Meyer, M. S., Hart, L. A., Speed, W. C., Shuster, A. and Pauls, D. L. (1997). 'Susceptibility loci for distinct components of developmental dyslexia on chromosomes 6 and 15.' **American Journal of Human Genetics,** 60(1), 27–39.

Grigorenko, E. L., Wood, F. B., Meyer, M. S., Pauls, J. E. D., Hart, L. A. and Pauls, D. L. (2001). 'Linkage studies suggest a possible locus for developmental dyslexia on chromosome 1p.' **American Journal of Medical Genetics,** 105(1), 120–129.

Gross-Glenn, K., Skottun, B. C., Glenn, W., Kushch, A., Lingua, R., Dunbar, M., Jallad, B., Lubs, H. A., Levin, B., Rabin, M., Parke, L. A. and Duara, R. (1995). 'Contrast sensitivity in dyslexia.' **Visual Neuroscience,** 12(1), 153–163.

Gustafson, S. (2001). 'Cognitive abilities and print exposure in surface and phonological types of reading disability.' **Scientific Studies of Reading,** 5(4), 351–375.

Gustafson, S. and Samuelsson, S. (1999). 'Intelligence and dyslexia: implications for diagnosis and intervention.' **Scandinavian Journal of Psychology,** 40(2), 127–134.

Guyer, B. P., Banks, S. R. and Guyer, K. E. (1993). 'Spelling improvement for college students who are dyslexic.' **Annals of Dyslexia,** 43, 186–193.

Guyer, B. P. and Sabatino, D. (1989). 'The effectiveness of a multisensory alphabetic phonetic approach with college students who are learning disabled.' **Journal of Learning Disabilities,** 22, 430–434.

Habib, M. (2000). 'The neurological basis of developmental dyslexia: an overview and working hypothesis.' **Brain,** 123(12), 2373–2399.

Habib, M. and Robichon, F. (2002). 'Neuroanatomical correlates of hemispheric specialization.' **Revue de Neuropsychologie,** 12(1), 87–127.

Habib, M., Robichon, F., Chanoine, V., Démonet, J.-F., Frith, C. and Frith, U. (2000). 'The influence of language learning on brain morphology: the "callosal effect" in dyslexics differs according to native language.' **Brain and Language,** 74(3), 520–524.

Haigler, K. O., Harlow, C., O'Connor, O. and Campbell, A. (1994). **Literacy Behind Prison Walls: profiles of the prison population from the National Adult Literacy Survey.** Washington, DC: US Department of Education.

Hari, R. and Renvall, H. (2001). 'Impaired processing of rapid stimulus sequences in dyslexia.' **Trends in Cognitive Sciences,** 5(12), 525–532.

Harm, M. W., McCandliss, B. D. and Seidenberg, M. S. (2003). 'Modeling the successes and failures of interventions for disabled readers.' **Scientific Studies of Reading,** 7(2), 155–182.

Harm, M. W. and Seidenberg, M. S. (1999). 'Phonology, reading acquisition, and dyslexia: insights from connectionist models.' **Psychological Review,** 106(3), 491–528.

Harrington, R. C., Cartwright-Hatton, S. and Stein, A. (2002). 'Randomised trials.' **Journal of Child Psychology and Psychiatry,** 43(6), 695–704.

Haslum, M. N. (1989). 'Predictors of dyslexia?' **The Irish Journal of Psychology,** 10(4), 622–630.

Hatcher, P., Hulme, C. and Ellis, A. W. (1994). 'Ameliorating early reading failure by integrating the teaching of reading and phonological skills: the phonological linkage hypothesis.' **Child Development,** 65, 41–57.

Hatcher, P. J. (2000). 'Sound links in reading and spelling with discrepancy-defined dyslexics and children with moderate learning difficulties.' **Reading and Writing,** 13(3–4), 257–272.

Hayduk, S., Bruck, M. and Cavanagh, P. (1996). 'Low-level visual processing skills of adults and children with dyslexia.' **Cognitive Neuropsychology,** 13(7), 975–1015.

Heath, S. M., Hogben, J. H. and Clark, C. D. (1999). 'Auditory temporal processing in disabled readers with and without oral language delay.' **Journal of Child Psychology and Psychiatry,** 40(4), 637–647.

Hecht, S. A., Burgess, S. R., Torgesen, J. K., Wagner, R. K. and Rashotte, C. A. (2000). 'Explaining social class differences in growth of reading skills from beginning kindergarten through fourth-grade: the role of phonological awareness, rate of access, and print knowledge.' **Reading and Writing,** 12(1–2), 99–127.

Heiervang, E., Hugdahl, K., Steinmetz, H., Smievoll, A. I., Stevenson, J., Lund, A., Ersland, L. and Lundervold, A. (2000). 'Planum temporale, planum parietale and dichotic listening in dyslexia.' **Neuropsychologia,** 38(13), 1704–1713.

Helenius, P., Salmelin, R., Richardson, U., Leinonen, S. and Lyytinen, H. (2002). 'Abnormal auditory cortical activation in dyslexia 100 msec after speech onset.' **Journal of Cognitive Neuroscience,** 14(4), 603–617.

Hendriks, A. W. and Kolk, H. H. J. (1997). 'Strategic control in developmental dyslexia.' **Cognitive Neuropsychology,** 14(3), 321–366.

Herrington, M. and Hunter-Carsch, M. (2001). 'A social interactive model of specific learning difficulties, e.g. dyslexia.' In M. Hunter-Carsch (Ed.), **Dyslexia: a psychosocial perspective** (pp. 107–133). London: Whurr.

Higgins, E. L. and Zvi, J. C. (1995). 'Assistive technology for postsecondary students with learning disabilities: from research to practice.' **Annals of Dyslexia,** 45, 123–142.

Hill, N. I., Bailey, P. J., Griffiths, Y. M. and Snowling, M. J. (1999). 'Frequency acuity and binaural masking release in dyslexic listeners.' **Journal of the Acoustical Society of America,** 106(6), L53–L58.

HM Prison Service. (1999). **Dyslexia Information Pack**. London: Author.

Ho, C. S.-H., Law, T. P.-S. and Ng, P. M. (2000). 'The phonological deficit hypothesis in Chinese developmental dyslexia.' **Reading and Writing,** 13(1–2), 57–79.

Ho, C. S. H. and Lai, D. N. C. (1999). 'Naming-speed deficits and phonological memory deficits in Chinese developmental dyslexia.' **Learning and Individual Differences,** 11(2), 173–186.

Holopainen, L., Ahonen, T. and Lyytinen, H. (2001). 'Predicting delay in reading achievement in a highly transparent language.' **Journal of Learning Disabilities,** 34(5), 401–413.

Horrobin, D. F., Glen, A. I. M. and Hudson, C. J. (1995). 'Possible relevance of phospholipid abnormalities and genetic interactions in psychiatric disorders: the relationship between dyslexia and schizophrenia.' **Medical Hypotheses,** 45, 605–613.

Hoskyn, M. and Swanson, H. L. (2000). 'Cognitive processing of low achievers and children with reading disabilities: a selective meta-analytic review of the published literature.' **School Psychology Review,** 29(1), 102–119.

Hsieh, L., Gandour, J., Wong, D. and Hutchins, G. D. (2001). 'Functional heterogeneity of inferior frontal gyrus is shaped by linguistic experience.' **Brain and Language,** 76(3), 227–252.

Huey, E. B. (1908). **The Psychology and Pedagogy of Reading, with a review of the history of reading and writing and of methods, texts, and hygiene in reading** (1968 MIT Press reprint, with foreword by John B. Carroll and introduction by Paul A Kolers. ed.). New York: The Macmillan Company.

Hulme, C. (1988). 'The implausibility of low-level visual deficits as a cause of children's reading difficulties.' **Cognitive Neuropsychology,** 5(3), 369–374.

Hulme, C. (2002). 'Phonemes, rimes, and the mechanisms of early reading development.' **Journal of Experimental Child Psychology,** 82, 58–64.

Hulme, C. and Roodenrys, S. (1995). 'Verbal working memory development and its disorders.' **Journal of Child Psychology and Psychiatry,** 36(3), 373–398.

Hurry, J. (1999). 'Children's reading levels.' **Journal of Child Psychology and Psychiatry,** 40(2), 143–159.

Hynd, G. W., Hall, J., Novey, E. S., Eliopulos, D., Black, K., Gonzalez, J. J., Edmonds, J. E., Riccio, C. and Cohen, M. (1995). 'Dyslexia and corpus callosum morphology'. **Archives of Neurology,** 52(1), 32–38.

Hynd, G. W. and Semrud-Clikeman, M. (1989). 'Dyslexia and brain morphology.' **Psychological Bulletin,** 106(3), 447–482.

Ito, M. (1993). 'New concepts in cerebellar function.' **Revue Neurologique,** 149(11), 596–599.

Ivry, R. and Lebby, P. C. (1998). 'The neurology of consonant perception: specialized module or distributed processors?' In M. Beeman & C. Chiarello (Eds.), **Right Hemisphere Language**

Comprehension: perspectives from cognitive neuroscience (pp. 3–25). Mahwah, NJ: Lawrence Erlbaum Associates.

Jackson, N. E. and Coltheart, M. (2001). **Routes to Reading Success and Failure: towards an integrated cognitive psychology of atypical reading**. Hove: Psychology Press.

Johnson, K. R. and Layng, T. V. J. (1992). 'Breaking the structuralist barrier: literacy and numeracy with fluency.' **American Psychologist,** 47(11), 1475–1490.

Johnson, S. P. (2003). 'The nature of cognitive development.' **Trends in Cognitive Sciences,** 7(3), 102–104.

Jorm, A. F., Share, D. L., Maclean, R. and Matthews, R. (1986a). 'Cognitive factors at school entry predictive of specific reading retardation and general reading backwardness: a research note.' **Journal of Child Psychology and Psychiatry,** 27(1), 45–54.

Jorm, A. F., Share, D. L., Matthews, R. and Maclean, R. (1986b). 'Behaviour problems in specific reading retarded and general reading backward children: a longitudinal study.' **Journal of Child Psychology and Psychiatry,** 27(1), 33–43.

Kaplan, B. J., Dewey, D. M., Crawford, S. G. and Wilson, B. N. (2001). 'The term **comorbidity** is of questionable value in reference to developmental disorders: data and theory.' **Journal of Learning Disabilities,** 34(6), 555–565.

Karmiloff-Smith, A. (1992). **Beyond Modularity: a developmental perspective on cognitive science**. Cambridge, MA: MIT Press.

Karmiloff-Smith, A. (1998). 'Development itself is the key to understanding developmental disorders.' **Trends in Cognitive Sciences,** 2(10), 389–398.

Karmiloff-Smith, A., Scerif, G. and Ansari, D. (2003). 'Double dissociations in developmental disorders? Theoretically misconceived, empirically dubious.' **Cortex,** 39(1), 161–163.

Kavale, K. A. and Forness, S. R. (2000). 'What definitions of learning disability say and don't say: a critical analysis.' **Journal of Learning Disabilities,** 33(3), 239–256.

Kerr, H. (2001). 'Learned helplessness and dyslexia: a carts and horses issue?' **Reading,** 35(2), 82–85.

Kirk, J. and Reid, G. (2001). 'An examination of the relationship between dyslexia and offending in young people and the implications for the training system.' **Dyslexia,** 7, 77–84.

Kirk, S. A., Gallagher, J. J. and Anastasiow, N. J. (1993). **Educating Exceptional Children** (Seventh ed.). Boston: Houghton Mifflin.

Kitz, W. R. and Nash, R. T. (1992). 'Testing the effectiveness of the Project Success Summer Program for adult dyslexics.' **Annals of Dyslexia,** 42, 3–24.

Klein, C. (1993). **Diagnosing Dyslexia: a guide to the assessment of adults with specific learning difficulties**. London: Adult Literacy & Basic Skills Unit.

Klein, C. (1998). **Dyslexia and Offending: Intervention for Change (Final Report on the Dyspel Pilot Project, February 1998)**. London: Dyspel.

Klein, R. M. and Farmer, M. E. (1995). 'Dyslexia and the temporal processing deficit: a reply to the commentaries.' **Psychonomic Bulletin & Review,** 2(4), 515–526.

Klicpera, C. and Klicpera, B. G. (2001). 'Does intelligence make a difference? Spelling and phonological abilities in discrepant and non-discrepant reading and spelling disabilities.' **Zeitschrift fur Kinder- und Jugendpsychiatrie und Psychotherapie,** 29(1), 37–49.

Kohl, H. (1988). **Reading, how to: a people's guide to alternatives to learning and testing**. Milton Keynes: Open University Press.

Kolinsky, R., Morais, J. and Verhaeghe, A. (1994). 'Visual separability: a study on unschooled adults.' **Perception,** 23, 471–486.

Kolvin, I., Miller, F. J. W., Scott, D. M., Gatzanis, S. R. M. and Fleeting, M. (1990). **Continuities of Deprivation? The Newcastle 1000 Family Study**. Aldershot: Avebury.

Korkman, M., Barron-Linnankoski, S. and Lahti-Nuuttila, P. (1999). 'Effects of age and duration of reading instruction on the development of phonological awareness, rapid naming, and verbal memory span.' **Developmental Neuropsychology,** 16(3), 415–431.

Kramer, J. H., Knee, K. and Delis, D. C. (2000). 'Verbal memory impairments in dyslexia.' **Archives of Clinical Neuropsychology,** 15(1), 83–93.

Kruidenier, J. (2002). **Research-Based Principles for Adult Basic Education Reading Instruction**. Portsmouth, NH: RMC Research Corporation [Accessed at http://www.nifl.gov/partnershipforreading/publications/adult.html on 1 September 2003].

Kuhl, P. K., Tsao, F.-M., Liu, H.-M., Zhang, Y. and de Boer, B. (2001). 'Language/culture/mind/brain: progress at the margins between disciplines.' **Annals of the New York Academy of Sciences,** 935, 136–174.

Kujala, T., Karma, K., Ceponiene, R., Belitz, S., Turkkila, P., Tervaniemi, M. and Naatanen, R. (2001). 'Plastic neural changes and reading improvement caused by audiovisual training in reading-impaired children.' **Proceedings of the National Academy of Sciences of the United States of America,** 98(18), 10509–10514.

LaBerge, D. and Samuels, S. J. (1974). 'Toward a theory of automatic information processing in reading.' **Cognitive Psychology,** 6, 293–323.

Lawton, D. (1968). **Social Class, Language and Education**. London: Routledge & Kegan Paul.

Lee, J. (2000). 'The challenge of dyslexia in adults.' In J. Townend & M. Turner (Eds.), **Dyslexia in Practice: a guide for teachers**. London: Kluwer Academic/Plenum Publishers.

Lee, J. (2002). **Making the Curriculum work for Learners with Dyslexia**. London: Basic Skills Agency.

Leonard, C. M., Lombardino, L. J., Walsh, K., Eckert, M. A., Mockler, J. L., Rowe, L. A., Williams, S. and DeBose, C. B. (2002). 'Anatomical risk factors that distinguish dyslexia from SLI predict reading skill in normal children.' **Journal of Communication Disorders,** 35(6), 501–531.

Leong, C. K. (1999). 'Phonological and morphological processing in adult students with learning/reading disabilities.' **Journal of Learning Disabilities,** 32(3), 224–238.

Levelt, W. J. M. (2001). 'Defining dyslexia.' **Science,** 292(5520), 1300–1301.

Levinson, S. C. (1983). **Pragmatics**. Cambridge: Cambridge University Press.

Leybaert, J. and Content, A. (1995). 'Reading and spelling acquisition in two different teaching methods: a test of the independence hypothesis.' **Reading and Writing,** 7(1), 65–88.

Liberman, A. M. (1998). 'When theories of speech meet the real world.' **Journal of Psycholinguistic Research,** 27(2), 111–122.

Liberman, A. M. and Whalen, D. H. (2000). 'On the relation of speech to language.' **Trends in Cognitive Sciences,** 4(5), 187–196.

Liberman, I. Y. and Liberman, A. M. (1992). 'Whole language versus code emphasis: underlying assumptions and their implications for reading instruction.' In P. B. Gough & L. C. Ehri & R. Treiman (Eds.), **Reading Acquisition** (pp. 343–366). Hillsdale, NJ: Lawrence Erlbaum Associates.

Lieberman, P. (2000). **Human Language and our Reptilian Brain: the subcortical bases of speech, syntax, and thought**. Cambridge, MA: Harvard University Press.

Livingston, R., Adam, B. S. and Bracha, H. S. (1993). 'Season of birth and neurodevelopmental disorders: summer birth is associated with dyslexia.' **Journal of the American Academy of Child and Adolescent Psychiatry,** 32(3), 612–616.

Livingstone, M. S., Rosen, G. D., Drislane, F. W. and Galaburda, A. M. (1991). 'Physiological and anatomical evidence for a magnocellular defect in developmental dyslexia.' **Proceedings of the National Academy of Sciences of the United States of America,** 88, 7943–7947.

Locke, A., Ginsborg, J. and Peers, I. (2002). 'Development and disadvantage: implications for the early years and beyond.' **International Journal of Language & Communication Disorders,** 37(1), 3–15.

Locke, J. L. (1997). 'A theory of neurolinguistic development.' **Brain and Language,** 58(2), 265–326.

Lovegrove, W. (1994). 'Visual deficits in dyslexia: evidence and implications.' In A. Fawcett & R. Nicolson (Eds.), **Dyslexia in Children: multidisciplinary perspectives** (pp. 113–135). London: Wheatsheaf Harvester.

Lovett, M. W. (1984). 'A developmental perspective on reading dysfunction: accuracy and rate criteria in the subtyping of dyslexic children.' **Brain & Language,** 22, 67–91.

Lovett, M. W., Lacerenza, L. and Borden, S. L. (2000a). 'Putting struggling readers on the PHAST track: a program to integrate phonological and strategy-based remedial reading instruction and maximise outcomes.' **Journal of Learning Disabilities,** 33(5), 458–476.

Lovett, M. W., Steinbach, K. A. and Frijters, J. C. (2000b). 'Remediating the core deficits of developmental reading disability: a double deficit perspective.' **Journal of Learning Disabilities,** 33(4), 334–358.

Lukatela, K., Carello, C., Shankweiler, D. and Liberman, I. Y. (1995). 'Phonological awareness in illiterates: observations from Serbo-Croatian.' **Applied Psycholinguistics,** 16(4), 463–487.

Luke, A. (1988). **Literacy, Textbooks and Ideology: postwar literacy instruction and the mythology of Dick and Jane.** London: The Falmer Press.

Lyon, G. R. and Moats, L. C. (1997). 'Critical conceptual and methodological considerations in reading intervention research.' **Journal of Learning Disabilities,** 30(6), 578–588.

MacKay, T. (1999). 'Can endemic reading failure in socially disadvantaged children be successfully tackled?' **Educational and Child Psychology,** 16(1), 22–29.

MacKay, T. and Watson, K. (1999). 'Literacy, social disadvantage and early intervention: enhancing reading achievement in primary school.' **Educational and Child Psychology,** 16(1), 30–36.

Mackintosh, N. J. (1998). **IQ and Human Intelligence**. Oxford: Oxford University Press.

Maguin, E., Loeber, R. and LeMahieu, P. G. (1993). 'Does the relationship between poor reading and delinquency hold for males of different ages and ethnic groups?' **Journal of Emotional and Behavioral Disorders,** 1(2), 88–100.

Maguire, E. A., Gadian, D. G., Johnsrude, I. S., Good, C. D., Ashburner, J., Frackowiak, R. S. J. and Frith, C. D. (2000). 'Navigation-related structural change in the hippocampi of taxi drivers.' **Proceedings of the National Academy of Sciences of the United States of America,** 97(8), 4398–4403.

Malmgren, K., Abbott, R. D. and Hawkins, J. D. (1999). 'LD and delinquency: rethinking the 'Link'.' **Journal of Learning Disabilities,** 32(3), 194–200.

Manis, F. R., Seidenberg, M. S., Doi, L. M., McBride-Chang, C. and Peterson, A. (1996). 'On the bases of two subtypes of developmental dyslexia.' **Cognition,** 58, 157–195.

Mann, V. A. (1987). 'Phonological awareness and alphabetic literacy.' **Cahiers de Psychologie Cognitive/European Bulletin of Cognitive Psychology,** 7(5), 476–481.

Mann, V. A. and Brady, S. (1988). 'Reading disability: the role of language deficiencies.' **Journal of Consulting and Clinical Psychology,** 56(6), 811–816.

Marcel, A. J. (1978). 'Prerequisites for a more applicable psychology of reading.' In M. M. Gruneberg & P. E. Morris & R. N. Sykes (Eds.), **Practical aspects of memory.** (pp. 531–542). London: Academic Press.

Marcus, D. (1997). **An investigation of the relationship of naming speed, processing speed, and reading in young, reading-impaired children.** Unpublished Master's thesis, Tufts University.

Marshall, C. M., Snowling, M. J. and Bailey, P. J. (2001). 'Rapid auditory processing and phonological ability in normal readers and readers with dyslexia.' **Journal of Speech, Language, and Hearing Research,** 44(4), 925–940.

Martin, R. C. (1995). 'Heterogeneity of deficits in developmental dyslexia and implications for methodology.' **Psychonomic Bulletin & Review,** 2(4), 494–500.

Mather, N., Bos, C. and Babur, N. (2001). 'Perceptions and knowledge of preservice and inservice teachers about early literacy instruction.' **Journal of Learning Disabilities,** 34(5), 472–482.

Mathiak, K., Hertrich, I., Grodd, W. and Ackermann, H. (2002). 'Cerebellum and speech perception: a functional magnetic resonance imaging study.' **Journal of Cognitive Neuroscience,** 14(6), 902–912.

Mattis, S., French, J. and Rapin, I. (1975). 'Dyslexia in children and adults: three independent neurological syndromes.' **Developmental Medicine and Child Neurology,** 17, 150–163.

Maughan, B., Pickles, A., Hagell, A., Rutter, M. and Yule, W. (1996). 'Reading problems and antisocial behaviour: developmental trends in comorbidity.' **Journal of Child Psychology and Psychiatry,** 37(4), 405–418.

Maughan, B. and Yule, W. (1994). Reading and Other Learning Disabilities. In M. Rutter & E. Taylor & L. Hersov (Eds.), **Child and Adolescent Psychiatry: modern approaches.** (pp. 647–665). Oxford: Blackwell Scientific Publications.

McAnally, K. I. and Stein, J. F. (1996). 'Auditory temporal coding in dyslexia.' **Proceedings of the Royal Society of London Series (B) – Biological Sciences,** 263(1373), 961–965.

McBride-Chang, C. and Ho, C. S.-H. (2000). 'Developmental issues in Chinese children's character acquisition.' **Journal of Educational Psychology,** 92(1), 52–55.

McBride-Chang, C. and Kail, R. V. (2002). 'Cross-cultural similarities in the predictors of reading acquisition.' **Child Development,** 73(5), 1392–1407.

McBride-Chang, C. and Manis, F. R. (1996). 'Structural invariance in the associations of naming speed, phonological awareness, and verbal reasoning in good and poor readers: a test of the double deficit hypothesis.' **Reading and Writing,** 8(4), 323–339.

McBride-Chang, C., Wagner, R. K. and Chang, L. (1997). 'Growth modeling of phonological awareness.' **Journal of Educational Psychology,** 89(4), 621–630.

McCrory, E. (2001). **A neurocognitive investigation of phonological processing in developmental dyslexia.** Unpublished PhD thesis, University of London.

McCrory, E. (2003). 'The neurocognitive basis of developmental dyslexia.' In R. S. J. Frackowiak & K. J. Friston & C. D. Frith & R. Dolan & C. J. Price (Eds.), **Human Brain Function** (Second ed., pp. 301–328). San Diego, CA: Academic Press.

McCrory, E., Frith, U., Brunswick, N. and Price, C. (2000). 'Abnormal functional activation during a simple word repetition task: a PET study of adult dyslexics.' **Journal of Cognitive Neuroscience,** 12(5), 753–762.

McGuinness, D. (1998). **Why Children Can't Read and what we can do about it: a scientific revolution in reading.** London: Penguin.

McKusick, V. A. (1994). **Mendelian Inheritance in Man: a catalogue of human genes and genetic disorders** (Eleventh ed.). Baltimore, MD: Johns Hopkins University Press.

McManus, I. C. (1999). 'Handedness, cerebral lateralization, and the evolution of language.' In M. C. Corballis & S. E. G. Lea (Eds.), **The Descent of Mind: psychological perspectives on hominid evolution** (pp. 194–217). Oxford: Oxford University Press.

Meek, M. (1991). **On Being Literate.** London: The Bodley Head.

Mesulam, M.-M. (1998). 'From sensation to cognition.' **Brain,** 121(6), 1013–1052.

Metsala, J. L. (1999). 'The development of phonemic awareness in reading-disabled children.' **Applied Psycholinguistics,** 20(1), 149–158.

Metsala, J. L. and Brown, G. D. A. (1998). 'Normal and dyslexic reading development: the role of formal models.' In C. Hulme & R. M. Joshi (Eds.). Mahwah, NJ: Lawrence Erlbaum Associates.

Metsala, J. L., Stanovich, K. E. and Brown, G. D. A. (1998). 'Regularity effects and the phonological deficit model of reading disabilities: a meta-analytic review.' **Journal of Educational Psychology,** 90(2), 279–293.

Meyer, M. S., Wood, F. B., Hart, L. A. and Felton, R. H. (1998). 'Selective predictive value of rapid automatised naming in poor readers.' **Journal of Learning Disabilities,** 31(2), 106–117.

Michel, G. F. and Moore, C. L. (1995). **Developmental Psychobiology: an interdisciplinary science.** Cambridge, MA: MIT Press.

Migden, S. D. (1990). 'Dyslexia and psychodynamics: a case study of a dyslexic adult.' **Annals of Dyslexia,** 40, 107–116.

Miles, T. R. (1982). **The Bangor Dyslexia Test.** Cambridge: Learning Development Aids.

Miles, T. R. (1983). **Dyslexia: The Pattern of Difficulties.** London: Granada.

Miles, T. R. and Miles, E. (1999). **Dyslexia: a hundred years on.** (Second ed.). Buckingham: Open University Press.

Miles, T. R., Wheeler, T. J. and Haslum, M. N. (1993). Picking out dyslexics from a population of 10-year-olds. **Literacy 2000: proceedings of a conference held by the Hornsby International Centre to mark ... the twenty-five years' involvement of Dr Bevé Hornsby in dyslexia, 16–19 September 1993.** (pp. 22–28). London: The Hornsby International Centre.

Miles, T. R., Wheeler, T. J. and Haslum, M. N. (1994). 'Dyslexia and the middle classes.' **Links 2,** 1(2), 17–19.

Miles, T. R., Wheeler, T. J. and Haslum, M. N. (2003). 'The existence of dyslexia without severe literacy problems.' **Annals of Dyslexia,** 53, 340–354.

Moats, L. C. (1994). 'The missing foundation in teacher education: knowledge of the structure of spoken and written language. '**Annals of Dyslexia,** 44, 81–102.

Moats, L. C. and Lyon, G. R. (1996). 'Wanted: teachers with knowledge of language.' **Topics in Language Disorders,** 16(2), 73–86.

Mody, M. (2003). 'Phonological basis in reading disability: a review and analysis of the evidence.' **Reading and Writing,** 16(1), 21–39.

Moffatt, S. D., Hampson, E. and Lee, D. H. (1998). 'Morphology of the planum temporale and corpus callosum in left handers with evidence of left and right hemisphere speech representation.' **Brain,** 121, 2369–2379.

Morais, J., Alegria, J. and Content, A. (1987). 'The relationships between segmental analysis and alphabetic literacy: an interactive view.' **Cahiers de Psychologie Cognitive/European Bulletin of Cognitive Psychology,** 7(5), 415–438.

Morais, J., Cary, L., Alegria, J. and Bertelson, P. (1979). 'Does awareness of speech as a sequence of phones arise spontaneously?' **Cognition,** 7, 323–331.

Morais, J., Content, A., Bertelson, P., Cary, L. and Kolinsky, R. (1988). 'Is there a critical period for the acquisition of segmental analysis?' **Cognitive Neuropsychology,** 5(3), 347–352.

Morgan, A. E. and Hynd, G. W. (1998). 'Dyslexia, neurolinguistic ability, and anatomical variation of the planum temporale.' **Neuropsychology Review,** 8(2), 79–93.

Morgan, W. (1997). 'Dyslexia and crime.' **Dyslexia,** 3, 247–248.

Morgan, W. P. (1896). 'A case of congenital word-blindness.' **British Medical Journal**(7 November 1896), 1378.

Morris, J. M. (1993). Phonicsphobia, **Literacy 2000: proceedings of a conference held by the Hornsby International Centre to mark ... the twenty-five years' involvement of Dr Bevé Hornsby in dyslexia, 16–19 September 1993.** London: The Hornsby International Centre.

Morris, R. (1963). **Success and Failure in Learning to Read**. London: Oldbourne.

Morris, R. D., Stuebing, K. K., Fletcher, J. M., Shaywitz, S. E., Lyon, G. R., Shankweiler, D. P., Katz, L., Francis, D. J. and Shaywitz, B. A. (1998). 'Subtypes of reading disability: variability around a phonological core.' **Journal of Educational Psychology,** 90(3), 347–373.

Mortimore, J. and Blackstone, T. (1982). **Disadvantage and Education**. London: Heinemann.

Mortimore, P., Sammons, P., Stoll, L., Lewis, D. and Ecob, R. (1988). **School Matters: the junior years.** Wells: Open Books.

Morton, J. and Frith, U. (1995). 'Causal modelling: a structural approach to developmental psychopathology.' In D. Cicchetti & D. J. Cohen (Eds.), **Developmental Psychopathology** (Vol. 1 Theory and Methods, pp. 357–390). New York: Wiley-Interscience.

Murphy, L. and Pollatsek, A. (1994). 'Developmental dyslexia: heterogeneity without discrete subgroups.' **Annals of Dyslexia,** 44, 120–146.

Närhi, V. and Ahonen, T. (1995). 'Reading disability with or without Attention Deficit Hyperactivity Disorder: do attentional problems make a difference?' **Developmental Neuropsychology,** 11(3), 337–349.

Nathan, L., Wells, B. and Donlan, C. (1998). 'Children's comprehension of unfamiliar regional accents: a preliminary investigation.' **Journal of Child Language,** 25, 343–365.

Nation, K. and Snowling, M. J. (1998). 'Semantic processing and the development of word-recognition skills: evidence from children with reading comprehension difficulties.' **Journal of Memory and Language,** 39(1), 85–101.

National Reading Panel. (2000). **Teaching Children to Read: an evidence-based assessment of the scientific research literature on reading and its implications for reading instruction. [Accessible at http://www.nichd.nih.gov/publications/nrp/report.htm]**. Washington, DC: National Institute of Child Health and Human Development.

Neisser, U., Boodoo, G., T J Bouchard, J., Boykin, A. W., Brody, N., Ceci, S. J., Halpern, D. F., Loehlin, J. C., Perloff, R., Sternberg, R. J. and Urbina, S. (1996). 'Intelligence: knowns and unknowns.' **American Psychologist,** 51(2), 77–101.

NICHD. (2000). **Emergent and Early Literacy Workshop: current status and research directions. [Accessed at www.nichd.nih.gov/crmc/c on 6 December 2002]**.

Nicholson, T. (1997). 'Closing the gap on reading failure: social background, phonemic awareness, and learning to read.' In B. A. Blachman (Ed.), **Foundations of Reading Acquisition and Dyslexia: implications for early intervention.** (pp. 381–407). Mahwah, NJ: Lawrence Erlbaum Associates.

Nicholson, T., Bailey, J. and McArthur, J. (1991). 'Context clues in reading: the gap between research and popular opinion.' **Journal of Reading, Writing, and Learning Disabilities International,** 7, 33–41.

Nicolson, R. I. (1996). 'Developmental dyslexia: past, present and future.' **Dyslexia,** 2(3), 190–207.

Nicolson, R. I. (2002). 'The dyslexia ecosystem.' **Dyslexia,** 8, 55–66.

Nicolson, R. I. and Fawcett, A. J. (1990). 'Automaticity: a new framework for dyslexia research?' **Cognition,** 35, 159–182.

Nicolson, R. I. and Fawcett, A. J. (1994). 'Comparison of deficits in cognitive and motor skills among children with dyslexia.' **Annals of Dyslexia,** 44, 147–164.

Nicolson, R. I. and Fawcett, A. J. (1999). 'Developmental dyslexia: the role of the cerebellum.' **Dyslexia,** 5, 155–177.

Nicolson, R. I., Fawcett, A. J. and Dean, P. (1995). 'Time estimation deficits in developmental dyslexia: evidence of cerebellar involvement.' **Proceedings of the Royal Society of London, Series B: Biological Sciences,** 259(1354), 43–47.

Nicolson, R. I., Fawcett, A. J. and Dean, P. (2001a). 'Developmental dyslexia: the cerebellar deficit hypothesis.' **Trends in Neurosciences,** 24(9), 508–511.

Nicolson, R. I., Fawcett, A. J. and Dean, P. (2001b). 'Dyslexia, development and the cerebellum.' **Trends in Neurosciences,** 24(9), 515–516.

Nicolson, R. I., Fawcett, A. J. and Miles, T. R. (1993). **Adult Dyslexia Screening Feasibility Study (Report OL176)**. Sheffield: Department of Employment.

Nicolson, R. I. and Reynolds, D. (2003a). 'Science, sense and synergy: response to commentators.' **Dyslexia,** 9(3), 167–176.

Nicolson, R. I. and Reynolds, D. (2003b). 'Sound findings and appropriate statistics: response to Snowling and Hulme.' **Dyslexia,** 9(2), 134–135.

Nittrouer, S. (1996). 'The relation between speech perception and phonemic awareness: evidence from low-SES children and children with chronic OM.' **Journal of Speech and Hearing Research,** 39, 1059–1070.

Nittrouer, S. (2001). 'Challenging the notion of innate phonetic boundaries.' **Journal of the Acoustical Society of America,** 110(3), 1598–1605.

Nittrouer, S. (2002). 'From ear to cortex: a perspective on what clinicians need to understand about speech perception and language processing.' **Language, Speech and Hearing Services in Schools,** 33(4), 237–252.

Nopola-Hemmi, J., Myllyluoma, B., Haltia, T., Taipale, M., Ollikainen, V., Ahonen, T., Voutilainen, A., Kere, J. and Widen, E. (2001). 'A dominant gene for developmental dyslexia on chromosome 3.' **Journal of Medical Genetics,** 38(10), 658–664.

Norris, J. A. and Hoffman, P. R. (2002). 'Phonemic awareness: a complex developmental process.' **Topics in Language Disorders,** 22(2), 1–34.

Oakland, T., Black, J. L., Stanford, G., Nussbaum, N. L. and Balise, R. R. (1998). 'An evaluation of the dyslexia training program: a multisensory method for promoting reading in students with reading disabilities.' **Journal of Learning Disabilities,** 31(2), 140–147.

Olson, D. R. (1994). **The World on Paper: the conceptual and cognitive implications of writing and reading.** Cambridge: Cambridge University Press.

Orton, S. T. (1925). 'Word-blindness' in school children. **Archives of Neurology and Psychiatry,** 14, 581–615.

Orton, S. T. (1937). **Reading, writing and speech problems in children: a presentation of certain types of disorders in the development of the language faculty**. New York, NY: Norton.

Ott, P. (1997). **How to Manage and Detect Dyslexia: a reference and resource manual**. Oxford: Heinemann.

Paradise, J. L., Dollaghan, C. A., Campbell, T. F., Feldman, H. M., Bernard, B. S., Colborn, D. K., Rockette, H. E., Janosky, J. E., Pitcairn, D. L., Sabo, D. L., Kurs-Lasky, M. and Smith, C. G. (2000). 'Language, speech sound production, and cognition in three-year-old children in relation to otitis media in their first three years of life.' **Pediatrics,** 105(5), 1119–1130.

Patterson, K. and Lambon Ralph, M. A. (1999). 'Selective disorders of reading?' **Current Opinion in Neurobiology,** 9, 235–239.

Paulesu, E., Démonet, J.-F., Fazio, F., McCrory, E., Chanoine, V., Brunswick, N., Cappa, S. F., Cossu, G., Habib, M., Frith, C. D. and Frith, U. (2001). 'Dyslexia: cultural diversity and biological unity.' **Science,** 291(5511), 2165–2167.

Paulesu, E., Frith, U., Snowling, M., Gallagher, A., Morton, J., Frackowiak, R. S. J. and Frith, C. D. (1996). 'Is developmental dyslexia a disconnection syndrome?' Evidence from PET scanning. **Brain,** 119, 143–157.

Pawson, R. and Tilley, N. (1997). **Realistic Evaluation**. London: Sage.

Peiffer, A. M., Rosen, G. D. and Fitch, R. H. (2002). 'Sex differences in rapid auditory processing deficits in ectopic BXSB/MpJ mice.' **NeuroReport,** 13(17), 2277–2280.

Pennington, B. F. (1991). 'Genetics of learning disabilities.' **Seminars in Neurology,** 11(1), 28–34.

Pennington, B. F. (1999). 'Toward an integrated understanding of dyslexia: genetic, neurological, and cognitive mechanisms.' **Development and Psychopathology,** 11, 629–654.

Pennington, B. F., Cardoso-Martins, C., Green, P. A. and Lefly, D. L. (2001). 'Comparing the phonological and double-deficit hypotheses for developmental dyslexia.' **Reading and Writing,** 14(7–8), 707–755.

Pennington, B. F., Gilger, J. W., Olson, R. K. and DeFries, J. C. (1992). 'The external validity of age- versus IQ-discrepancy definitions of reading disability: lessons from a twin study.' **Journal of Learning Disabilities,** 25(9), 562–573.

Perfetti, C. A., Georgi, M. C. and Beck, I. (1993). 'Implications of the Pittsburgh Study for issues of risk.' In H. Grimm & H. Skowronek (Eds.), **Language acquisition problems and reading disorders: aspects of diagnosis and intervention.** (pp. 193–218). Berlin: Walter de Gruyter.

Perfetti, C. A. and Marron, M. A. (1995). **Learning to Read: Literacy Acquisition by Children and Adults.** Philadelphia: National Center on Adult Literacy [Accessed at http://literacy.org/search/detailed.html on 6 August 2003].

Petersson, K. M., Reis, A., Askelof, S., Castro-Caldas, A. and Ingvar, M. (2000). 'Language processing modulated by literacy: a network analysis of verbal repetition in literate and illiterate subjects.' **Journal of Cognitive Neuroscience,** 12(3), 364–382.

Pickle, J. M. (1998). 'Historical trends in biological and medical investigations of reading disabilities: 1850–1915.' **Journal of Learning Disabilities,** 31(6), 625–635.

Pinker, S. (1994). **The Language Instinct: how the mind creates language**. New York: HarperCollins.

Plaut, D. C., McClelland, J. L., Seidenberg, M. S. and Patterson, K. (1996). 'Understanding normal and impaired word reading: computational principles in quasi-regular domains.' **Psychological Review,** 103(1), 56–115.

Plomin, R., DeFries, J. C., McClearn, G. E. and McGuffin, P. (2001). **Behavioural Genetics** (Fourth ed.). New York: Worth Publishers.

Pogorzelski, S. and Wheldall, K. (2002). 'Do differences in phonological processing performance predict gains made by older low-progress readers following intensive literacy intervention?' **Educational Psychology,** 22(4), 413–427.

Posner, M. I., DiGirolamo, G. J. and Fernandez-Duque, D. (1997). 'Brain mechanisms of cognitive skills. '**Consciousness and Cognition,** 6, 267–290.

Postman, N. (1970). 'The politics of reading.' **Harvard Educational Review,** 40(2), 244–252.

Price, C. J. (2000). 'The anatomy of language: contributions from functional neuroimaging.' **Journal of Anatomy,** 197, 335–359.

Pulvermüller, F. (1999). 'Words in the brain's language.' **Behavioral and Brain Sciences,** 22(2), 253–336.

Pulvermüller, F. (2003). **The Neuroscience of Language: on brain circuits of words and serial order**. Cambridge: Cambridge University Press.

Pumfrey, P. (2001). 'Specific Developmental Dyslexia (SDD): 'Basics to back' in 2000 and beyond?' In M. Hunter-Carsch (Ed.), **Dyslexia: a psychosocial perspective** (pp. 137–159). London: Whurr.

Pumfrey, P. D. and Reason, R. (1991). **Specific Learning Difficulties (Dyslexia): Challenges and Responses.** Windsor: NFER-Nelson.

Purcell-Gates, V. (1995). **Other People's Words: the cycle of low literacy.** Cambridge, MA: Harvard University Press.

Putnins, A. L. (1999). 'Literacy, numeracy and non-verbal reasoning skills of South Australian young offenders.' **Australian Journal of Education,** 43(2), 157–171.

Quartz, S. R. and Sejnowski, T. J. (1997). 'The neural basis of cognitive development: a constructivist manifesto.' **Behavioral and Brain Sciences,** 20(4), 537–596.

Rack, J. (1994). 'Dyslexia: the phonological deficit hypothesis.' In R. I. Nicolson & A. J. Fawcett (Eds.), **Dyslexia in Children: multidisciplinary perspectives**. Hemel Hempstead: Harvester Wheatsheaf.'

Rack, J. (1997). 'Issues in the assessment of developmental dyslexia in adults: theoretical and applied perspectives.' **Journal of Research in Reading,** 20(1), 66–76.

Rack, J. (2003). 'The who, what, why and how of intervention programmes: comments of the DDAT evaluation.' **Dyslexia,** 9(3), 137–139.

Rack, J. and Hatcher, J. (2002). **SPELLIT Summary Report, August 2002**. Staines: Dyslexia Institute [Accessed at www.dyslexia-inst.org.uk/spellitsum.htm on 12 January 2003].

Rack, J. P., Snowling, M. J. and Olson, R. K. (1993). 'The nonword reading deficit in developmental dyslexia: a review.' **Reading Research Quarterly,** 27(1), 28–53.

Rae, C., Harasty, J. A., Dzendrowskyj, T. E., Talcott, J. B., Simpson, J. M., Blamire, A. M., Dixon, R. M., Lee, M. A., Thompson, C. H., Styles, P., Richardson, A. J. and Stein, J. F. (2002). 'Cerebellar morphology in developmental dyslexia.' **Neuropsychologia,** 40(8), 1285–1292.

Rae, C., Lee, M. A., Dixon, R. M., Blamire, A. M., Thompson, C. H., Styles, P., Talcott, J., Richardson, A. J. and Stein, J. F. (1998). 'Metabolic abnormalities in developmental dyslexia detected by 1H magnetic resonance spectroscopy.' **Lancet,** 351(9119), 1849–1852.

Ramus, F., Pidgeon, E. and Frith, U. (2003a). 'The relationship between motor control and phonology in dyslexic children.' **Journal of Child Psychology and Psychiatry,** 44(5), 712–722.

Ramus, F., Rosen, S., Dakin, S. C., Day, B. L., Castellote, J. M., White, S. and Frith, U. (2003b). 'Theories of developmental dyslexia: insights from a multiple case study of dyslexic adults.' **Brain,** 126, 841–865.

Rapin, I. (2002). 'Diagnostic dilemmas in developmental disabilities: fuzzy margins at the edges of normality. An essay prompted by Thomas Sowell's new book: 'The Einstein Syndrome'.' **Journal of Autism and Developmental Disorders,** 32(1), 49–57.

Rashid, F. L., Morris, M. K. and Morris, R. (2001). 'Naming and verbal memory skills in adults with attention deficit hyperactivity disorder and reading disability.' **Journal of Clinical Psychology,** 57(6), 829–838.

Ravenette, A. T. (1968). **Dimensions of Reading Difficulties**. Oxford: Pergamon Press.

Rayner, K. (1998). 'Eye movements in reading and information processing: twenty years of research.' **Psychological Bulletin,** 124(3), 372–422.

Rayner, K., Foorman, B. R., Perfetti, C. A., Pesetsky, D. and Seidenberg, M. S. (2001). 'How psychological science informs the teaching of reading.' **Psychological Science in the Public Interest,** 2(2), 31–74.

Raz, I. S. and Bryant, P. E. (1990). 'Social background, phonological awareness, and children's reading.' **British Journal of Developmental Psychology,** 8, 209–226.

Read, C., Yun-Fei, Z., Hong-Yin, N. and Bao-Qing, D. (1987). 'The ability to manipulate speech sounds depends on knowing alphabetic writing.' In P. Bertelson (Ed.), **The Onset of Literacy: cognitive processes in reading acquisition.** (pp. 31–44). Cambridge, MA: The MIT Press.

Redecker, C., Lutzenburg, M., Gressens, P., Evrard, P., Witte, O. W. and Hagemann, G. (1998). 'Excitability changes and glucose metabolism in experimentally induced focal cortical dysplasias.' **Cerebral Cortex,** 8(7), 623–634.

Rée, J. (1999). **I See a Voice: a philosophical history of language, deafness and the senses**. London: HarperCollins.

Rego, L. L. B. and Bryant, P. E. (1993). 'The connection between phonological, syntactic and semantic skills and children's reading and spelling.' **European Journal of Psychology of Education,** 8(3), 235–246.

Reichle, E. D., Rayner, K. and Pollatsek, A. (in press). 'The E-Z model of eye movement control in reading: comparisons to other models.' **Behavioral and Brain Sciences**.

Renvall, H. and Hari, R. (2002). 'Auditory cortical responses to speech-like stimuli in adults.' **Journal of Cognitive Neuroscience,** 14(5), 757–768.

Reynolds, D., Nicolson, R. I. and Hambly, H. (2003). 'Evaluation of an exercise-based treatment for children with reading difficulties.' **Dyslexia,** 9(1), 48–71.

Riccio, C. A. and Hynd, G. W. (2000). 'Measurable biological substrates to verbal-performance differences in Wechsler scores.' **School Psychology Quarterly,** 15(4), 386–399.

Riccio, C. A., Kessler, R. H. and Ross, C. M. (1998). 'Phonological processing and rapid naming in adult students with dyslexia.' **Archives of Clinical Neuropsychology,** 13(1), 124–125.

Rice, M. (2000). 'The extent and nature of reading problems in the prison population.' **Prison Service Journal**(129), 2–10.

Richards, I. L., Moores, E., Witton, C., Reddy, P. A., Rippon, G., Talcott, J. B. and Rochelle, K. S. H. (2003). 'Science, sophistry and 'commercial sensitivity': comments on 'evaluation of an exercise-based treatment for children with reading difficulties', by Reynolds, Nicolson and Hambly.' **Dyslexia,** 9(3), 146–150.

Richards, I. L., Witton, C., Moores, E., Reddy, P. A., Rippon, G. and Talcott, J. B. (2002). Comments on 'The Dyslexia Ecosystem': a reply to Nicolson. **Dyslexia,** 8, 226–233.

Richardson, A. J. and Ross, M. A. (2000). 'Fatty acid metabolism in neurodevelopmental disorder: a new perspective on associations between attention-deficit/hyperactivity disorder, dyslexia, dyspraxia and the autistic spectrum.' **Prostaglandins Leukotrienes and Essential Fatty Acids,** 63(1–2), 1–9.

Richman, N., Stevenson, J. and Graham, P. J. (1982). **Pre-school to School: a behavioural study**. London: Academic Press.

Rie, E. D. (1987). 'Soft signs in learning disabilities.' In D. E. Tupper (Ed.), **Soft Neurological Signs** (pp. 201–224). Orlando, FL: Grune & Stratton, Inc.

Robichon, F., Bouchard, P., Démonet, J.-F. and Habib, M. (2000). 'Developmental dyslexia: re-evaluation of the corpus callosum in male adults.' **European Neurology,** 43(4), 233–237.

Robichon, F., Levrier, O., Farnarier, P. and Habib, M. (2000). 'Developmental dyslexia: atypical cortical asymmetries and functional significance.' **European Journal of Neurology,** 7, 35–46.

Rodgers, B. (1983). 'The identification and prevalence of specific reading retardation.' **British Journal of Educational Psychology.,** 53, 369–373.

Rosen, S. and Manganari, E. (2001). 'Is there a relationship between speech and nonspeech auditory processing in children with dyslexia?' **Journal of Speech, Language, and Hearing Research,** 44, 720–736.

Rozin, P. and Gleitman, L. R. (1977). The structure and acquisition of reading II: the reading process and the acquisition of the alphabetic principle. In A. S. Reber & D. L. Scarborough (Eds.), **Toward a Psychology of Reading: the proceedings of the CUNY conferences** (pp. 55–141). Hillsdale, NJ: Lawrence Erlbaum Associates.

Rumsey, J. M., Casanova, M., Mannheim, G. B., Patronas, N., DeVaughn, N., Hamburger, S. D. and Aquino, T. (1996). 'Corpus callosum morphology, as measured with MRI, in dyslexic men.' **Biological Psychiatry,** 39, 769–775.

Rumsey, J. M., Donohue, B. C., Brady, D. R., Nace, K., Giedd, J. N. and Andreason, P. (1997a). 'A magnetic resonance imaging study of planum temporale asymmetry in men with developmental dyslexia.' **Archives of Neurology,** 54(12), 1481–1489.

Rumsey, J. M., Nace, K., Donohue, B., Wise, D., Maisog, J. M. and Andreason, P. (1997b). 'A positron emission tomographic study of impaired word recognition and phonological processing in dyslexic men.' **Archives of Neurology,** 54(5), 562–578.

Rutter, M. (1978). 'Prevalence and types of dyslexia.' In A. L. Benton & D. Pearl (Eds.), **Dyslexia: an appraisal of current knowledge.** (pp. 5–28). New York: Oxford University Press.

Rutter, M. (2002). 'Nature, nurture, and development: from evangelism through science towards policy and practice.' **Child Development,** 73(1), 1–21.

Rutter, M., Tizard, J. and Whitmore, K. (Eds.). (1970). **Education, Health and Behaviour.** London: Longman.

Rutter, M., Yule, B., Quinton, D., Rowlands, O., Yule, W. and Berger, M. (1975). 'Attainment and adjustment in two geographical areas: III – some factors accounting for area differences.' **British Journal of Psychiatry,** 126, 520–533.

Rutter, M. and Yule, W. (1975). 'The concept of specific reading retardation.' **Journal of Child Psychology and Psychiatry,** 16, 181–197.

Saarelma, K., Renvall, H., Jousmaki, V., Kovala, T. and Hari, R. (2002). 'Facilitation of the spinal H-reflex by auditory stimulation in dyslexic adults.' **Neuroscience Letters,** 327(3), 213–215.

Sabatini, J. P. (2002). 'Efficiency in word reading of adults: ability group comparisons.' **Scientific Studies of Reading,** 6(3), 267–298.

Sameroff, A. J. (1995). General systems theories and developmental psychopathology. In D. Cicchetti & D. J. Cohen (Eds.), **Developmental Psychopathology** (Vol. I Theory and Methods, pp. 659–695). New York: John Wiley & Sons, Inc.

Sameroff, A. J. and Chandler, M. J. (1975). Reproductive risk and the continuum of caretaking casualty. In F. D. Horowitz (Ed.), **Review of Child Development Research** (Vol. IV, pp. 187–244). Chicago, IL: University of Chicago Press.

Samuelsson, S., Finnström, O., Leijon, I. and Mård, S. (2000). 'Phonological and surface profiles of reading difficulties among very low birth weight children: converging evidence for the developmental lag hypothesis.' **Scientific Studies of Reading,** 4(3), 197–217.

Samuelsson, S., Herkner, B. and Lundberg, I. (2003). 'Reading and writing difficulties among prison inmates: a matter of experiential factors rather than dyslexic problems.' **Scientific Studies of Reading,** 7(1), 53–73.

Saugstad, L. F. (1999). 'A lack of cerebral lateralization in schizophrenia is within the normal variation in brain maturation but indicates late, slow maturation.' **Schizophrenia Research,** 39(3), 183–196.

Scarborough, H. S. (1984). 'Continuity between childhood dyslexia and adult reading.' **British Journal of Psychology,** 75, 329–348.

Schatschneider, C., Carlson, C. D., Francis, D. J., Foorman, B. R. and Fletcher, J. M. (2002). 'Relationship of rapid automatized naming and phonological awareness in early reading development: implications for the double-deficit hypothesis.' **Journal of Learning Disabilities,** 35(5), 245–256.

Schatschneider, C., Francis, D. J., Foorman, B. R., Fletcher, J. M. and Mehta, P. (1999). 'The dimensionality of phonological awareness: an application of item response theory.' **Journal of Educational Psychology,** 91(3), 439–449.

Schlaug, G. (2001). 'The brain of musicians: a model for functional and structural adaptation.' **Annals of the New York Academy of Sciences (Biological Foundations of Music),** 930, 281–299.

Seidenberg, M. S. (1992). 'Dyslexia in a computational model of word recognition in reading.' In P. B. Gough & L. C. Ehri & R. Treiman (Eds.), **Reading Acquisition**. Hillsdale, NJ: Lawrence Erlbaum Associates.

Seidenberg, M. S., Bruck, M., Fornarolo, G. and Backman, J. (1986). 'Who is dyslexic? Reply to Wolf.' **Applied Psycholinguistics,** 7, 77–84.

Seymour, P. H. K. (1986). **Cognitive Analysis of Dyslexia**. London: Routledge & Kegan Paul.

Shankweiler, D. (1999). 'Words to meanings.' **Scientific Studies of Reading,** 3, 113–127.

Shapleske, J., Rossell, S. L., Woodruff, P. W. R. and David, A. S. (1999). 'The planum temporale: a systematic, quantitative review of its structural, functional and clinical significance.' **Brain Research Reviews,** 29(1), 26–49.

Share, D. L. (1995). 'Phonological recoding and self-teaching: sine qua non of reading acquisition.' **Cognition,** 55, 151–218.

Share, D. L., Jorm, A. F., Maclean, R. and Matthews, R. (1984). 'Sources of individual differences in reading acquisition.' **Journal of Educational Psychology,** 76(6), 1309–1324.

Share, D. L., McGee, R., McKenzie, D., Williams, S. and Silva, P. A. (1987). 'Further evidence relating to the distinction between specific reading retardation and general reading backwardness.' **British Journal of Developmental Psychology,** 5, 35–44.

Shaywitz, S. E., Escobar, M. D., Shaywitz, B. A., Fletcher, J. M. and Makuch, R. (1992). 'Evidence that dyslexia may represent the lower tail of a normal distribution of reading ability.' **The New England Journal of Medicine,** 326(2), 145–150.

Shaywitz, S. E., Shaywitz, B. A., Pugh, K. R., Fulbright, R. K., Constable, R. T., Mencl, W. E., Shankweiler, D. P., Liberman, A. L., Skudlarski, P., Fletcher, J. M., Katz, L., Marchione, K. E., Lacadie, C., Gatenby, C. and Gore, J. C. (1998). ''Functional disruption in the organisation of the brain for reading in dyslexia.' **Proceedings of the National Academy of Sciences of the United States of America,** 95(5), 2636–2641.

Sheehan-Holt, J. K. and Smith, M. C. (2000). 'Does basic skills education affect adults' literacy proficiencies and reading practices?' **Reading Research Quarterly,** 35(2), 226–243.

Siegel, L. S. (1992). 'An evaluation of the discrepancy definition of dyslexia.' **Journal of Learning Disabilities,** 25(10), 618–629.

Silveri, M. C. and Misciagna, S. (2000). 'Language, memory, and the cerebellum.' **Journal of Neurolinguistics,** 13(2–3), 129–143.

Simmerman, S. and Swanson, H. L. (2001). 'Treatment outcomes for students with learning disabilities: how important are internal and external validity?' **Journal of Learning Disabilities,** 34(3), 221–236.

Singleton, C. and Simmons, F. (2001). 'An evaluation of Wordshark in the classroom.' **British Journal of Educational Technology,** 32(3), 317–330.

Singleton, C. and Stuart, M. (2003). 'Measurement mischief: a critique of Reynolds, Nicolson and Hambly (2003).' **Dyslexia,** 9(3), 151–160.

Singleton, C., Thomas, K. and Horne, J. (2000). 'Computer-based cognitive assessment and the development of reading.' **Journal of Research in Reading,** 23(2), 158–180.

Skottun, B. C. (2000a). 'The magnocellular deficit theory of dyslexia: the evidence from contrast sensitivity.' **Vision Research,** 40(1), 111–127.

Skottun, B. C. (2000b). 'On the conflicting support for the magnocellular-deficit theory of dyslexia: response to Stein, Talcott and Walsh (2000).' **Trends in Cognitive Sciences,** 4(6), 211–212.

Skottun, B. C. and Parke, L. A. (1999). 'The possible relationship between visual deficits and dyslexia: examination of a critical assumption.' **Journal of Learning Disabilities,** 32(1), 2–5.

Slaghuis, W. L., Lovegrove, W. J. and Davidson, J. A. (1993). 'Visual and language processing deficits are concurrent in dyslexia.' **Cortex,** 29(4), 601–615.

Smart, D., Prior, M., Sanson, A. and Oberklaid, F. (2001). 'Children with reading difficulties: a six-year follow-up from early primary school to secondary school.' **Australian Journal of Psychology,** 53(1), 45–53.

Smith, F. (1978). **Reading**. Cambridge: Cambridge University Press.

Smith, F. (1997). **Reading Without Nonsense**. New York, NY: Teachers College, Columbia University.

Smith, S. D., Kelley, P. M., Askew, J. W., Hoover, D. M., Deffenbacher, K. E., Gayán, J., Brower, A. M. and Olson, R. K. (2001). 'Reading disability and chromosome 6p21.3: evaluation of MOG as a candidate gene.' **Journal of Learning Disabilities,** 34(6), 512–519.

Smith, S. D., Pennington, B. F., Kimberling, W. J. and Ing, P. S. (1990). 'Familial dyslexia: use of genetic linkage data to define subtypes.' **Journal of the American Academy of Child and Adolescent Psychiatry,** 29(2), 204–213.

Snowling, M., Bishop, D. V. M. and Stothard, S. E. (2000b). 'Is preschool language impairment a risk factor for dyslexia in adolescence?' **Journal of Child Psychology and Psychiatry,** 41(5), 587–600.

Snowling, M. and Nation, K. (1997). 'Language, phonology and learning to read.' In C. Hulme & M. Snowling (Eds.), **Dyslexia: biology, cognition and intervention**. London: Whurr.

Snowling, M. J. (1991). 'Developmental reading disorders.' **Journal of Child Psychology and Psychiatry,** 32(1), 49–77.

Snowling, M. J. (1996). 'Contemporary approaches to the teaching of reading.' **Journal of Child Psychology and Psychiatry,** 37(2), 139–148.

Snowling, M. J. (1998). 'Reading development and its difficulties.' **Educational and Child Psychology,** 15(2), 44–58.

Snowling, M. J. (2000). **Dyslexia: a cognitive developmental perspective** (2nd ed.). Oxford: Basil Blackwell.

Snowling, M. J., Adams, J. W., Bowyer-Crane, C. and Tobin, V. (2000a). 'Levels of literacy among juvenile offenders: the incidence of specific reading difficulties.' **Criminal Behaviour and Mental Health,** 10, 229–241.

Snowling, M. J., Bryant, P. E. and Hulme, C. (1996a). 'Theoretical and methodological pitfalls in making comparisons between developmental and acquired dyslexia: Some comments on A. Castles & M. Coltheart (1993).' **Reading and Writing,** 8(5), 443–451.

Snowling, M. J., Goulandris, N. and Defty, N. (1996b). 'A longitudinal study of reading development in dyslexic children.' **Journal of Educational Psychology,** 88(4), 653–669.

Snowling, M. J. and Hulme, C. (2003). 'A critique of claims from Reynolds, Nicolson & Hambly (2003) that DDAT is an effective treatment for children with reading difficulties – 'Lies, damned lies and (inappropriate) statistics?' **Dyslexia,** 9(2), 127–133.

Social Exclusion Unit. (2002). **Reducing Re-offending by Ex-prisoners**. London: Author.

Sodoro, J., Allinder, R. M. and Rankin-Erickson, J. L. (2002). 'Assessment of phonological awareness: review of methods and tools.' **Educational Psychology Review,** 14(3), 223–260.

Solan, H. A. (1999). 'Visual deficits and dyslexia (letter).' **Journal of Learning Disabilities,** 32(4), 282–283.

Sonuga-Barke, E. J. S. (2002). 'Psychological heterogeneity in AD/HD: a dual pathway model of behaviour and cognition.' **Behavioural Brain Research,** 130, 29–36.

Spear-Swerling, L. (in press). A road map for understanding reading disability and other reading problems. In R. Ruddell & N. Unrau (Eds.), **Theoretical Models and Processes of Reading, Vol. 5**. Newark, DE: International Reading Association.

Spear-Swerling, L. and Sternberg, R. J. (1994). 'The road not taken: an integrative theoretical model of reading disability.' **Journal of Learning Disabilities,** 27(2), 91–103,122.

Spear-Swerling, L. and Sternberg, R. J. (1996). **Roads to Reading Disability: When Poor Readers Become 'Learning Disabled'**. Boulder, CO: Westview Press.

Spear-Swerling, L. and Sternberg, R. J. (1998). 'Curing our 'epidemic' of learning disabilities. **Phi Delta Kappan,** 79(5), 397–401.

Spinelli, D., Angelelli, P., De Luca, M., Di Pace, E., Judica, A. and Zoccolotti, P. (1997). 'Developmental surface dyslexia is not associated with deficits in the transient visual system.' **NeuroReport,** 8(8), 1807–1812.

Sprenger-Charolles, L., Cole, P., Lacert, P. and Serniclaes, W. (2000). 'On subtypes of developmental dyslexia: evidence from processing time and accuracy scores.' **Canadian Journal of Experimental Psychology – Revue Canadienne de Psychologie Expérimentale,** 54(2), 87–104.

Sprenger-Charolles, L., Lacert, P., Bechennec, D., Cole, P. and Serniclaes, W. (2001). 'Stability across sessions and across languages of dyslexia subtypes.' **Approche Neuropsychologique des Apprentissages Chez l'Enfant,** 13(2–3), 115–128.

Sroufe, L. A. (1997). 'Psychopathology as an outcome of development.' **Development and Psychopathology,** 9, 251–268.

Stanovich, K. E. (1986). 'Matthew effects in reading: Some consequences of individual differences in the acquisition of literacy.' **Reading Research Quarterly,** 21(4), 360–407.

Stanovich, K. E. (1988). 'Explaining the differences between the dyslexic and the garden-variety poor reader: the phonological core variable-difference model.' **Journal of Learning Disabilities,** 21(10), 590–604, 612.

Stanovich, K. E. (1994). 'Annotation: does dyslexia exist?' **Journal of Child Psychology and Psychiatry,** 35(4), 579–595.

Stanovich, K. E. (1996). 'Toward a more inclusive definition of dyslexia.' **Dyslexia,** 2(3), 154–166.

Stanovich, K. E. (1999). 'The sociometrics of learning disabilities.' **Journal of Learning Disabilities,** 32(4), 350–361.

Stanovich, K. E. (2000). **Progress in Understanding Reading: scientific foundations and new frontiers**. New York: The Guilford Press.

Stanovich, K. E., Siegel, L. S. and Gottardo, A. (1997). 'Converging evidence for phonological and surface subtypes of reading disability.' **Journal of Educational Psychology,** 89(1), 114–127.

Steele, J. (1998). 'Cerebral asymmetry, cognitive laterality, and human evolution.' **Cahiers de Psychologie Cognitive/Current Psychology of Cognition,** 17(6), 1202–1214.

Stein, J. (2001). 'The magnocellular theory of developmental dyslexia.' **Dyslexia,** 7, 12–36.

Stein, J. (2003). 'Evaluation of an exercise-based treatment for children with reading difficulties.' **Dyslexia,** 9(2), 124–126.

Stein, J. and Talcott, J. (1999). 'Impaired neuronal timing in developmental dyslexia: the magnocellular hypothesis.' **Dyslexia,** 5, 59–77.

Stein, J., Talcott, J. and Walsh, V. (2000). 'Controversy about the visual magnocellular deficit in developmental dyslexics.' **Trends in Cognitive Sciences,** 4(6), 209–211.

Stein, J. F. (1994). 'Developmental dyslexia, neural timing and hemispheric lateralisation.' **International Journal of Psychophysiology,** 18, 241–249.

Stein, J. F. (2002). 'Commentary: the dyslexia ecosystem.' **Dyslexia,** 8, 178–179.

Stein, J. F. and McAnally, K. (1995). 'Auditory temporal processing in developmental dyslexics.' **The Irish Journal of Psychology,** 16(3), 220–228.

Stein, J. F. and Walsh, V. (1997). 'To see but not to read: the magnocellular theory of dyslexia.' **Trends in Neuroscience,** 20.

Sternberg, R. J. (Ed.). (2000). **Handbook of Intelligence**. Cambridge: Cambridge University Press.

Stewart, I. and Silva, P. A. (1996). Otitis media with effusion. In P. A. Silva & W. R. Stanton (Eds.), **From Child to Adult: the Dunedin Multidisciplinary Health and Development Study** (pp. 113–129). Auckland: Oxford University Press.

Stordy, B. J. (2000). 'Dark adaptation, motor skills, docoahexaenoic acid, and dyslexia.' **American Journal of Clinical Nutrition,** 71(1), 323S-326S.

Strucker, J. (1995). **Patterns of Reading in Adult Basic Literacy.** Unpublished EdD thesis, Harvard University.

Stuart, G. W., McAnally, K. I. and Castles, A. (2001). 'Can contrast sensitivity functions in dyslexia be explained by inattention rather than a magnocellular deficit?' **Vision Research,** 41(24), 3205–3211.

Stuart, M. (1998). 'Let the Emperor retain his underclothes: a response to Scholes (1998) 'The case against phonemic awareness'.' **Journal of Research in Reading,** 21(3), 189–194.

Stubbs, M. (1980). **Language and Literacy: the sociolinguistics of reading and writing**. London: Routledge & Kegan Paul.

Studdert-Kennedy, M. (2002). 'Deficits in phoneme awareness do not arise from failures in rapid auditory processing.' **Reading and Writing,** 15, 5–14.

Stuebing, K. K., Fletcher, J. M., LeDoux, J. M., Lyon, G. R., Shaywitz, S. E. and Shaywitz, B. A. (2002). 'Validity of IQ-discrepancy definitions of reading disabilities: a meta-analysis.' **American Educational Research Journal,** 39(2), 469–518.

Swan, D. and Goswami, U. (1997). 'Picture naming deficits in developmental dyslexia: the phonological representations hypothesis.' **Brain and Language,** 56, 334–353.

Swanson, H. L. (2003). 'Age-related differences in learning disabled and skilled readers' working memory.' **Journal of Experimental Child Psychology,** 85(1), 1–31.

Swanson, H. L. and Sachse-Lee, C. (2001). 'A subgroup analysis of working memory in children with reading disabilities: domain-general or domain-specific deficiency?' **Journal of Learning Disabilities,** 34(3), 249–263.

Tannock, R., Martinussen, R. and Frijters, J. (2000). 'Naming speed performance and stimulant effects indicate effortful semantic processing deficits in attention-deficit/hyperactivity disorder.' **Journal of Abnormal Child Psychology,** 28(3), 237–252.

Taylor, H. G., Satz, P. and Friel, J. (1979). 'Developmental dyslexia in relation to other childhood reading disorders: significance and clinical utility.' **Reading Research Quarterly,** 15, 84–101.

Taylor, K. E., Higgins, C. J., Calvin, C. M., Hall, J. A., Easton, T., McDaid, A. M. and Richardson, A. J. (2000). 'Dyslexia in adults is associated with clinical signs of fatty acid deficiency.' **Prostaglandins Leukotrienes and Essential Fatty Acids,** 63(1–2), 75–78.

Taylor, K. E., Richardson, A. J. and Stein, J. F. (2001). 'Could platelet activating factor play a role in developmental dyslexia?' **Prostaglandins Leukotrienes and Essential Fatty Acids,** 64(3), 173–180.

Thelen, E. and Smith, L. B. (1994). **A Dynamic Systems Approach to the Development of Cognition and Action**. Cambridge, MA: MIT Press.

Thomas, M. (2000). 'Albert Einstein and LD: an evaluation of the evidence.' **Journal of Learning Disabilities,** 33(2), 149–157.

Thomas, M. and Karmiloff-Smith, A. (2002). 'Are developmental disorders like cases of brain damage? Implications from connectionist modelling.' **Behavioral and Brain Sciences,** 25(6), 727–787.

Thompson, G. B. and Johnston, R. S. (2000). 'Are nonword and other phonological deficits indicative of a failed reading process?' **Reading and Writing,** 12(1–2), 63–97.

Thomson, M. (2002). 'Dyslexia and diagnosis.' **The Psychologist,** 15(11), 551.

Thomson, M. E. (1999). 'Subtypes of dyslexia: a teaching artefact?' **Dyslexia,** 5, 127–137.

Tønnessen, F. E. (1997). 'How can we best define 'dyslexia'?' **Dyslexia,** 3, 78–92.

Tønnessen, F. E., Lokken, A., Hoien, T. and Lundberg, I. (1993). 'Dyslexia, left-handedness, and immune disorders.' **Archives of Neurology,** 50, 411–416.

Torgerson, C., Brooks, G., Porthouse, J., Burton, M., Robinson, A., Watt, I. and Wright, K. (2002). **A Systematic Review and Meta-Analysis of Randomised Controlled Trials Evaluating Interventions in Adult Literacy and Numeracy**. London: National Research and Development Centre for Adult Literacy and Numeracy.

Torgesen, J. K. (1989). 'Why IQ is relevant to the definition of learning disabilities.' **Journal of Learning Disabilities,** 22(8), 484–486.

Torgesen, J. K., Alexander, A. W., Wagner, R. K., Rashotte, C. A., Voeller, K. K. S. and Conway, T. (2001). 'Intensive remedial instruction for children with severe reading disabilities: immediate and long-term outcomes from two instructional approaches.' **Journal of Learning Disabilities,** 34(1), 33–58.

Torgesen, J. K., Wagner, R. K., Rashotte, C. A., Rose, E., Lindamood, P., Conway, T. and Garvan, C. (1999). 'Preventing reading failure in young children with phonological processing disabilities: group and individual responses to instruction.' **Journal of Educational Psychology,** 91(4), 579–593.

Tough, J. (1977). **The Development of Meaning: a study of children's use of language.** London: Allen & Unwin.

Tough, J. (1982). 'Language, poverty, and disadvantage in school.' In L. Feagans & D. C. Farran (Eds.), **The Language of Children Reared in Poverty: Implications for evaluation and intervention.** (pp. 3–18). New York, NY: Academic Press.

Treiman, R. (2000). 'The foundations of literacy.' **Current Directions in Psychological Science,** 9, 89–92.

Tressoldi, P. E., Stella, G. and Faggella, M. (2001). 'The development of reading speed in Italians with dyslexia: a longitudinal study.' **Journal of Learning Disabilities,** 34(5), 414–417.

Troia, G. A. (1999). 'Phonological awareness intervention research: a critical review of the experimental methodology.' **Reading Research Quarterly,** 34(1), 28–52.

Tunmer, W. E. and Chapman, J. W. (1996). 'A developmental model of dyslexia: can the construct be saved?' **Dyslexia,** 2(3), 179–189.

Turic, D., Robinson, L., Duke, M., Morris, D. W., Webb, V., Hamshere, M., Milham, C., Hopkin, E., Pound, K., Fernando, S., Grierson, A., Easton, M., Williams, N., Van Den Bree, M., Chowdhury, R., Gruen, J., Stevenson, J., Krawczak, M., Owen, M. J., O'Donovan, M. C. and Williams, J. (2003). 'Linkage disequilibrium mapping provides further evidence of a gene for reading disability on chromosome 6p.21.3–22.' **Molecular Psychiatry,** 8(2), 176–185.

Turner, M. (1990). **Sponsored Reading Failure: an object lesson.** Warlingham: IPSET Education Unit.

Turner, M., Sercombe, L. and Cuffe-Fuller, A. (2000). 'Dyslexia and crime.' **Dyslexia Review,** 12(1), 4–5.

Tyler, S. and Elliott, C. D. (1988). 'Cognitive profiles of groups of poor readers and dyslexic children on the British Ability Scales.' **British Journal of Psychology,** 79(4), 493–508.

van der Wissel, A. and Zegers, F. E. (1985). 'Reading retardation revisited.' **British Journal of Developmental Psychology,** 3, 3–9.

Van Orden, G. C., Pennington, B. F. and Stone, G. O. (2001). 'What do double dissociations prove?' **Cognitive Science,** 25(1), 111–172.

Vellutino, F. R. (1979). **Dyslexia: theory and research.** Cambridge, MA: MIT Press.

Vellutino, F. R. (2001). 'Further analysis of the relationship between reading achievement and intelligence: response to Naglieri.' **Journal of Learning Disabilities,** 34(4), 306–310.

Vellutino, F. R., Scanlon, D. M. and Lyon, G. R. (2000). 'Differentiating between difficult-to-remediate and readily remediated poor readers: more evidence against the IQ-achievement discrepancy definition of reading disability.' **Journal of Learning Disabilities,** 33(3), 223–238.

Vellutino, F. R., Scanlon, D. M., Sipay, E. R., Small, S. G., Pratt, A., Chen, R. and Denckla, M. B. (1996). 'Cognitive profiles of difficult-to-remediate and readily-remediated poor readers: early intervention as a vehicle for distinguishing between cognitive and experiential deficits as basic causes of specific reading disability.' **Journal of Educational Psychology,** 88(4), 601–638.

Vellutino, F. R., Scanlon, D. M. and Spearing, D. (1995). 'Semantic and phonological coding in poor and normal readers.' **Journal of Experimental Child Psychology,** 59(1), 76–123.

Ventura, P., Kolinsky, R., Brito-Mendes, C. and Morais, J. (2001). 'Mental representations of the syllable internal structure are influenced by orthography.' **Language and Cognitive Processes,** 16(4), 393–418.

Vernon, M. D. (1957). **Backwardness in Reading: a study of its nature and origin**. Cambridge: Cambridge University Press.

Vernon-Feagans, L., Hurley, M. and Yont, K. (2002). 'The effect of otitis media and daycare quality on mother/child bookreading and language use at 48 months of age.' **Journal of Applied Developmental Psychology,** 23(2), 113–133.

Vidyasagar, T. R. (2001). 'From attentional gating in macaque primary visual cortex to dyslexia in humans.' **Vision from Neurons to Cognition,** 134, 297–312.

Viise, N. M. (1996). 'A study of the spelling development of adult literacy learners compared with that of the classroom children.' **Journal of Literacy Research,** 28(4), 561–587.

Vincent, A., Deacon, R., Dalton, P., Salmond, C., Blamire, A. M., Pendlebury, S., Johansen-Berg, H., Rajagopalan, B., Styles, P. and Stein, J. (2002). 'Maternal antibody-mediated dyslexia? Evidence for a pathogenic serum factor in a mother of two dyslexic children shown by transfer to mice using behavioural studies and magnetic resonance spectroscopy.' **Journal of Neuroimmunology,** 130(1–2), 243–247.

von Karolyi, C., Winner, E., Gray, W. and Sherman, G. F. (2003). 'Dyslexia linked to talent: global visual-spatial ability.' **Brain and Language,** 85(3), 427–431.

von Plessen, K., Lundervold, A., Duta, N., Heiervang, E., Klauschen, F., Smievoll, A. I., Ersland, L. and Hugdahl, K. (2002). 'Less developed corpus callosum in dyslexic subjects: a structural MRI study.' **Neuropsychologia,** 40(7), 1035–1044.

Waber, D. P., Wolff, P. H., Forbes, P. W. and Weiler, M. D. (2000). 'Rapid automatized naming in children referred for evaluation of heterogeneous learning problems: how specific are naming speed deficits to reading disability?' **Child Neuropsychology,** 6(4), 251–261.

Wada, J. A., Clarke, R. and Hamm, A. (1975). 'Cerebral hemispheric asymmetry in humans: cortical speech zones in 100 adult and 100 infant brains.' **Archives of Neurology,** 32, 239–246.

Wadsworth, S. J., Corley, R. P., Hewitt, J. K. and DeFries, J. C. (2001). 'Stability of genetic and environmental influences on reading performance at 7, 12, and 16 years of age in the Colorado Adoption Project.' **Behavior Genetics,** 31(4), 353–359.

Wadsworth, S. J., DeFries, J. C., Fulker, D. W., Olson, R. K. and Pennington, B. F. (1995). 'Reading performance and verbal short-term memory: a twin study of reciprocal causation.' **Intelligence,** 20, 145–167.

Wadsworth, S. J., Olson, R. K., Pennington, B. F. and DeFries, J. C. (2000). 'Differential genetic etiology of reading disability as a function of IQ.' **Journal of Learning Disabilities,** 33(2), 192–199.

Walker, D., Greenwood, C., Hart, B. and Carta, J. (1994). 'Prediction of school outcomes based on early language production and socieconomic factors.' **Child Development,** 65(2), 606–621.

Wallace, I. F., Gravel, J. S., Schwartz, R. G. and Ruben, R. j. (1996). 'Otitis media, communication style of primary caregivers, and language skills of 2 year olds: a preliminary report.' **Journal of Developmental and Behavioral Pediatrics,** 17(1), 27–35.

Wallach, L., Wallach, M. A., Dozier, M. G. and Kaplan, N. E. (1977). 'Poor children learning to read do not have trouble with auditory discrimination but do have trouble with phoneme recognition.' **Journal of Educational Psychology,** 69(1), 36–39.

Walton, P. D. and Walton, L. M. (2002). 'Beginning reading by teaching in rime analogy: effects on phonological skills, letter-sound knowledge, working memory, and word-reading strategies.' **Scientific Studies of Reading,** 6(1), 79–115.

Waring, S., Prior, M., Sanson, A. and Smart, D. (1996). 'Predictors of 'recovery' from reading disability.' **Australian Journal of Psychology,** 48(3), 160–166.

Weatherall, D. J. (1991). **The New Genetics and Clinical Practice** (Third ed.). Oxford: Oxford University Press.

West, T. G. (1997). **In the Mind's Eye: visual thinkers, gifted people with dyslexia and other learning difficulties, computer images and the ironies of creativity.** (Second ed.). Amherst, NY: Prometheus.

Wijsman, E. M., Peterson, D., Leutenegger, A. L., Thomson, J. B., Goddard, K. A. B., Hsu, L., Berninger, V. W. and Raskind, W. H. (2000). 'Segregation analysis of phenotypic components of learning disabilities. 1. Nonword memory and digit span.' **American Journal of Human Genetics,** 67(3), 631–646.

Wilsher, C. R. (2002). 'A miracle cure? 'Tonight with Trevor McDonald', ITV, 21/01/02.' **Dyslexia,** 8, 116–117.

Wimmer, H. and Goswami, U. (1994). 'The influence of orthographic consistency on reading development: word recognition in English and German children.' **Cognition,** 51(1), 91–103.

Wimmer, H., Mayringer, H. and Landerl, K. (2000). 'The double-deficit hypothesis and difficulties in learning to read a regular orthography.' **Journal of Educational Psychology,** 92(4), 668–680.

Winner, E., von Karolyi, C., Malinsky, D., French, L., Seliger, C., Ross, E. and Weber, C. (2001). 'Dyslexia and visual-spatial talents: compensation **vs** deficit model.' **Brain and Language,** 76(2), 81–110.

Wise, R. J. S., Scott, S. K., Blank, S. C., Mummery, C. J., Murphy, K. and Warburton, E. A. (2001). 'Separate neural subsystems within 'Wernicke's area'.' **Brain,** 124, 83–95.

Wolf, M. and Bowers, P. G. (1999). 'The double-deficit hypothesis for the developmental dyslexias.' **Journal of Educational Psychology,** 91(3), 415–438.

Wolf, M. and Bowers, P. G. (2000). 'Naming-speed processes and developmental reading disabilities: an introduction to the Special Issue on the double-deficit hypothesis.' **Journal of Learning Disabilities,** 33(4), 322–324.

Wolf, M., Bowers, P. G. and Biddle, K. (2000a). 'Naming-speed processes, timing, and reading: a conceptual review.' **Journal of Learning Disabilities,** 33(4), 387–407.

Wolf, M., Miller, L. and Donnelly, K. (2000b). 'Retrieval, automaticity, vocabulary elaboration, orthography (RAVE-O): a comprehensive, fluency-based reading intervention program.' **Journal of Learning Disabilities,** 33(4), 375–386.

Wolff, P. H. (2002). 'Timing precision and rhythm in developmental dyslexia.' **Reading and Writing,** 15, 179–206.

Wood, F. B. and Grigorenko, E. L. (2001). 'Emerging issues in the genetics of dyslexia: a methodological preview.' **Journal of Learning Disabilities,** 34(6), 503–511.

World Federation of Neurology. (1968). **Report of Research Group on Dyslexia and World Illiteracy.** Dallas, TX: Author.

World Health Organisation. (1992). **The ICD-10 Classification of Mental and Behavioural Disorders**. Geneva: WHO.

Worthy, J. and Viise, N. M. (1996). 'Morphological, phonological, and orthographic differences between the spelling of normally achieving children and basic literacy adults.' **Reading and Writing,** 8(April), 139–159.

Wright, S. F., Fields, H. and Newman, S. P. (1996). 'Dyslexia: stability of definition over a five-year period.' **Journal of Research in Reading,** 19(1), 46–60.

Yap, R. and van der Leij, A. (1994). 'Automaticity deficits in word reading.' In A. Fawcett & R. Nicolson (Eds.), **Dyslexia in Children: multidisciplinary perspectives** (pp. 77–106). London: Harvester Wheatsheaf.

Yule, W. and Rutter, M. (1976). Epidemiology and social implications of specific reading retardation. In R. M. Knights & D. J. Bakker (Eds.), **The Neuropsychology of Learning Disorders** (pp. 25–39). Baltimore, MD: University Park Press.

Yule, W., Rutter, M., Berger, M. and Thompson, J. (1974). 'Over- and under-achievement in reading: distribution in the general population.' **British Journal of Educational Psychology,** 44, 1–12.

Zabell, C. and Everatt, J. (2002). 'Surface and phonological subtypes of adult developmental dyslexia.' **Dyslexia,** 8, 160–177.

Zeffiro, T. and Eden, G. (2001). 'The cerebellum and dyslexia: perpetrator or innocent bystander?' **Trends in Neurosciences,** 24(9), 512–513.

Zera, D. A. (2001). 'A reconceptualization of learning disabilities via a self-organizing systems paradigm.' **Journal of Learning Disabilities,** 34(1), 79–94.

Zera, D. A. and Lucian, D. G. (2001). 'Self-organization and learning disabilities: a theoretical perspective for the interpretation and understanding of dysfunction.' **Learning Disability Quarterly,** 24(2), 107–118.

Ziman, J. (2000). **Real Science: what it is, and what it means**. Cambridge: Cambridge University Press.

Appendix 1
Some definitions of dyslexia

Caveat 1 'A complete explanation of any kind of individual difference in reading behaviour requires three things: a description of the reading performance that can be compared with performances of other readers; at least one hypothesis as to its proximal cause, which must be at the cognitive level; at least one hypothesis as to the distal cause or causes which brought about the cognitive condition ... At least one such distal cause must be at the biological level' (*page* 17). Jackson, N. E. and Coltheart, M. (2001). **Routes to Reading Success and Failure: towards an integrated cognitive psychology of atypical reading**. Hove: Psychology Press.

Caveat 2 A good definition of dyslexia provides 'operational criteria which pick out all those —and only those—who would be recognised as dyslexic by the dyslexia community' (*page* 57). Miles, T. R. (2001). Editorial. **Dyslexia**, 7, 57–61.

Caveat 3 'Rod Nicolson's choice of the word 'ecosystem' to describe the dyslexia community is imaginative and apposite because the essence of ecosystems is vicious competition for scarce resources ... competitive viciousness characterises the dyslexia ecosystem' (*page* 178). Stein, J. F. (2002). Commentary: the dyslexia ecosystem. **Dyslexia**, 8, 178–179.

Caveat 4 'Of the many definitions that exist, there are very few that make sense in the context of the workplace experience of adult dyslexics' (*page* 2). Fitzgibbon, G. and O'Connor, B. (2002). **Adult Dyslexia: a guide for the workplace**. Chichester: John Wiley & Sons.

Caveat 5 'Dyslexia may perplexia'. Marion Welchman.

Advocacy Group Definitions

British Dyslexia Association

Dyslexia is best described as a combination of abilities and difficulties that affect the learning process in one or more of reading, spelling, writing. Accompanying weaknesses may be identified in areas of speed of processing, short-term memory, sequencing and organisation, auditory and/or visual perception, spoken language and motor skills. It is particularly related to mastering and using written language, which may include alphabetic, numeric and musical notation.

Some dyslexics have outstanding or creative skills. Others have strong oral talents. Some have no outstanding talents. They all have strengths.

Dyslexia can occur despite normal intellectual ability and teaching. It is independent of socio-economic or language background.

Accessed at www.bda-dyslexia.org.uk on 4 October 2002.

This definition is similar to the Bangor Dyslexia Unit's definition of dyslexia (which is accessible at www.dyslexia.bangor.ac.uk/what_is_dyslexia.html).

Or, alternatively,

> The word 'dyslexia' has been coined from the Greek and literally means 'difficulty with words'. The old way of describing it was 'word blindness'—an inability to read letters and numbers in the right order—but that's far from the whole picture.
>
> Dyslexic people can experience difficulties with organisation and short-term memory. In addition to problems with reading, spelling and writing, dyslexic people may:
>
> - confuse directions, muddling left and right or up and down;
> - find it hard to remember a list, dates or times;
> - have difficulties following a sequence—days of the week or a map of the London Underground, a-b-c, 1–2–3.

From 'Dyslexia', a BDA leaflet published in 1999.

Or, alternatively,

> Dyslexia is thought by many researchers to be an organic difference in the learning centre of the brain. Dyslexic people experience difficulty in processing language, both written and oral. Many may also confuse directions, sequences, verbal labels, letters and words or numbers that may look or sound similar. It tends to run in families.
>
> There is more and more evidence gathered from brain imaging techniques that dyslexic people process information differently from other people.

From 'Reading Together', a volunteer resource pack published by the BDA in 1999.

> *Note* 'There is no single brain center for reading, writing, or comprehension. There are only networks of highly specific mechanisms dedicated to the individual operations that comprise a complex task' (*page* 133). Alfonso Caramazza, in **Conversations in the Cognitive Neurosciences**. Cambridge, MA: The MIT Press.

British Dyslexics

> Our own simple definition of dyslexia is 'intelligent, bright or even gifted individuals, that for no obvious reason, struggle to learn through the medium of written or spoken language'.

Accessed at www.dyslexia.uk.com on 4 October 2002.

Dyslexia Institute

> Dyslexia causes difficulties in learning to read, write and spell. Short-term memory, mathematics, concentration, personal organisation and sequencing may also be affected.

Dyslexia usually arises from a weakness in the processing of language-based information. Biological in origin, it tends to run in families, but environmental factors also contribute.

Dyslexia can occur at any level of intellectual ability. It is not the result of poor motivation, emotional disturbance, sensory impairment or lack of opportunities, but it may occur alongside any of these.

The effects of dyslexia can be largely overcome by skilled specialist teaching and the use of compensatory strategies.

Accessed at www.dyslexia-inst.org.uk on 4 October 2002.

International Dyslexia Association (formerly the Orton Dyslexia Society)

Dyslexia is one of several distinct learning disabilities. It is a specific language-based disorder of constitutional origin characterised by difficulties in single word decoding, usually reflecting insufficient phonological processing abilities. These difficulties in single word decoding are often unexpected in relation to age and other cognitive and academic abilities; they are not the result of generalised developmental disability or sensory impairment. Dyslexia is manifest by variable difficulty with different forms of language, often including, in addition to problems in reading, a conspicuous problem with acquiring proficiency in writing and spelling.

Accessed at http://interdys.org on 17 October 2002.

Consortium Definition

US National Joint Committee on Learning Disabilities (1988), in Hammill, D. D. (1990). On defining learning disabilities: an emerging consensus. **Journal of Learning Disabilities**, 23(2), 74–84.

Learning disabilities is a general term that refers to a heterogeneous group of disorders manifested by significant difficulties in the acquisition and use of listening, speaking, reading, writing, reasoning, or mathematical abilities. These disorders are intrinsic to the individual, presumed to be due to central nervous system dysfunction, and may occur across the life span. Problems in self-regulatory behavior, social perception and social interaction may exist with learning disabilities but do not by themselves constitute a learning disability. Although learning disabilities may occur concomitantly with other handicapping conditions (for example, sensory impairment, mental retardation, serious emotional disturbance) or with extrinsic influences (such as cultural differences, insufficient or inappropriate instruction), they are not the result of those conditions or influences (*page* 77).

Note 1 ' ... of the current viable definitions, the one by the NJCLD is probably the best descriptive statement about the nature of learning disabilities' (*page* 82).

Note 2 ' ... many elements included in definitions of LD, if not invalid, are, at least, questionable' (*page* 250). Kavale, K. A. and Forness, S. R. (2000). 'What definitions of learning disability say and don't say: a critical analysis'. **Journal of Learning Disabilities**, 33(3), 239–256.

Note 3 'We believe that children come to school with individual differences in specific cognitive abilities that render some children more susceptible than others to school failure. Nevertheless, whether or not children actually fail may depend a great deal on their experiences in school. With the right kinds of educational experiences, a given child's vulnerability to school failure might never be realised, or at least might be greatly ameliorated' (*page* 400). Spear-Swerling, L. and Sternberg, R. J. (1998). Curing our 'epidemic' of learning disabilities. **Phi Delta Kappan**, 79(5), 397–401.

Practitioner Definitions

Academy of Orton-Gillingham Practitioners and Educators

The word dyslexia is derived from the Greek *dys*, difficulty with and *lex* (from *legein*, to speak), having to do with words. We encounter words in their many forms when we speak, read, spell and write, as well as in mathematics and in organising, understanding and expressing thought. A definition, based on information from neuroscientific and linguistic research, is *difficulty in the use and processing of linguistic/symbolic codes— alphabetic letters representing speech sounds, or numeric symbols representing numbers or quantities.* Such difficulty is reflected in the language continuum that includes spoken language, written language, and language comprehension.

Children and adults with dyslexia typically fail to master the basic elements of the language system of their culture despite traditional classroom teaching. Since language is the necessary tool upon which subsequent academic learning is based, people with dyslexia often encounter difficulty in all educational endeavors.

Dyslexia has its genesis in human biology. While not the result of neurological damage, it is the product of neurological development. Dyslexia commonly runs in families and varies from mild to severe. Most importantly, the use of the Orton-Gillingham approach by a skilled and experienced teacher can significantly moderate the language learning and processing problems that arise from dyslexia. Indeed, the approach, used early enough and by qualified practitioners, has every likelihood of eliminating the emergence of notable reading and writing problems.

Accessed at www.ortonacademy.org on 17 October 2002.

Note 'In order to understand how difficult it can be to make any difference with an intervention, it is useful to understand that even well-designed interventions based on over 35 hours teaching over a year using a well-tried method, the Orton-Gillingham approach, can achieve an effect size of as little as 0.04 improvement in reading in comparison with a control group who received normal teaching.' Fawcett, A. (2002). *Reading Remediation: an evaluation of traditional phonologically-based interventions. A review for the Department for Education and Skills, British Dyslexia Association and the Dyslexia Institute.* [Accessed at **www.dfes.gov.uk/sen/documents/** Dyslexia_3rd_review.htm on 2 December 2002].

British Psychological Society. (1999). **Dyslexia, Literacy and Psychological Assessment** (Report of a Working Party of the Division of Educational and Child Psychology). Leicester: Author.

Dyslexia is evident when accurate and fluent word reading and/or spelling develops very incompletely or with great difficulty. (*Recommended 'working definition' of dyslexia that separates description from causal explanations. It focuses on learning at the 'word' level and implies that the problem is severe and persistent despite appropriate learning opportunities.*)

Note 1 This report could be seriously misleading for practising educational psychologists' (*Abstract*). Thomson, M. (2003). 'Monitoring dyslexics' intelligence and attainments: a follow-up study'. **Dyslexia**, 9(1), 3–17.

Note 2 'This definition is so general that it could easily be applied to any child who has poor literacy skills, regardless of their origin. Such contributions simply reinforce false stereotypes and contribute to misunderstandings' (*page* 9). Fitzgibbon, G. and O'Connor, B. (2002). **Adult Dyslexia: a guide for the workplace**. Chichester: John Wiley & Sons.

Note 3 '... the report's definition of dyslexia, as 'word-reading developing incompletely or with great difficulty' has given rise, in my view, to the misunderstanding that 'diagnosis' is not important. On the contrary, it is crucially important for deciding on the most appropriate intervention.' Thomson, M. (2002). 'Dyslexia and diagnosis'. **The Psychologist**, 15(11), 551.

Note 4 'The recent tautologous definition offered by the Working Party of the British Psychological Society ... focuses entirely on literacy difficulties. There are clear advantages in this approach ... However, there are also profound weaknesses ... First, there is a tendency to view difficulties through a school-based literacy rather than a "New Literacy Studies" lens ... A second weakness is that if primary and secondary causal factors are not distinguished, inappropriate teaching approaches may be produced ... A third weakness is that in side-stepping the question of distinguishing between causal factors and their effects, it becomes difficult to answer the common question of whether all those with persistent literacy difficulties are dyslexic ... Finally, the literacy focus encourages a view of dyslexia as solely a literacy problem ... ' (*page* 111). Herrington, M. and Hunter-Carsch, M. (2001). A social interactive model of specific learning difficulties, e.g. dyslexia. In M. Hunter-Carsch (Ed.), **Dyslexia: a psychosocial perspective**. London: Whurr.

Note 5 'We used the term "working" to show that developments in research and practice were ongoing while we needed a starting point for the report. It was something to work with and not necessarily the final word. And it was particularly important to recognise that the descriptive *working* definition was not an *operational* definition'. Reason, R. (2001). 'Letter to the Editor'. **Dyslexia**, 7, 174.

Note 6 ' ... a good operational definition of "dyslexia" will stick to symptoms' (*page* 84). Tønnessen, F. E. (1997). 'How can we best define 'dyslexia'?' **Dyslexia**, 3, 78–92.

Gersons-Wolfensberger, D. C. M. and Ruijssenaars, W. A. J. J. M. (1997). Definition and treatment of dyslexia: a report by the Committee of Dyslexia of the Health Council of the Netherlands. **Journal of Learning Disabilities**, 30(2), 209–213.

Dyslexia is present when the automatisation of word identification (reading) and/or word spelling does not develop or does so very incompletely or with great difficulty (page 209).

Note 1 The JLD paper is an adapted version of the executive summary of the report, which had appeared (in Dutch) as Publication No. 1995/15 of the Health Council of the Netherlands.

Note 2 The committee stipulated that a working definition 'should be descriptive (with no explanatory elements), specific enough to identify dyslexia within the whole of severe reading and spelling problems, general enough to allow for various scientific explanatory models and developments those models might undergo, operationalisable for the purposes of research into people and groups, directive for statements concerning the need for intervention and finally, applicable to the various groups involved' (*page* 209).

Note 3 The authors, who were secretary and chairman of the committee, add that 'In all cases a partial (and sometimes principal) role is played by a person-bound factor ' (*page* 209).

Hornsby, B. (1995). **Overcoming Dyslexia: a straightforward guide for families and teachers**. (Second ed.). London: Optima.

Perhaps the simplest modern definition of dyslexia is that it is difficulty in learning how to read and write—particularly in learning to spell correctly and to express your thoughts on paper—which affects those who have had normal schooling and do not show backwardness in other subjects. This definition is helpful in so far as it describes what every dyslexic has in common, but it does not tell the whole story (*page* 3).

Note ' ... the presence of literacy problems should no longer be regarded as a necessary condition for a diagnosis of dyslexia' (*Abstract*). Miles, T. R., Wheeler, T. J. and Haslum, M. N. (2002). Dyslexia without literacy problems? (*Unpublished manuscript*).

Klein, C. (1993). **Diagnosing Dyslexia: a guide to the assessment of adults with specific learning difficulties**. London: Adult Literacy & Basic Skills Unit.

In this book both ['specific learning difficulties' and 'dyslexia'] are used interchangeably to refer to written language processing difficulties affecting visual, auditory and/or motor processing in reading, writing and spelling (*page* 5).

Note 1 'If the term *dyslexia* were to be taken as synonymous with *specific reading difficulties*, then the overlap between the groups would be more considerable than the cognitive analysis of their difficulties suggests. The use of the two terms interchangeably is therefore misleading' (*pages* 597–598). Snowling, M., Bishop, D. V. M. and Stothard, S. E. (2000). 'Is preschool language impairment a risk factor for dyslexia in adolescence?' **Journal of Child Psychology and Psychiatry**, 41(5), 587–600.

Note 2 '*Dyslexia* is a generic term typically used to refer to children who are severely impaired in reading. It is also known as *specific reading disability*, the two terms being used interchangeably' (*page* 7). Vellutino, F. R. (1979). **Dyslexia: theory and research**. Cambridge, MA: MIT Press.

Critchley, M. and Critchley, E. A. (1978). **Dyslexia Defined**. London: Heinemann Medical Books.

Developmental dyslexia [is] a learning disability which initially shows itself by difficulty in learning to read and later by erratic spelling and by lack of facility in manipulating written as opposed to spoken words. The condition is cognitive in essence and usually genetically determined. It is not due to intellectual inadequacy or to lack of socio-cultural opportunity, or to emotional factors, or to any known structural brain defect. It probably represents a specific maturational defect which tends to lessen as the child grows older and is capable of considerable improvement, especially when appropriate remedial help is afforded at the earliest opportunity (*page* 149).

Research Definitions

Fletcher, J. M., Foorman, B. R., Boudousquie, A., Barnes, M. A., Schatschneider, C. and Francis, D. J. (2002). Assessment of reading and learning disabilities: a research-based intervention-oriented approach. **Journal of School Psychology**, 40(1), 27–63.

> Dyslexia is one of several distinct learning disabilities. It is a specific language-based disorder characterised by difficulties in the development of accurate and fluent single word decoding skills, usually associated with insufficient phonological processing and rapid naming abilities. These difficulties in single word decoding are often unexpected in relation to age and other cognitive and academic abilities; they are not the result of generalised developmental disability or sensory impairment. Dyslexia is manifest by variable difficulty with different forms of language, often including, in addition to problems in reading, a conspicuous problem with acquiring proficiency in writing and spelling. Reading comprehension problems are common, reflecting decoding and fluency problems (*page* 43).

Fisher, S. E., Francks, C., Marlow, A. J., MacPhie, I. L., Newbury, D. F., Cardon, L. R., Ishikawa-Brush, Y., Richardson, A. J., Talcott, J. B., Gayan, J., Olson, R. K., Pennington, B. F., Smith, S. D., DeFries, J. C., Stein, J. F. and Monaco, A. P. (2002). Independent genome-wide scans identify a chromosome 18 quantitative-trait locus influencing dyslexia. **Nature Genetics**, 30(1), 86–91.

> Developmental dyslexia is defined as a specific and significant impairment in reading ability that cannot be explained by deficits in intelligence, learning opportunity, motivation or sensory acuity. It is one of the most frequently diagnosed disorders in childhood, representing a major educational and social problem. It is well established that dyslexia is a significantly heritable trait with a neurobiological basis. The etiological mechanisms remain elusive, however, despite being the focus of intensive multidisciplinary research (*page* 86).

Berninger, V. W. (2001). Understanding the 'lexia' in dyslexia: a multidisciplinary team approach to learning disabilities. **Annals of Dyslexia**, 51, 23–48.

> Developmental dyslexia is defined as uneven development (dissociation) between word reading and higher-level processes in the functional reading system. Dyslexics may struggle with word reading because of deficits in phonological processes, orthographic-phonological connections and/or fluency (rate, automaticity, or executive coordination) (*Abstract*).

Grigorenko, E. L. (2001). Developmental dyslexia: an update on genes, brains, and environments. **Journal of Child Psychology and Psychiatry**, 42(1), 91–125.

> ... a complex biologically-rooted behavioral condition resulting from impairment of reading-related processes (phonological skills, automatised lexical retrieval and verbal short-term memory, in any combination) and manifested in difficulties related to the

mastery of reading up to the level of population norms under the condition of adequate education and a normal developmental environment (*page* 94).

Stein, J. (2001). The magnocellular theory of developmental dyslexia. *Dyslexia,* 7, 12–36.

Low literacy is termed 'developmental dyslexia' when reading is significantly behind that expected from the intelligence quotient (IQ) in the presence of other symptoms—incoordination, left-right confusions, poor sequencing—that characterise it as a neurological syndrome (*page* 12).

Gilger, J. W. (2001). 'Current issues in the neurology and genetics of learning-related traits and disorders'. **Journal of Learning Disabilities**, 34(6), 490–491.

People with reading disability 'do not have clear and unitary neurological, physical, or psychiatric problems that would explain their inability to acquire literacy skills' (*pages* 490–491).

Snowling, M. J. (2000). **Dyslexia: a cognitive developmental perspective** (2nd ed.). Oxford: Basil Blackwell.

Dyslexia is a specific form of language impairment that affects the way in which the brain encodes the phonological features of spoken words. The core deficit is in phonological processing and stems from poorly specified phonological representations. Dyslexia specifically affects the development of reading and spelling skills but its effects can be modified through development leading to a variety of behavioural manifestations ... the impairment in dyslexia does not affect reading directly but affects the development of the spoken language substrate that is critical for learning to read ... it has its origins in early spoken language skills ... (*pages* 213–214).

Snowling, M., Bishop, D. V. M. and Stothard, S. E. (2000). 'Is preschool language impairment a risk factor for dyslexia in adolescence?' **Journal of Child Psychology and Psychiatry**, 41(5), 587–600.

For simplicity, we use the term 'developmental dyslexia' to designate unexpected difficulties in learning to read ... We regard this as a synonym for 'specific reading retardation' (*page* 587).

Raskind, W. H., Hsu, L., Berninger, V. W., Thomson, J. B. and Wijsman, E. M. (2000). 'Familial aggregation of dyslexia phenotypes'. **Behavior Genetics**, 30(5), 385–396.

Dyslexia is a specific reading disability in which affected individuals have unexpected difficulty in learning how to read and spell words (*page* 385).

Aaron, P. G., Joshi, M. and Williams, K. A. (1999). 'Not all reading disabilities are alike'. **Journal of Learning Disabilities**, 32(2), 120–137.

Reading disability, in the present context, is not used as a synonym for dyslexia or specific reading disability but does include dyslexia as one of its several possible manifestations. Also implied in this definition is the belief that certain varieties of reading disability are caused by etiological factors that are cognitively distinct from each other. It has to be noted that this way of describing reading disability is not universally accepted (*page* 120).

Cossu, G. (1999). 'Biological constraints on literacy acquisition'. **Reading and Writing: An Interdisciplinary Journal**, 11, 213–237.

For the most part ... the term 'developmental dyslexia' is used to mean difficulties in single word decoding (*page* 215).

Stanovich, K. E. (1999). 'The sociometrics of learning disabilities'. **Journal of Learning Disabilities**, 32(4), 350–361.

Its proximal cause is difficulties with word recognition skills due to weak grapheme-phoneme coding skills ... because of segmental language difficulties (lack of phonological awareness) (page 351).

Frith, U. (1999). 'Paradoxes in the definition of dyslexia'. **Dyslexia**, 5, 192–214.

Defining dyslexia at a single level of explanation—biological, cognitive or behavioural—will always lead to paradoxes. For a full understanding of dyslexia we need to link together the three levels and consider the impact of cultural factors which can aggravate or ameliorate the condition. The consensus is emerging that dyslexia is a neurodevelopmental disorder with a biological origin, which impacts on speech processing with a range of clinical manifestations (page 211).

Rack, J. (1997). 'Issues in the assessment of developmental dyslexia in adults: theoretical and applied perspectives'. **Journal of Research in Reading**, 20(1), 66–76.

Narrowly defined dyslexia is developmental phonological dyslexia, the most common and best understood pattern, sometimes also called 'classic developmental dyslexia'. Broadly-defined dyslexia is difficulty in acquiring literacy skills which is related to any underlying specific learning difficulty, not solely phonological processing difficulty (*page* 67).

Padget, S. Y., Knight, D. F. and Sawyer, D. J. (1996). 'Tennessee meets the challenge of dyslexia'. **Annals of Dyslexia**, 46, 51–72.

Dyslexia is a language-based learning disorder that is biological in origin and primarily interferes with the acquisition of print literacy (reading, writing and spelling). Dyslexia is characterised by poor decoding and spelling abilities as well as deficit in phonological awareness and/or phonological manipulation. These primary characteristics may co-occur with spoken language difficulties and deficits in short-term memory. Secondary characteristics may include poor reading comprehension (due to the decoding and memory difficulties) and poor written expression, as well as difficulty organising information for study and retrieval (*page* 55).

Tunmer, W. E. and Chapman, J. W. (1996). 'A developmental model of dyslexia: can the construct be saved?' **Dyslexia**, 2(3), 179–189.

The term dyslexia has been used to refer to children who *unexpectedly* fail to learn to read. These are children who satisfy standard exclusionary criteria, which include factors such as intellectual impairment, gross neurological disorders, severe physical disabilities, sensory deficits, attentional problems, emotional and social difficulties, poor motivation, inadequate early language environment, socio-economic disadvantage, poor school attendance and inadequate or inappropriate school instruction. These factors would be expected to cause problems in reading and in other areas as well, whereas the key assumption underlying the concept of dyslexia is that the cause, or triggering mechanism, for the condition is reasonably specific to the reading task. In actual practice, however, dyslexia is normally defined as a discrepancy between reading achievement and intellectual potential as measured by standardised intelligence tests. Most of the factors mentioned previously are generally ignored (*page* 179).

It may be possible to define dyslexia as the condition that arises from not being able to respond appropriately to formal reading instruction, despite access to linguistic and environmental opportunities, because of an initial weakness in phonological processing that is due to an executive dysfunction (i.e. a deficit or delay in metacognitive functioning) and/or a deficiency in the phonological processing module (*pages* 186–187).

Nicolson, R. I. (1996). 'Developmental dyslexia: past, present and future'. **Dyslexia**, 2(3), 190–207.

Dyslexia is not just a difficulty in learning to read (though this is the most important educational symptom). Dyslexia is present from birth, involves neurophysiological and neuroanatomical abnormalities and has strong genetic components (*page* 191).

Stanovich, K. E. (1996). 'Toward a more inclusive definition of dyslexia'. **Dyslexia**, 2(3), 154–166.

If we have decided to keep the term 'dyslexia' in our conceptual lexicon, then all children with problems in phonological coding resulting from segmental language problems are dyslexic (page 161).

Miles, T. R. (1996). Peer review commentary 'Are dyslexics different? I & II'. **Dyslexia**, 2, 88–91.

With regard to the issue of definition, I see no point in using the word 'dyslexia' at all unless the concept is basically the same as that advocated by the early pioneers ... Hinshelwood, Hallgren, and Hermann spoke of 'word blindness' and Orton of 'strephosymbolia' but they were clearly referring to the same concept (*page* 89) ... If one is interested in specific developmental dyslexia it is important not to tie this concept definitionally to 'poor reading' but to concentrate instead on exploring how the different manifestations of the syndrome arise and how they interact (*page* 90).

Note 'We would defend the use of minimal criteria which only require that a dyslexic be of average or above-average intelligence and have unexpected reading difficulties which cannot easily be attributed to problems of perception, emotion, education, etc. That may be out of line with some historic approaches, but it is very much *in line* with current research practice' (*page* 4). Ellis, A. W., McDougall, S. J. P. and Monk, A. F. (1997). Are dyslexics different? III. Of course they are! **Dyslexia**, 3(1), 2–8.

Farmer, M. E. and Klein, R. M. (1995). 'The evidence for a temporal processing deficit linked to dyslexia: a review'. **Psychonomic Bulletin & Review**, 2(4), 460–493.

Learning to read calls upon many cognitive processes and involves many areas of the brain. A breakdown in any of the contributing processes or areas may thus lead to an inability to learn to read in the normal way. A difficulty in learning to read, or dyslexia, should not be viewed as a condition in itself, but as a symptom of a breakdown in one or more of the various processes involved (*page* 460).

Maughan, B. and Yule, W. (1994). Reading and Other Learning Disabilities. In M. Rutter & E. Taylor & L. Hersov (Eds.), **Child and Adolescent Psychiatry; modern approaches**. Oxford: Blackwell Scientific Publications.

There are two important respects in which the concept of dyslexia seems to be mistaken: firstly, the supposition that it is a distinct unitary condition; and secondly, that the presence of a biological condition means that environmental influences are unimportant. Quite the converse is true. Children with a biological impairment may be more vulnerable to environmental adversities and reading difficulties are best seen as the outcome of an interaction between constitutional deficits and environmental hazards (page 651).

Badian, N. A. (1994). 'Do dyslexic and other poor readers differ in reading-related cognitive skills?' **Reading and Writing: An Interdisciplinary Journal**, 6, 45–63.

... a significant weakness in word recognition and nonword reading accompanied by deficits in both orthographic and phonological processing, manifested as failure in automatic visual recognition and phonological recoding of graphic stimuli (*page* 61).

Aaron, P. G. (1989). **Dyslexia & Hyperlexia**. Boston, MA: Kluwer Academic Publishers.

... a form of reading disorder found in individuals who have average or superior listening comprehension but whose reading performance is compromised by deficient phonological skills (*page* 153).

Thomson, M. E. (1989). **Developmental Dyslexia** (2nd ed.). London: Cole & Whurr.

Developmental dyslexia is a severe difficulty with the written form of language independent of intellectual, cultural and emotional causation. It is characterised by the individual's reading, writing and spelling attainments being well below the level expected based on intelligence and chronological age (page 3).

Baddeley, A. D., Ellis, N. C., Miles, T. R. and Lewis, V. J. (1982). 'Developmental and acquired dyslexia: a comparison'. **Cognition**, 11, 185–199.

... a particular pattern of difficulties involving inconsistency between reading/spelling performance and intelligence level in the absence of sensory defects or primary emotional disturbance (page 187).

Note 1 The 'definition of dyslexia—poor reading in relation to intelligence—is out of line with traditional definitions' (*page* 88). Miles, T. R. (1996). Peer review commentary 'Are dyslexics different? I & II'. **Dyslexia**, 2, 79–100.

Note 2 'In line with traditional usage, only those picked out by the 'imbalance' criteria should be described as 'dyslexic'; a more appropriate term for [poor reading in relation to intelligence] is 'specific reading retardation' (*Abstract*). Miles, T. R., Wheeler, T. J. and Haslum, M. N. (1994). **More dyslexic boys after all?** Paper given to 1994 BDA conference, Manchester.

Vellutino, F. R. (1979). **Dyslexia: theory and research**. Cambridge, MA: MIT Press.

Dyslexia is a generic term typically used to refer to children who are severely impaired in reading. It is also known as specific reading disability, the two terms being used interchangeably. Many investigators believe that dyslexia is a developmental disorder associated with some form of neurological dysfunction, but it is not a well-defined entity and is not clearly identified with any specific neurological abnormalities. Indeed reading problems in any given child can be caused by a number of interacting contingencies, including such extrinsic factors as environmental experiences, lack of attendance at school, poor motivation and deficiencies in organismic variables that are prerequisite to learning in general, for example, sensory and intellectual functions (page 7).

Rutter, M. (1978). Prevalence and types of dyslexia. In A. L. Benton & D. Pearl (Eds.), **Dyslexia: an appraisal of current knowledge**. New York: Oxford University Press.

... the term 'dyslexia' ... constitutes a hypothesis regarding the supposed existence of a nuclear group or groups of disorders of reading and/or spelling caused by constitutional factors, probably genetic in origin. Or, alternatively, it refers to a more heterogeneous group of reading disabilities characterised by the fact that reading/spelling attainment is far below that expected on the basis of the child's age or IQ. If the latter usage is employed, it is probably preferable to use the terms 'specific reading retardation' and 'specific spelling retardation' which involve no theoretical assumptions (page 27).

World Federation of Neurology. (1968). Report of a research group on developmental dyslexia and world illiteracy. Bulletin of the Orton Society, 18, 21–22. (Definition accessed at http://www.bda-dyslexia.org.uk/ on 21 November 2002)

... a disorder manifested by a difficulty in learning to read despite conventional instruction, adequate intelligence and socio-cultural opportunity. It is dependent upon fundamental cognitive difficulties which are frequently of a constitutional character.

Note 'As a piece of logic this definition is a nonstarter ... it suggests that if all the known causes of reading disability can be ruled out, the unknown (in the form of dyslexia) should be invoked. A counsel of despair, indeed' (*page* 12). Rutter, M. (1978). Prevalence and types of dyslexia. In A. L. Benton & D. Pearl (Eds.), **Dyslexia: an appraisal of current knowledge**. New York: Oxford University Press.

Tansley, A. E. (1967). **Reading and Remedial Reading**. London: Routledge and Kegan Paul.

Inability to read, sometimes called dyslexia, is a secondary disorder resulting from primary causes. The diagnosis should attempt to break down the dyslexia into component elements so as to isolate the principal cause. Thus all sensory channels and their integration must be investigated; perceptual activity, which cannot in practice be isolated from sensation, must be analysed; psycholinguistic processes must be tested (*page* 85).

Morgan, W. P. (1896). 'A case of congenital word-blindness'. **British Medical Journal** (7 November 1896), 1378.

> Percy's visual memory for words is defective or absent; which is equivalent to saying that he is what Kussmaul has termed 'word blind' ... This case is evidently congenital, and due most probably to defective development of that region of the brain, disease of which in adults produces practically the same symptoms—that is, the left angular gyrus.

> *Note* 'This explanation assumed (a) that functions are localised similarly in the brain in both adults and children, (b) that such localisations are innate (although it is certainly peculiar to hypothesise an innate brain mechanism for reading, which is a cultural artefact) and (c) that there is little developmental plasticity available to compensate for an early localised lesion. Subsequent work ... has shown that these assumptions are clearly wrong for spoken language and it is doubtful that they hold for written language' (*page* 639). Pennington, B. F. (1999). Toward an integrated understanding of dyslexia: genetic, neurological and cognitive mechanisms. **Development and Psychopathology**, 11, 629–654.

> *Note* 'The functional neuroanatomy of reading disorders in children is still enigmatic and, for the most part, as speculative as it was a century ago' (*page* 214). Cossu, G. (1999). Biological constraints on literacy acquisition. **Reading and Writing: An Interdisciplinary Journal**, 11, 213–237.

Hinshelwood, J. (1895). Word-blindness and visual memory. **The Lancet** (21 December 1895), 1564–1570.

> There are different forms of word-blindness which must be carefully distinguished from one another. The case just reported is really one of letter-blindness—i.e. the inability to recognise individual letters (page 1565) ... A lesion on one side of the brain, in the vast majority of cases on the left side, may completely obliterate the visual word memories and make the individual word-blind (page 1568).

Crossword definition

1 Across in *Quick Crossword* 10,155 (*The Guardian*, 20 November 2002).

Dyslexia (4–9)

The answer is, of course, | W | O | R | D | B | L | I | N | D | N | E | S | S |

Official definitions

Department of Education and Science (1975). *A Language for Life: Report of the Committee of Enquiry appointed by the Secretary of State for Education under the Chairmanship of Sir Alan Bullock.* London: HMSO.

> '... *not susceptible to precise operational definition*' (page *587*)

Note 'No reasons are given for this curious and dogmatic statement' (*page* 184). Miles, T. R. (1983). **Dyslexia: The Pattern of Difficulties**. London: Granada.

Department for Education and Skills (2002). *Dyslexia and related specific learning difficulties.* [Accessed at www.dfes.gov.uk/curriculum_literacy/access/dyslexia on 28 November 2002.]

> Dyslexia is most commonly described as a difficulty with processing written language ... Others may experience similar difficulties to dyslexic people ... The kinds, patterns and levels of difficulty will vary according to the type(s) of difficulty and the degree of impact within individual learning contexts (sic).

(*Adult Literacy Core Curriculum*)

Dictionary definitions

OED

> **dyslexia**   a difficulty in reading due to affection of the brain (1886–8)

> *Note* The word 'dyslexia' first appeared in: Berlin, R. (1884). Über Dyslexie. **Archiv für Psychiatrie**, 15, 276–278.

Chambers Dictionary (1998 edition)

> **dyslexia**   word-blindness, great difficulty in learning to read or spell, unrelated to intellectual competence and of unknown cause.

Parliamentary Written Answer

> **Mr. Beggs:** To ask the Secretary of State for Education and Skills what arrangements are in place to assist pupils/students with specific learning disabilities, with particular reference to dyslexia, when they are completing tests or examinations; and if he will make a statement.

> **Mr. Stephen Twigg:** ... The arrangements for dyslexic candidates taking public examinations are determined by the relevant awarding bodies. The most common arrangement permitted for such candidates is additional time in which to complete the examination. The use of readers, writers and word processors are also permitted in exceptional circumstances. Appropriate evidence must support each case and the decision rests with the awarding body.

(Hansard, 19 November 2002)

Appendix 2
An analysis of dyslexia definitions

				Behaviour specific to literacy								
		Age discrepant	IQ discrepant	Reading Accuracy deficit	Reading fluency deficit	Spelling accuracy deficit	Writing deficit	Comprehension deficit	Non-specific behaviour	Cognitive impairment	Intrinsic	Lifelong
Advocates	BDA 1		•	•		•	•			•	•	
	BDA 2			•		•	•			•	•	
	BDA 3									•	•	•
	BD		•	•				•				
Practitioners	DI		•	•		•	•			•		
	IDA	•	•	•		•	•				•	
	NJCLD	•		•			•	•	•	•		•
	Orton-Gillingham	•		•		•	•	•		•		
	BPS	•	•	•	•	•						
	CDHCN	•		•		•					•	
	Hornsby	•	•	•		•	•					
	Klein	•		•		•	•			•		
Scholars	Fletcher (2002)	•	•	•	•			•				
	Fisher (2002)		•	•							•	
	Grigorenko (2001)	•		•	•					•	•	
	Stein (2001)		•	•						•		
	Snowling (2000)			•					•			
	Snowling et al. (2000)	•	•	•						•		
	Raskind (2000)	•	•	•								
	Cossu (1999)			•								
	Stanovich (1999)			•						•		
	Frith (1999)			•		•	•			•	•	
	Padget (1996)	•		•		•	•	•		•		
	Nicolson (1996)	•		•								
	Stanovich (1996)			•						•	•	
	Badian (1994)			•	•					•	•	
	WFN (1968)	•	•	•						•		
Government	DfES (2002)			•								

Appendix 3
Some research criteria used in studies of dyslexia

Caveat: ' ... the majority of research investigations seeking to elucidate the characteristics of dyslexia ... have yielded findings that are difficult to interpret, replicate, and generalise' (*page* 7). Lyon, G. R. (1995). 'Toward a definition of dyslexia'. **Annals of Dyslexia**, 45, 3–27.

Study	Construct group(s)	Selection criteria
Bourassa, D. and Treiman, R. (*2003*). 'Spelling in children with dyslexia: analyses from the Treiman-Bourassa early spelling test'. **Scientific Studies of Reading**, *7(4), 309-333.*	Dyslexic (*vs.* younger, spelling-level matched non-dyslexic) children	*For dyslexia*: Prior classification by their schools as developmentally dyslexic and then full-scale standard IQ score of at least 85, performance below the 25th percentile for their age group on both spelling and reading subtests of the Wide Range Achievement Test-3 (based on the combined performance across the two forms of each subtest) and performance below the fourth-grade level on the spelling subtests of the Wide Range Achievement Test-3, based on the combined performance across the two forms.
Pogorzelski, S. and Wheldall, K. (2002). 'Do differences in phonological processing performance predict gains made by older low-progress readers following intensive literacy intervention?' **Educational Psychology**, 22(4), 413–427.	Dyslexic (*vs.* garden variety) low-progress readers	*For the study*: attendance at a programme for children who were at least two years behind in reading accuracy, socially disadvantaged and at serious risk of disaffection from school. *For dyslexia*: severe reading disability as defined by the Phonological Assessment Battery, i.e. scores falling one SD below the mean on at least three out of the nine subtests.
Chiappe, P., Stringer, R., Siegel, L. S. and Stanovich, K. E. (2002). 'Why the timing deficit hypothesis does not explain reading disability in adults'. **Reading and Writing**, 15, 73–107.	Reading-disabled (*vs.* age-matched and reading-level matched normally-reading) children	*For reading disability*: reading at or below the 25th percentile on the reading subtest of the Wide Range Achievement Test-3, which is an untimed confrontational naming task.
Heiervang, E., Stevenson, J. and Hugdahl, K. (2002). 'Auditory processing in children with dyslexia.' **Journal of Child Psychology and Psychiatry**, 43(7), 931–938.	Dyslexic (*vs.* normal control) children	*For dyslexia*: At the first stage, a score below the 10th percentile on a spelling test administered by teachers; at the second stage, a mean score of at least 2 SD below the mean age level on five reading tasks from a standardised battery of computerised reading tests.

Study	Construct group(s)	Selection criteria
Zabell, C. and Everatt, J. (2002). 'Surface and phonological subtypes of adult developmental dyslexia'. **Dyslexia**, 8, 160–177.	Dyslexic (*vs.* non-dyslexic) adults	*For the study:* current or recent university student status. *For dyslexia:* Educational Psychological Assessments confirming a diagnosis of dyslexia based on poor performance on measures of literacy and phonological processing in the absence of known general intellectual deficits, perceptual impairments and psycho-emotional dysfunction and self-reported difficulty in learning to read.
Pisecco, S., Baker, D. B., Silva, P. A. and Brooke, M. (2001). 'Boys with reading disabilities and/or ADHD: distinctions in early childhood'. **Journal of Learning Disabilities**, 34(2), 98–106.	Reading-disabled only (*vs.* RD/ADHD, ADHD only, and normal comparison) children	*For reading disability:* a reading score at least 1.5 SD below the male sample's average reading score.
Kirk, J. and Reid, G. (2001). 'An examination of the relationship between dyslexia and offending in young people and the implications for the training system'. **Dyslexia**, 7, 77–84.	Dyslexic (*vs.* non-dyslexic) young offenders	*For dyslexia:* 'positive' indicators of dyslexia as calculated by the computerised self-assessment screening test for dyslexia, QuickScan (normed on university students).
Curtin, S., Manis, F. R. and Seidenberg, M. S. (2001). 'Parallels between the reading and spelling deficits of two subgroups of developmental dyslexics'. **Reading and Writing**, 14(5–6), 515–547.	Phonological and surface dyslexic children *vs.* normal readers	*For poor readers:* initially, teacher nomination based on estimates that subjects were in the bottom quartile for reading; subsequently, classification by difficulty with either nonword reading or exception word reading.
de Martino, S., Espesser, R., Rey, V. and Habib, M. (2001). 'The 'temporal processing deficit' hypothesis in dyslexia: new experimental evidence'. **Brain and Cognition**, 46(1–2), 104–108.	Phonological dyslexic *vs.* normal control children	*For dyslexia:* normal IQ; no neurological, auditory or visual disorders of any kind; no attention deficit; and a two-year lag in reading ability.
Facoetti, A., Turatto, M., Lorusso, M. L. and Mascetti, G. G. (2001). 'Orienting of visual attention in dyslexia: evidence for asymmetric hemispheric control of attention'. **Experimental Brain Research**, 138(1), 46–53.	Dyslexic children *vs.* normal readers	*For dyslexia:* absence of spoken language impairment; full-scale IQ >85 as measured by WISC-R; no known gross behavioural or emotional problems; normal or corrected-to-normal vision and hearing; normal visual field; absence of ADHD; right manual preference.

Study	Construct group(s)	Selection criteria
Griffiths, Y. M. and Snowling, M. J. (2001). 'Auditory word identification and phonological skills in dyslexic and average readers'. **Applied Psycholinguistics**, 22(3), 419–439.	Dyslexic *vs.* average readers in late childhood and early adolescence	*For dyslexia*: an IQ of >85 on WISC-III; a reading standard score below 87 and a standard score for spelling below 85 on Wechsler's WORD tests of single-word reading and spelling; and a WISC-III vocabulary scaled score of at least 8.
Gustafson, S. (2001). 'Cognitive abilities and print exposure in surface and phonological types of reading disability'. **Scientific Studies of Reading**, 5(4), 351–375.	Surface and phonological reading-disabled children	*For reading disability*: children in Grades 4 through 6 who received special instruction in reading because of reading difficulties at the time of the study, excluding those with gross neurological disturbances and those whose first language was different from the language of instruction.
Wadsworth, S. J., Olson, R. K., Pennington, B. F. and DeFries, J. C. (2000). 'Differential genetic etiology of reading disability as a function of IQ'. **Journal of Learning Disabilities**, 33(2), 192–199.	Reading-disabled children with full-scale WISC IQ scores above and below 100	*For reading disability*: a positive school history of reading problems; an RD classification computed from reading and spelling subtests of the PIAT; no evidence of emotional or behavioural problems; no uncorrected visual or auditory acuity deficit; but without exclusion on the basis of IQ.
Moores, E. and Andrade, J. (2000). 'Ability of dyslexic and control teenagers to sustain attention and inhibit responses'. **European Journal of Cognitive Psychology**, 12(4), 520–540.	Dyslexic adolescents *vs.* age-matched controls	*For dyslexia*: normal or above-normal full-scale IQ on WISC-III; no known primary emotional, behavioural, or socio-economic problems; reading age or spelling age at least eighteen months behind chronological age at initial diagnosis; no evidence of ADHD.
Patel, T. K. and Licht, R. (2000). 'Verbal and affective laterality effects in P-dyslexic, L-dyslexic and normal children'. **Child Neuropsychology**, 6(3), 157–174.	Perceptual (P-type) and linguistic (L-type) dyslexic *vs.* normal control children	*For dyslexia*: righthandedness; failure to acquire normal reading proficiency despite conventional instruction, socio-cultural opportunity, average intelligence and freedom from gross sensory, emotional or neurological handicaps; and a lag in reading ability of at least one and a half years at age 9 to 12.
Temple, E., Poldrack, R. A., Protopapas, A., Nagarajan, S., Salz, T., Tallal, P., Merzenich, M. M. and Gabrieli, J. D. E. (2000). Disruption of the neural response to rapid acoustic stimuli in dyslexia: evidence from functional MRI. **Proceedings of the National Academy of Science USA**, 97(25), 13907–13912.	Dyslexic *vs.* normal adults	*For dyslexia*: a history of developmental dyslexia, confirmed by standardised reading tests of real word reading and nonword reading; good physical health; and freedom from any history of neurologic disease.

Study	Construct group(s)	Selection criteria
Habib, M., Robichon, F., Chanoine, V., Démonet, J.-F., Frith, C. and Frith, U. (2000). 'The influence of language learning on brain morphology: the 'callosal effect' in dyslexics differs according to native language'. **Brain and Language**, 74(3), 520–524.	Dyslexic *vs.* normal monolingual adult male university students	*For dyslexia*: poor performance on timed and untimed word and nonword reading, digit naming, word auditory span, and spoonerism tasks.
Sprenger-Charolles, L., Colé, P., Lacert, P. and Serniclaes, W. (2000). 'On subtypes of developmental dyslexia: evidence from processing time and accuracy scores'. **Canadian Journal of Experimental Psychology - Revue Canadienne de Psychologie Expérimentale**, 54(2), 87–104.	Phonological and surface dyslexics *vs.* age-matched average-reading and younger reading-level controls	*For dyslexia*: not coming from an underprivileged home; absence of language, motor, or psychological disorders; average or above-average non-verbal and verbal IQ; reading score more than 2 SD below the mean on the reading-aloud subtest of a standardised test battery at age 10 years.
Robichon, F., Bouchard, P., Démonet, J.-F. and Habib, M. (2000). 'Developmental dyslexia: re-evaluation of the corpus callosum in male adults'. **European Neurology**, 43(4), 233–237.	Dyslexic *vs.* age-matched adult male controls	*For dyslexia*: pre-screening criteria of righthandedness; childhood history of at least two years school retardation; familial occurrence of dyslexia or reading impairment in at least one first-degree relative; diagnosis of dyslexia and speech therapy by professionals serving children in France. These criteria were qualified by: IQ not less than lower level of age range or 90 by Raven or WAIS-R; no histories of epileptic seizures, neurological or psychiatric illnesses, or hyperactivity (with or without attention deficit disorder).
Wimmer, H., Mayringer, H. and Raberger, T. (1999). 'Reading and dual-task balancing: evidence against the automatization deficit explanation of developmental dyslexia'. **Journal of Learning Disabilities**, 32(5), 473–478.	Dyslexic *vs.* non-dyslexic children	*For dyslexia*: initial teacher nomination, refined by a nonverbal IQ above 90 and a reading speed below the 16th percentile for either individual words or a short passage of text.
Fagerheim, T., Raeymaekers, P., Tønnessen, F. E., Pedersen, M., Tranebjærg, L. and Lubs, H. A. (1999). 'A new gene (DYX3) for dyslexia is located on chromosome 2'. **Journal of Medical Genetics**, 36, 664–669.	A large Norwegian family in which dyslexia is inherited as an autosomal dominant trait	*For dyslexia*: timed and untimed tests of reading ordinary words; a test of nonword reading; sound-blending tests for familiar words and nonwords; spelling from dictation; with the same cut-points for both adults and children.

Study	Construct group(s)	Selection criteria
Cohen, M. J., Morgan, A. M., Vaughn, M., Riccio, C. A. and Hall, J. (1999). 'Verbal fluency in children: developmental issues and differential validity in distinguishing children with Attention-Deficit Hyperactivity Disorder and two subtypes of dyslexia'. **Archives of Clinical Neuropsychology**, 14(5), 433–443.	Dyslexic *vs.* ADHD and normal control children	*For dyslexia*: normal intelligence and a IQ/achievement discrepancy of at least 20 standard score points in either reading recognition or reading comprehension or both.

Note Although this table could be extended, it is probably long enough to make its point.

Appendix 4
A general model of reading and influences on reading development

Figure 2.5 in Jackson, N. E. and Coltheart, M. (2001). **Routes to Reading Success and Failure: towards an integrated cognitive psychology of atypical reading.** Hove: Psychology Press.

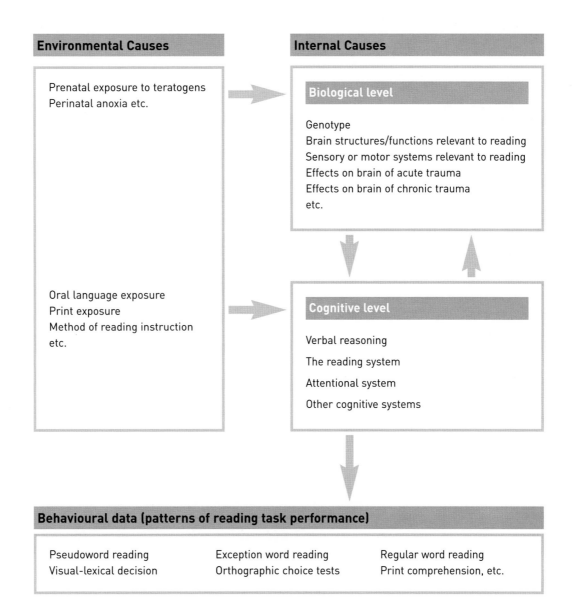

Environmental Causes

Prenatal exposure to teratogens
Perinatal anoxia etc.

Oral language exposure
Print exposure
Method of reading instruction
etc.

Internal Causes

Biological level

Genotype
Brain structures/functions relevant to reading
Sensory or motor systems relevant to reading
Effects on brain of acute trauma
Effects on brain of chronic trauma
etc.

Cognitive level

Verbal reasoning

The reading system

Attentional system

Other cognitive systems

Behavioural data (patterns of reading task performance)

Pseudoword reading
Visual-lexical decision

Exception word reading
Orthographic choice tests

Regular word reading
Print comprehension, etc.

Appendix 5
Referral items in 'screening' checklists

Note These items may fall into three groups, which are seldom adequately distinguished: those differentiating between competent and poor readers, those differentiating between people with and without learning disabilities and those differentiating between dyslexics and ordinary poor readers.

Checklist item	US National Adult Literacy and Learning Disabilities Center (2002)	Vinegrad (1994)	Ott (1997)	Direct Learning (2002)	Adult Dyslexia Organisation (2002)	British Dyslexia Association	Dyslexia Institute (2002)	Everatt & Smyth (2002)
1 Performs similar tasks differently from day to day	•		•					
2 Can read well but not write well, or write well but not read well	•							
3 Can learn information presented in one way, but not in another	•							
4 Has a short attention span, is impulsive and/or easily distracted	•							
5 Has difficulty telling or understanding jokes	•							
6 Misinterprets language, has poor comprehension of what is said	•							
7 Has difficulty with social skills, may misinterpret social cues	•							
8 Finds it difficult to memorise information	•	•	•		•	•	•	•
9 Has difficulty in following a schedule, being on time, or meeting deadlines	•	•	•	•	•	•	•	•
10 Gets lost easily, either driving and/or in large buildings	•							
11 Has trouble reading maps	•	•	•		•	•	•	•
12 Often misreads or miscopies	•		•					•
13 Confuses similar letters or numbers, reverses them, or confuses their order	•	•		•	•	•	•	
14 Has difficulty in reading the newspaper, following small print and/or following columns	•		•					
15 Can explain things orally, but not in writing	•							
16 Has difficulty in writing ideas on paper	•							
17 Reverses or omits letters, words, or phrases when writing	•		•					
18 Has difficulty completing forms correctly	•	•	•	•	•	•	•	•

Checklist item	US National Adult Literacy and Learning Disabilities Center (2002)	Vinegrad (1994)	Ott (1997)	Direct Learning (2002)	Adult Dyslexia Organisation (2002)	British Dyslexia Association	Dyslexia Institute (2002)	Everatt & Smyth (2002)
19 Has persistent problems with sentence structure, writing mechanics and organising written work	•							
20 Experiences continuous problems with spelling the same word differently in one document	•							
21 Has trouble dialling phone numbers and reading addresses	•		•	•				•
22 Has difficulty with mathematics, mathematics language and mathematics concepts	•		•					
23 Reverses numbers, e.g. in chequebook and has difficulty balancing a chequebook	•	•	•	•	•	•	•	•
24 Confuses right and left, up and down	•	•	•	•	•		•	•
25 Has difficulty following directions, especially multiple directions	•		•					•
26 Poorly coordinated	•							•
27 Unable to tell you what has just been said	•		•					
28 Hears sounds, words, or sentences imperfectly or incorrectly	•							
29 Dislikes reading aloud	•	•	•		•		•	•
30 Takes longer than expected to read a page of a book		•	•	•	•		•	•
31 Finds it hard to remember the sense of what has been read		•	•		•		•	•
32 Dislikes reading long books		•	•		•		•	•
33 Spells poorly		•	•	•	•		•	•
34 Writes illegibly		•			•		•	•
35 Becomes confused when speaking in public		•	•		•		•	•
36 Has difficulty in taking telephone messages for others		•	•	•	•		•	•
37 Scrambles the sounds in long words		•	•	•	•		•	•
38 Has difficulty in reciting months forwards		•		•	•		•	
39 Has difficulty in reciting months backwards		•			•		•	
40 Written vocabulary limited by spelling ability								•
41 Does not read for pleasure								•
42 Finds it difficult to learn to speak a foreign language								•

Checklist item	US National Adult Literacy and Learning Disabilities Center (2002)	Vinegrad (1994)	Ott (1997)	Direct Learning (2002)	Adult Dyslexia Organisation (2002)	British Dyslexia Association	Dyslexia Institute (2002)	Everatt & Smyth (2002)
43 Finds it difficult to learn to write a foreign language								•
44 Finds it difficult to recite the alphabet								•
45 Finds it difficult to separate the syllables of a word								•
46 Finds it difficult to understand spoonerisms								•
47 Finds it difficult to understand malapropisms								•
48 Finds it difficult to understand rhyming slang								•
49 Loses place or jumps lines when reading			•					
50 Finds that words jump around on the page								•
51 Finds vision blurred when trying to look at fine details								•
52 Confuses morphologically similar words when speaking								•
53 Confuses orthographically similar words when reading								•
54 Confuses semantically similar words								•
55 Misplaces personal possessions			•					
56 Has difficulty with mental arithmetic			•					
57 Thinks laterally or creatively								•

Appendix 6
An analysis of referral items in dyslexia screening checklists

Note 1 The diversity of these items challenges the claim of specificity.
Note 2 More than one item in this list indicates a need to resolve the ambiguity between concepts and percepts.

Function	Checklist item	Observations
Auditory perception	Hears sounds, words, or sentences imperfectly or incorrectly (28)	A difficulty in auditory perception might have a distal explanation in either childhood glue ear (*otitis media* with effusion) or later impairment through injury of some kind. On the other hand, there might be a cognitive difficulty because of impaired processing speed.
Visual perception	Finds that words jump around on the page (50)	Might indicate a problem with either low-level oculomotor factors (such as unstable vergence) or higher-level cognitive processes.
	Finds vision blurred when trying to look at fine details (51)	Might indicate a need to wear spectacles.
Phonological processing	Finds it difficult to separate the syllables of a word (45)	Might be a conceptual or a perceptual problem.
	Finds it difficult to understand spoonerisms (46)	Might be a conceptual or a perceptual problem. Production of spoonerisms also involves verbal working memory.
	Finds it difficult to understand malapropisms (47)	Might be a conceptual or a perceptual problem.
	Finds it difficult to understand rhyming slang (48)	Might be a conceptual or a perceptual problem.
Reading/ decoding	Has difficulty in reading the newspaper, following small print and/or following columns (14)	Difficulty with small print might indicate a need to wear spectacles. Difficulty in following columns might indicate a need to improve oculomotor control. Otherwise, difficulty in reading the newspaper might indicate a problem with decoding, a problem with general or vocabulary knowledge, or a problem with syntax.
	Has trouble reading addresses (21)	If the addresses are handwritten, this could represent a need to become more familiar with handwriting, in addition to any problems with word recognition or decoding.

Function	Checklist item	Observations
Reading/ decoding cont.	Dislikes reading aloud (29)	Might indicate a word recognition or decoding problem, or social self-consciousness.
	Takes longer than expected to read a page of a book (30)	As there is no representative 'page' and no representative 'reader', this is a necessarily subjective judgement. There might be a problem with reading rate despite accurate word recognition and decoding, or a conceptual difficulty with a complex text, or progress slowed by puzzling misreadings.
	Dislikes reading long books (32)	Similarly, this might indicate a problem with reading rate despite accurate word recognition and decoding, or a conceptual difficulty with a complex text, or progress slowed by puzzling misreadings.
	Does not read for pleasure (41)	Once again, this might indicate a problem with reading rate despite accurate word recognition and decoding, or a conceptual difficulty with a complex text, or progress slowed by puzzling misreadings.
	Loses place or jumps lines when reading (49)	Might indicate a problem with verbal short-term memory, or a problem with oculomotor control.
	Confuses morphologically similar words when speaking (52)	
	Confuses orthographically similar words when reading (53)	Might be a temporary characteristic of a relatively inexperienced reader.
	Confuses semantically similar words (54)	Might be a temporary characteristic of a relatively inexperienced reader.
Spelling/ encoding	Experiences continuous problems with spelling the same word differently in one document (20)	Might indicate lack of systematic learning or teaching.
	Spells poorly (33)	Ambiguous, as some spelling errors indicate a partial mastery of the alphabetic system (such as the regularisation of irregular words, or failure to observe rules for consonant doubling) while others might indicate fundamental misunderstanding or lack of knowledge.

Function	Checklist item	Observations
Comprehension of spoken language	Has difficulty telling or understanding jokes (5)	Might indicate inability to recognise wordplay (which, in turn, might be of more than one kind).
	Misinterprets language, has poor comprehension of what is said (6)	Might indicate deficits in general or vocabulary knowledge, insensitivity to prosody, or difficulty with more complex syntax.
Writing	Can explain things orally, but not in writing (15)	Might indicate problems with spelling, motor control, or the formal structuring of thought.
	Has difficulty in writing ideas on paper (16)	Might indicate problems with spelling, motor control, or the formal structuring of thought.
	Has difficulty in completing forms correctly (18)	Might indicate difficulty with reading, eyesight, spelling, writing, knowledge of the conventions (or badly-designed forms).
	Has persistent problems with sentence structure, writing mechanics and organising written work (19)	These are three separate problems, as in the notes to 15 and 16 above.
	Writes illegibly (34)	Might indicate genuine difficulty in fine motor control, want of adequate instruction, or lack of motivation.
	Written vocabulary limited by spelling ability (40)	Might indicate a defensive response to insensitive treatment in school.
Long-term or explicit memory	Has difficulty in reciting months forwards (38)	Serial recall might be compromised if the items were not learned in serial order.
	Finds it difficult to recite the alphabet (44)	Serial recall might be compromised if the items were not learned in serial order.
	Misplaces personal possessions (55)	
Verbal short-term memory	Can learn information presented in one way but not in another (3)	Ambiguous, in that 'assimilation' and 'retention' might not be simple cognitive functions, but generally perceived as a 'learning style' issue, where there is a preference for visual over verbal presentation.
	Finds it difficult to memorise information (8)	

Function	Checklist item	Observations
Verbal short-term memory cont.	Has trouble dialling phone numbers (21)	
	Has difficulty following directions, especially multiple directions (25)	
	Unable to tell you what has just been said (27)	The problem might be also attentional or linguistic
	Finds it hard to remember the sense of what has been read (31)	A failure of conceptual, not verbal, recall but might originate in a verbal short-term memory failure.
	Becomes confused when speaking in public (35)	But so do many people. Practice makes perfect.
	Has difficulty in taking telephone messages for others (36)	Might also entail problems with speech perception, spelling and writing.
Verbal working memory	Has difficulty in reciting months backwards (39)	
	Has difficulty with mental arithmetic (56)	
Attention	Has a short attention span, is impulsive and/or easily distracted (4)	Poor readers might have deficits in one or more of the functions of sustained attention, selective attention, attentional switching and auditory-verbal working memory.
Social cognition	Has difficulty in telling or understanding jokes (5)	Might involve misunderstanding of interpersonal dynamics.
	Has difficulty with social skills, might misinterpret social cues (7)	Might entail linguistic deficits (vocabulary or affective prosody) or difficulty in interpreting facial expression, stance and gesture.
Motor control	Poorly coordinated (26)	Might indicate cerebellar dysfunction.
	Scrambles the sounds in long words (37)	Might indicate impaired inter-hemispheric communication.
Miscellaneous	Day-to-day variability in performance (1)	Effortful work of any kind requires full concentration and even slight fatigue might lead to marked performance decrements.
	Can read well but not write well, or vice versa (2)	The former is likely to be more common than the latter.

Function	Checklist item	Observations
Miscellaneous cont.	Has difficulty in following a schedule, being on time, or meeting deadlines (9)	There might be several problems here, including over-reliance on prospective memory, difficulty in keeping a complete and accessible written record and poor time perception.
	Gets lost easily, either driving or in large buildings (10)	Might be inability to read the wording on signs or a spatial orientation problem independent of reading.
	Has trouble reading maps (11)	Might be a spatial orientation problem, or unfamilarity with the genre, or reading difficulty.
	Often misreads or miscopies (12)	Might entail both word recognition and verbal short-term memory problems.
	Confuses similar letters or numbers, reverses them, or confuses their order (13)	Might indicate that rules are still being learned, rather than any difficulty in learning.
	Reverses or omits letters, words or phrases when writing (17)	There might be several problems here, in which verbal short-term memory and excessive haste might be implicated.
	Reverses numbers, for example in a chequebook and has difficulty balancing a chequebook (23)	There might be at least two problems here: number reversal might indicate lack of experience in writing numerals; balancing books is both an arithmetic and a planning task and calls on verbal working memory.
	Confuses right and left, up and down (24)	Might indicate difficulty in accessing long-term memory.
	Thinks laterally or creatively (57)	If sequential thinking is an outcome of literacy, then lateral thinking might be necessitated by lack of literacy; creative thinking might be an adaptive strategy in people who become accustomed from an early age to devising solutions to problems where no help is forthcoming from others.

Appendix 7
A 'road map' for understanding patterns of reading disability.

From: Spear-Swerling, L. (in press). A road map for understanding reading disability and other reading problems: Origins, prevention and intervention. In R. Ruddell & N. Unrau (Eds.), **Theoretical Models and Processes of Reading**, vol. 5. Newark, DE: International Reading Association.

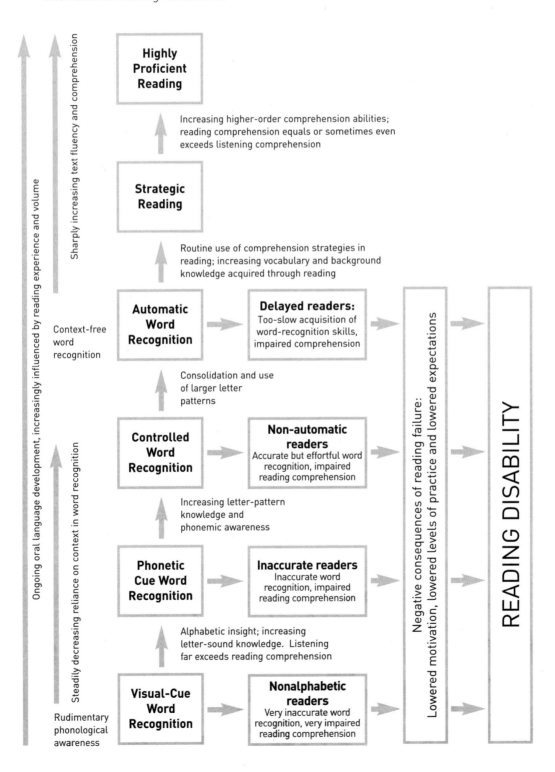

Appendix 8
Screening for dyslexic adults

'Methods for diagnosing dyslexia in adults vary and the appropriateness and validity of many tests is contentious.' **Department for Education and Skills (2002).** Dyslexia and related specific learning difficulties. *Accessed at* www.dfes.gov.uk/curriculum_literacy/access/dyslexia *on 28 November 2002.*

'One would be hard pressed to find a clear consensus within the dyslexia community to such fundamental questions as how best dyslexia is diagnosed' *(page* 56). Nicolson, R. I. (2002). The dyslexia ecosystem. **Dyslexia**, 8, 55–66.

'The diagnosis of dyslexia is itself a theory, distinguishing reading failure arising ultimately from internal rather than solely external reasons, but a rather unspecified one ... ' *(page* 558). Frith, U. (2001). What framework should we use for understanding developmental disorders? **Developmental Neuropsychology**, 20(2), 555–563.

'The incidence of SDD is either 4% (severe) or 10% (mild) according to estimates by some organisations, including the British Dyslexia Association ... Such estimates of prevalence are both theoretically and technically contentious' *(page* 153). Pumfrey, P. (2001). Specific Developmental Dyslexia (SDD): 'Basics to back' in 2000 and beyond? In M. Hunter-Carsch (Ed.), **Dyslexia: a psychosocial perspective**. London: Whurr.

'Any attempt to determine the prevalence of dyslexia should be treated with caution' *(page* 27). Miles, T. R. and Miles, E. (1999). **Dyslexia: a hundred years on**. (Second ed.). Buckingham: Open University Press.

'With a developmental condition such as dyslexia, there is an increased probability of secondary symptoms arising with increasing age. Given that there can also be interactive effects, the job of disentangling and understanding the causes and consequences of a person's pattern of difficulties is usually very difficult and sometimes impossible ... The more secondary difficulties there are, the harder it becomes to detect the dyslexia' *(page* 68). Rack, J. (1997). Issues in the assessment of developmental dyslexia in adults: theoretical and applied perspectives. **Journal of Research in Reading**, 20(1), 66–76.

'If there is, for any age and IQ, an uninterrupted gradation from good reading to bad, then the question of where to draw the line is an entirely arbitrary one. Therefore, to ask how prevalent dyslexia is in the general population will be as meaningful, and as meaningless, as asking how prevalent obesity is. The answer will depend entirely on where the line is drawn' *(page* 172). Ellis, A. W. (1985). The cognitive neuropsychology of developmental (and acquired) dyslexia: a critical survey. **Cognitive Neuropsychology**, 2(2), 169–205.

An epidemiological study has three options, broadly speaking, for determining the prevalence of a disability. It can ask respondents a single question of the kind 'Do you have *X*?' with three response options: 'yes', 'no', and 'I don't know'. It can employ a screening instrument alone and infer the prevalence of the condition from the instrument's known positive predictive value (although there might be a degree of circularity in this approach, since the positive predictive value for a population can only be determined in an epidemiological study). Or it can employ a screening instrument and follow up all people who screen 'positive' with a diagnostic examination to determine whether or not they are true positives.

Would any of these options work for dyslexia?

The single question method must be ruled out immediately. The advocacy groups might submit that historic failure to ascertain the nature of difficulties in learning to read means that an unknowable number of adults could be unaware that they are dyslexic. Although the evidence is anecdotal, it would be sufficient to establish the submission in principle. Answers to a single question could thus under-estimate the prevalence of dyslexia in an epidemiological study.

But the single question can be ruled out for a second reason. As we have shown, there is widespread confusion about the concept of dyslexia. This confusion has led to the mis-identification of 'ordinary poor readers' as 'dyslexics'. If, on the one hand, it is conceded that all poor readers are to be described (and for whatever reason) as 'dyslexic', then an epidemiological study needs to employ only mainstream methods of ascertaining the prevalence of poor reading at the single-word level and it can dispense with any question about 'dyslexia'. If, on the other hand, it is argued that 'dyslexics' are qualitatively different from 'ordinary poor readers', then the answers to a single question would over-estimate the prevalence of dyslexia severalfold. As the main body of this review has shown, tests of single word or pseudoword reading have no discriminative validity.

We do not know whether over- and under-estimates would cancel out. Even if they were to cancel out, an estimate of prevalence obtained in this way would be useless for either univariate or multivariate analysis, as the identified sample would omit some true positives and contain some false positives.

This leaves the screening instrument, either on its own or supplemented by a diagnostic assessment. There are two techniques in screening. One technique is to use a behavioural checklist, in order to elicit self-reports of behaviours that merit further investigation. Implicit in this technique is the possibility that two people who achieve scores of, say, eight out of twenty might not overlap at all. This does not necessarily matter if the checklist is used only to determine the need for further referral, but it could matter very much if the checklist is misused as a substitute for diagnosis. Also implicit in the use of checklists is the probability of quantitative differences between individual self-assessments, in that one person's positive response to a question does not necessarily indicate the same severity of impairment that a second person's positive response might indicate.

An alternative technique is to use a battery of objective tests of cognitive ability. By using tests such as these, researchers can be more confident that identical scores represent comparable degrees of impairment. Beyond that, the scores need to be interpreted: there may be quite different explanations why two people achieve the same score on a test. In other words, a test may be used to assess the current performance level but not to make a diagnosis in the absence of inferences from other sources of information.

Screening tests, whether behavioural checklists, cognitive test batteries or hybrid methods, have one purpose: to reduce the time and expense of diagnosis. In theory, the outcome of a screening test entails referral of true and false positives and non-referral of true and false negatives. Tests are therefore required to be sensitive to the condition under investigation by including as high a proportion of true positives as possible and to be specific to that condition by excluding as high a proportion of true negatives as possible. In a rule-of-thumb fashion, the tests serve a purpose, but it is improbable that they do so with equal efficiency. That is to say, their predictive values are likely to differ, in that one test may yield a higher proportion than another test of 'test positives' who are found to be 'true positives'.

One complication is that the predictive value of any screening test is unlikely to be a constant. It may vary strikingly according to the context in which it is used, so that an acceptably high predictive value for a clinic population (where the condition screened for is relatively common and where the test might have demonstrated its usefulness) may become an unacceptably low predictive value when the same test is used in a general population survey (where the condition screened for is relatively uncommon).

A further complication is that the test might have been normed in a way that makes it unsuitable for use in an epidemiological study. For example, it might omit to take age or maturational effects into account where there should be norms for different age-groups. Or it might omit to take sex differences into account where there should be norms for each sex. Or it might need variant forms to take cultural or linguistic differences into account. Where timed tests are used, it might be that norms derived from a high-achieving sample of university students are unsuitable for use with a sample of low-achieving young adults. This will be the case where reaction times are assessed, where failure to take the difference into account would refer an excessive proportion of people whose attainments, however low, could be expected on the basis of their general ability.

What criteria would a screening instrument need to satisfy in order to offer an adequate way of assessing the prevalence of dyslexia in an epidemiological study? A counsel of perfection would require a predictive value so high that the instrument would be, in effect, a diagnostic test. Unless and until such a test becomes available, a realistic set of criteria must prioritise optimal predictive value and availability of demographically-adjusted norms. There might be a trade-off between these two criteria.

If or when a screening instrument has been identified on realistic criteria, a decision can be made as to whether the data obtained through its use could be entered into any analyses. It is unlikely that any screened individuals could be identified as dyslexics for the purpose of data analysis, for the reasons already stated. However, it is possible that self-reported behaviours or scores on test items could be included in data analyses with no less confidence than applies to self-report in general.

If the desired unit of analysis is the dyslexic individual, then it is essential to supplement any screening test data. This might be done in two ways.

If the screening instrument is a behavioural checklist, the conventional wisdom would follow it with a full-scale diagnostic assessment by an educational psychologist. The feasibility of this procedure in a large-scale epidemiological survey would first need to be established. It is a moot point, in any case, whether full-scale diagnostic assessment could succeed in identifying dyslexic individuals to an acceptable level of accuracy, given the inutility of reading-related methods and the invalidity of IQ-discrepancy methods, for discriminating between dyslexics and ordinary poor readers. If full-scale diagnostic assessment were to take place at the second stage, neither construct validity nor test-retest reliability would be of over-riding importance in the screening test, but face validity, acceptability and ease of administration would be of primary importance. The risk of false negatives is evident, although it cannot be quantified

Alternatively, if the chosen screening instrument is a cognitive test battery, it might be acceptable to supplement test scores with a structured interview, which could be undertaken by the survey interviewer. Additional criteria for the screening instrument would then be face validity, acceptability, and ease of administration within the time constraints of the survey. However, of over-riding importance would be construct validity and test-retest reliability. This method of identification would, of necessity, be inferential, but perhaps no more so than any method likely to be employed by an educational psychologist.

Suggested strategy

It would be possible for those contemplating research of this kind to assess their options and then to pursue a course of action without reference to any other body. That would be an honourable position, but a hazardous one. Alternatively, intending researchers could set out criteria for a screening instrument and invite interested parties to propose for consideration any instruments known to them which meet those criteria. Suggestions made in response to this request could be reviewed and a decision whether (and, if so, how) to proceed could be taken on the basis of the review.

Appendix 9
Some recommended reading for literacy teachers

Abadzi, H. (1994). **What We Know about Acquisition of Adult Literacy: Is There Hope? (World Bank Discussion Papers No. 245)**. Washington, DC: World Bank.

Adams, M. J. (1990). **Beginning to Read: thinking and learning about print**. Cambridge, MA: The MIT Press.

Altick, R. D. (1957). **The English Common Reader: A Social History of the Mass Reading Public 1800–1900**. Chicago, IL: The University of Chicago Press.

Altmann, G. T. M. (1997). **The Ascent of Babel: an exploration of language, mind and understanding**. Oxford: Oxford University Press.

Bruner, J. (1983). **Child's Talk: learning to use language**. Oxford: Oxford University Press.

Bryant, P. and Bradley, L. (1985). **Children's Reading Problems: psychology and education**. Oxford: Basil Blackwell.

Byrne, B. (1998). **The Foundation of Literacy: the child's acquisition of the alphabetic principle**. Hove: Psychology Press.

Carr, T. H. and Levy, B. A. (Eds.). (1990). **Reading and its Development: component skills approaches.** San Diego, CA: Academic Press, Inc.

Chall, J. S., Jacobs, V. A. and Baldwin, L. E. (1990). **The Reading Crisis: why poor children fall behind**. Cambridge, MA: Harvard University Press.

Corballis, M. C. (2002). **From Hand to Mouth: the origins of language**. Princeton, NJ: Princeton University Press.

Cornoldi, C. and Oakhill, J. (Eds.). (1996). **Reading Comprehension Difficulties: processes and intervention**. Mahwah, NJ: Lawrence Erlbaum Associates.

Crystal, D. (1997). **The Cambridge Encyclopedia of Language** (Second ed.). Cambridge: Cambridge University Press.

Goswami, U. and Bryant, P. (1990). **Phonological Skills and Learning to Read.** Hove: Lawrence Erlbaum Associates.

Gough, P. B., Ehri, L. C. and Treiman, R. (Eds.). (1992). **Reading Acquisition**. Hillsdale, NJ: Lawrence Erlbaum Associates.

Graff, H. J. (1995). **The Labyrinths of Literacy: reflections on literacy past and present** (Revised and expanded ed.). Pittsburgh, PA: University of Pittsburgh Press.

Harris, M. and Hatano, G. (Eds.). (1999). **Learning to Read and Write: a cross-linguistic perspective**. Cambridge: Cambridge University Press.

Jackson, N. E. and Coltheart, M. (2001). **Routes to Reading Success and Failure: towards an integrated cognitive psychology of atypical reading**. Hove: Psychology Press.

Jusczyk, P. W. (1997). **The Discovery of Spoken Language**. Cambridge, MA: The MIT Press.

Kruidenier, J. (2002). **Research-Based Principles for Adult Basic Education Reading Instruction**. Portsmouth, NH: RMC Research Corporation **[Accessible at www.nifl.gov/partnershipforreading/publications/adult.html]**.

Levine, K. (1986). **The Social Context of Literacy**. London: Routledge & Kegan Paul.

Locke, J. L. (1993). **The Child's Path to Spoken Language**. Cambridge, MA: Harvard University Press.

Manguel, A. (1996). **A History of Reading**. London: HarperCollins.

National Reading Panel. (2000). **Teaching Children to Read: an evidence-based assessment of the scientific research literature on reading and its implications for reading instruction.** Washington, DC: National Institute of Child Health and Human Development. **[Accessible at www.nichd.nih.gov/publications/nrp/report.htm]**.

Olson, D. R. (1994). **The World on Paper: the conceptual and cognitive implications of writing and reading.** Cambridge: Cambridge University Press.

Perfetti, C. A. and Marron, M. A. (1995). **Learning to Read: Literacy Acquisition by Children and Adults.** Philadelphia: National Center on Adult Literacy. **[Accessible at literacy.org/search/detailed.html]**.

Purcell-Gates, V. (1995). **Other People's Words: the cycle of low literacy.** Cambridge, MA: Harvard University Press.

Rayner, K., Foorman, B. R., Perfetti, C. A., Pesetsky, D. and Seidenberg, M. S. (2001). 'How psychological science informs the teaching of reading'. **Psychological Science in the Public Interest,** 2(2), 31–74. **[Accessible at www.psychologicalscience.org/newsresearch/publications/journals/pspi2_2.html]**

Rée, J. (1999). **I See a Voice: a philosophical history of language, deafness and the senses**. London: HarperCollins.

Snow, C., Burns, M. S. and Griffin, P. (Eds.). (1998). **Preventing Reading Difficulties in Young Children (Committee on the Prevention of Reading Difficulties in Young Children, Commission on Behavioral and Social Sciences and Education, National Research Council)**. Washington, DC: National Academy Press. **[Accessible at http://bob.nap.edu/html/prydc]**

Snowling, M. J. (2000). **Dyslexia: a cognitive developmental perspective**. Oxford: Basil Blackwell.

Spear-Swerling, L. and Sternberg, R. J. (1998). **Off Track: when poor readers become 'learning disabled'.** Oxford: Westview Press.

Spear-Swerling, L. (in press). 'A road map for understanding reading disability and other reading problems'. In R. Ruddell & N. Unrau (Eds.), **Theoretical Models and Processes of Reading**, Vol. 5. Newark, DE: International Reading Association.

Stanovich, K. E. (2000). **Progress in Understanding Reading: scientific foundations and new frontiers**. New York: The Guilford Press.

Street, B. V. (1984). **Literacy in Theory and Practice**. Cambridge: Cambridge University Press.

Tomasello, M. (1999). **The Cultural Origins of Human Cognition**. Cambridge, MA: Harvard University Press.

Vincent, D. (1989). **Literacy and Popular Culture: England 1750–1914**. Cambridge: Cambridge University Press.

Appendix 10
Anatomy and Functions of the Brain

Mapped areas

Serious enquirers are recommended to consult Martin's *Atlas* for a full description of the areas of the human brain referred to in this review. Serious enquirers with crayons will find that *The Human Brain Coloring Book* is also helpful. Less detail, but much additional interest, is given in the *Cambridge Encyclopedia of Language*. As a stop-gap, this appendix indicates the location of most of the areas concerned, first by reference to Brodmann's mapping in Figure A and the table below it and then by reference to Martin's *Atlas*, from which Figures B, C, and D have been taken.

Areas not mapped

Three areas mentioned in the text, each occurring bilaterally, are not mapped here. One is the *insula*, an area of the cortex folded within the lateral sulcus and concealed by the superior temporal gyrus. The second unmapped area is the *planum temporale*, a triangular landmark (rather than a discrete structure) located within the superior planes of the left and right temporal lobe just posterior to Heschl's gyrus (Brodmann Area 42) within the depth of the sylvian fissure. The third unmapped area is the non-cortical *thalamus* or 'inner chamber' of the brain, a processing station for all sensory pathways. Its point of adhesion is marked in Figure D (the sources for which are to be found on pages 438 and 489 of Martin's *Atlas*).

Supplementary references

Brodmann, K. (1925). **Vergleichende Lokalisationslehre der Grosshirnrinde in ihren Prinzipien dargestellt auf Grund des Zellenbaues** (Second ed.). Leipzig: Barth.

Crystal, D. (1997). **The Cambridge Encyclopedia of Language** (Second ed.). Cambridge: Cambridge University Press.

Diamond, M. C., Scheibel, A. B. and Elson, L. M. (1985). **The Human Brain Coloring Book**. New York: HarperCollins.

Martin, J. H. (1996). **Neuroanatomy: Text and Atlas**. Stamford, CT: Appleton & Lange.

Table 3. Locations and functions of Brodmann's areas

Brodmann area	Functional area	Location	Function
1, 2, 3	Primary somatic sensory cortex	Postcentral gyrus	Touch
4	Primary motor cortex	Precentral gyrus	Voluntary movement control
5	Tertiary somatic sensory cortex; posterior parietal association area	Superior parietal lobule	Stereognosia
6	Supplementary motor cortex; supplementary eye field; premotor cortex; frontal eye fields	Precentral gyrus and rostral adjacent cortex	Limb and eye movement planning
7	Posterior parietal association area	Superior parietal lobule	Visuomotor; perception
8	Frontal eye fields	Superior, middle frontal gyri, medial frontal lobe	Saccadic eye movements
9, 10, 11, 12	Prefrontal association cortex; frontal eye fields	Superior middle frontal gyri, medial frontal lobe	Thought, cognition, movement planning
13, 14, 15, 16	Insular cortex (part)		
17	Primary visual cortex	Banks of calcarine fissure	Vision
18	Secondary visual cortex	Medial and lateral occipital gyri	Vision, depth
19	Tertiary visual cortex, middle temporal visual area	Medial and lateral occipital gyri	Vision, colour, motion, depth
20	Visual inferotemporal area	Inferior temporal gyrus	Form vision
21	Visual inferotemporal area	Middle temporal gyrus	Form vision
22	Higher-order auditory cortex	Superior temporal gyrus	Hearing, speech
23, 24, 25, 26, 27	Limbic association cortex	Cingulate gyrus, subcallosal area, retrosplenial area and parahippocampal gyrus	Emotions
28	Primary olfactory cortex; limbic association cortex	Parahippocampal gyrus	Smell, emotions
29, 30, 31, 32, 33	Limbic association cortex	Cingulate gyrus and retrosplenial area	Emotions
34, 35, 36	Primary olfactory cortex; limbic assocation cortex	Temporal pole	Smell, emotions
37	Parietal-temporal-occipital association cortex; middle temporal visual area	Middle and inferior temporal gyri at junction temporal and occipital lobes	Perception, vision, reading, speech

Brodmann area	Functional area	Location	Function
38	Primary olfactory cortex; limbic assocation cortex	Temporal pole	Smell, emotions
39	Parietal-temporal-occipital association cortex	Inferior parietal lobule (angular gyrus)	Perception, vision, reading, speech
40	Parietal-temporal-occipital association cortex	Inferior parietal lobule (supramarginal gyrus)	Perception, vision, reading, speech
41	Primary auditory cortex	Heschl's gyri and superior temporal gyrus	Hearing
42	Secondary auditory cortex	Heschl's gyri and superior temporal gyrus	Hearing
43	Gustatory cortex (?)	Insular cortex, frontoparietal operculum	Taste
44	Broca's area; lateral premotor cortex	Inferior frontal gyrus (frontal operculum)	Speech, movement, planning
45	Prefrontal association cortex	Inferior frontal gyrus (frontal operculum)	Thought, cognition, planning, behaviour
46	Prefrontal association cortex (dorsolateral prefrontal cortex)	Middle frontal gyrus	Thought, cognition, planning behaviour, aspects of eye movement control
47	Prefrontal association cortex (frontal operculum)	Inferior frontal gyrus	Thought, cognition, planning, behaviour

Source: Table 3–2 in Martin, J. H. (1996). **Neuroanatomy: Text and Atlas** (Second edition). Stamford, CT: Appleton & Lange.

Figure A: *Brodmann's areas*

Source: Brodmann, K. (1909). **Vergleichende Lokalisationslehre der Grosshirnrinde in ihren Prinzipien dargestellt auf Grund des Zellenbaues**. Leipzig: Barth.

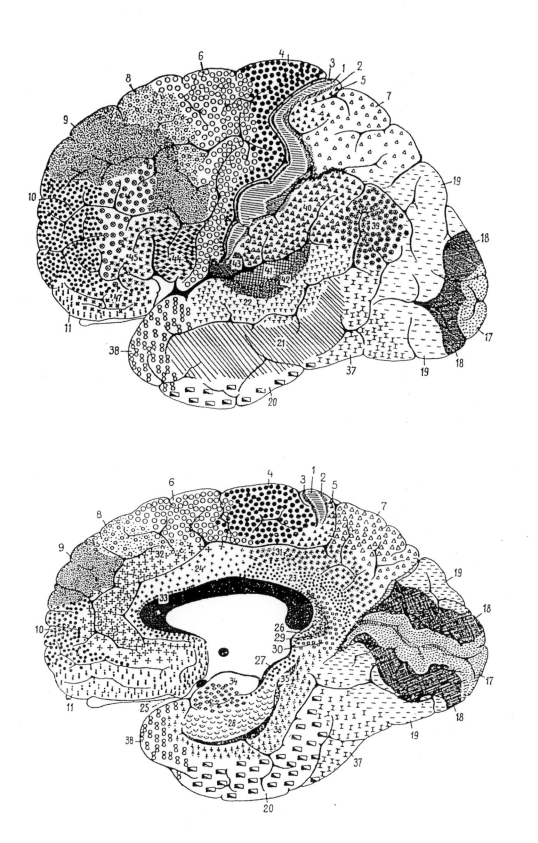

Figure B: *Lateral Surface of the Left Cerebral Hemisphere, Cerebellum (C), Brain Stem and Rostral Spinal Cord (S), indicating the Frontal (F), Parietal (P), Temporal (T) and Occipital (O) Lobes*

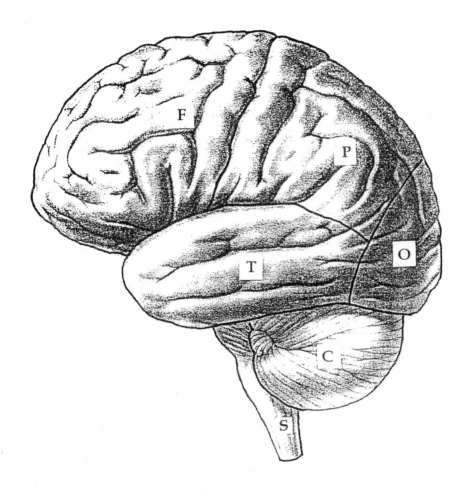

Adapted from: Figure A1–1 in Martin, J. H. (1996). **Neuroanatomy: Text and Atlas**. Stamford, CT: Appleton & Lange.

Figure C: *Lateral View of the Left Cerebral Hemisphere and Rostral View of the Cerebral Cortex, with Main Features*

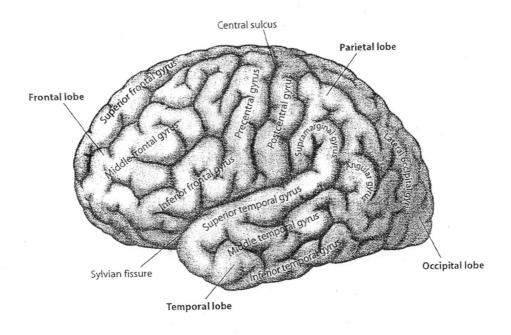

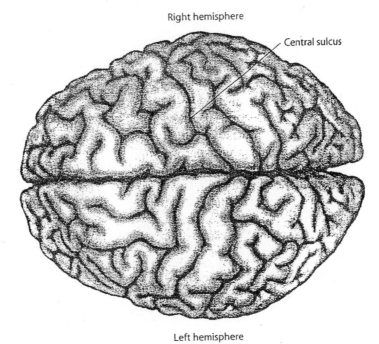

Source: Figure 2.22 in Martin, J. H. (1996). **Neuroanatomy: Text and Atlas**. Stamford, CT: Appleton & Lange.

Figure D: *Cortical Surface of the Left Cerebral Hemisphere and Mid-Sagittal Section, Showing the Main Features*

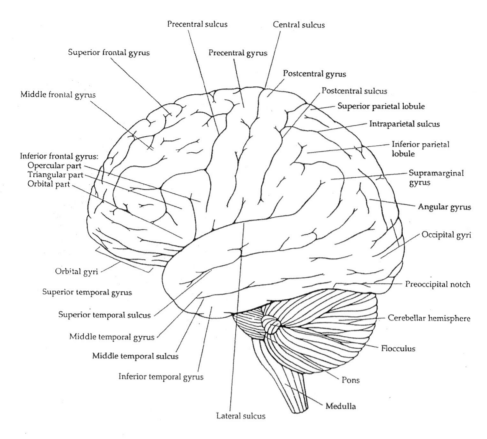

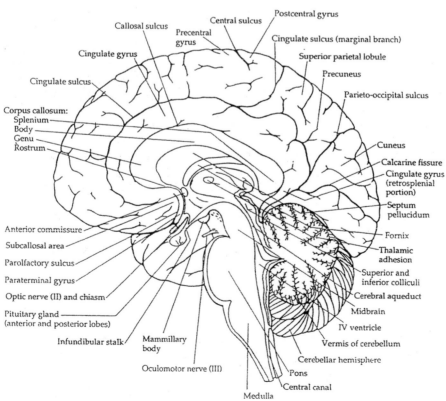

Source: Pages 483 and 489 in Martin, J. H. (1996). **Neuroanatomy: Text and Atlas**. Stamford, CT: Appleton & Lange.